I N T E G R A T I N G
Social Welfare Policy
— & —
Social Work Practice

INTEGRATING
Social Welfare Policy
&
Social Work Practice

KATHLEEN MCINNIS-DITTRICH
Marquette University

BROOKS/COLE PUBLISHING COMPANY
PACIFIC GROVE, CALIFORNIA

ITP™ The trademark ITP is used under license.

A CLAIREMONT BOOK —

Brooks/Cole Publishing Company
A Division of Wadsworth, Inc.

Printed in the United States of America
10 9 8 7 6 5 4 3 2 1

Library of Congress Cataloging-in-Publication Data

McInnis-Dittrich, Kathleen, [date]
   Integrating social welfare policy & social work practice /
Kathleen McInnis-Dittrich.
     p. cm.
   Includes bibliographical references and index.
   ISBN 0-534-17430-2
   1. Public welfare—United States.   2. United States—Social
policy. I. Title. II. Title: Integrating social welfare policy
and social work practice.
   HV95.M34   1993
   361.973—dc20   93-4781
                                CIP

Sponsoring Editor: *Claire Verduin*
Marketing Representative: *Eileen Murphy*
Editorial Associate: *Gay C. Bond*
Production Editor: *Laurel T. Jackson*
Manuscript Editor: *Joanne Tenenbaum*
Permissions Editor: *Karen Wootten*
Interior and Cover Design: *Terri Wright*
Art Coordinator: *Lisa Torri*
Interior Illustration: *Hierographics*
Typesetting: *Bookends Typesetting*
Cover Printing: *Color Dot Graphics, Inc.*
Printing and Binding: *The Maple-Vail Book Mfg. Group*

To Bill,
whose love is the anchor in my life

Contents

1 The Social Work Practitioner and Social Welfare Policy   **1**

DIRECT SERVICES AND SOCIAL WELFARE POLICY:
AN UNNATURAL DIVISION, 3

THE SOCIAL SERVICE AGENCY AS THE CONTEXT
FOR PRACTICE, 3
The Myth of Autonomous Practice, 4

A PATCHWORK SYSTEM OF SOCIAL SERVICES
AS THE CONTEXT FOR PRACTICE, 6
Institutional Social Welfare Services, 6
A Residual System of Social Welfare, 7
Reconciling Value Differences, 9

EVALUATING POLICY AND CHANGING IT, 9
Social Work as a Political Profession, 10
Our Clients' Lack of Political Power, 11
Social Work Ethics Are Political, 12

SUMMARY, 13

DISCUSSION QUESTIONS, 13

SUGGESTED PROJECTS, 14

NOTES, 14

IMPORTANT TERMS AND CONCEPTS, 15

2 Implementing Social Welfare Policy: The Internal Environment of the Social Service Agency 16

PRIMARY AND SECONDARY SETTINGS FOR SOCIAL WORK
  PRACTICE, 17
  Social Work Values versus Other Professional Values, 19
  The Marginality of Token Status, 19
  The Devaluation of Social Work, 19
  Role Ambiguity, 20
ELEMENTS OF THE INTERNAL ORGANIZATIONAL ENVIRONMENT, 20
THE DAVIS COUNTY MENTAL HEALTH
  CENTER (DCMHC), 21
  Social Service Agency Goals, 21
  Goal Displacement, 24
  How Do Goal Ambiguity and Conflict Affect the Practitioner? 25
ORGANIZATIONAL TECHNOLOGY, 26
  The Knowledge Base of Social Work, 26
  People: The Raw Material of Social Work Technology, 27
  The Sequence of Activities in Social Work Technology, 27
AUTHORITY AND POWER, 28
  The Functions of Authority and Power, 28
  Manifestations of Authority and Power, 29
  Authority and Power Issues Unique to
    Social Service Agencies, 31
DECISION MAKING, 33
  Bounded Rationality, 33
  The Organization as the Decision Environment, 34
  The Importance of Decision Making to Job Satisfaction, 34
MENTAL HEALTH AND SURVIVING IN THE ORGANIZATION, 35
THE PRACTITIONER'S VIEW, 35
SUMMARY, 35
DISCUSSION QUESTIONS, 37
SUGGESTED PROJECTS, 37
IMPORTANT TERMS AND CONCEPTS, 38

3 The External Environment of Social Service Agencies 39

THE POTENTIAL CLIENT POPULATION, 41
  Referrals, 42
  Advertising, 42

HUMAN RESOURCES, 43
  Legislative Mandates, 45
  Availability of Staff, 46
  Unionization of Professional Staff, 47
  The Agency's Reputation, 47
THE AGENCY'S ECONOMIC AND FINANCIAL ENVIRONMENT, 48
  The Local Economy, 48
  Budget Allocations, 49
  Diversification of Resources, 50
INTERORGANIZATIONAL RELATIONSHIPS, 52
  Conditions for Interorganizational Cooperation, 52
  Developing Coalitions, 53
RELATIONSHIPS WITH REGULATORY AGENCIES, 54
  The Delegation Doctrine, 54
  Prospective and Retrospective Rule Making, 54
THE SOCIOCULTURAL ENVIRONMENT, 56
  Community Values and Agency Goals, 57
  Client Values, 58
  Resource Dependency, 58
THE PRACTITIONER'S VIEW, 58
SUMMARY, 58
DISCUSSION QUESTIONS, 60
SUGGESTED PROJECTS, 61
IMPORTANT TERMS AND CONCEPTS, 61

4 The Current Social Welfare System: A Patchwork of Programs 62

PUBLIC AND PRIVATE SOCIAL SERVICE AGENCIES, 63
  Public Agencies, 64
  Private Nonprofit Social Service Agencies, 67
  How Do Public and Private Agencies Differ? 68
  The Private For-Profit Agencies, 71
  For-Profit Structures within Nonprofit Agencies, 72
A FRAGMENTED SYSTEM, 74
  Universal versus Means-Tested Programs, 76
  Cash and In-Kind Programs, 77
  Federal, State, and Local Administration, 78
  Implications for the Social Work Practitioner, 79
SUMMARY, 79
DISCUSSION QUESTIONS, 80

SUGGESTED PROJECTS, 80
NOTES, 81
IMPORTANT TERMS AND CONCEPTS, 81

5 Developing Social Welfare Policy:
A Political Process   82

WHAT MAKES THE POLICY-MAKING
    PROCESS POLITICAL? 83
    Values Determine Problem Definition and Intervention, 83
    Most Policy Is Made in the Legislative Arena, 85
THE INFLUENCE OF THE MEDIA, 89
    Editorial Policy, 90
    Investigative Reporting, 90
    Community Service Programming, 92
THE COURT SYSTEM, 93
    The Nature of Court Decision Making, 93
    The Structure of the Court System, 94
    How the Court System Is Political, 95
    How the Court System Determines Social Welfare Policy, 95
SUMMARY, 96
DISCUSSION QUESTIONS, 96
SUGGESTED PROJECTS, 96
NOTES, 97
IMPORTANT TERMS AND CONCEPTS, 97

6 The Policy-Making Process:
The Problem-Solving Approach   98

THE COMMUNITY OF CABLETON, 99
STEP 1: ASSESSING THE PROBLEM, 100
    Needs Assessments, 100
    Defining the Problem and Setting Goals, 103
    Identifying Resources and Obstacles, 105
STEP 2: EXPLORING ALTERNATIVES, 105
STEP 3: DEVELOPING AN ACTION PLAN, 108
STEP 4: IMPLEMENTING THE ACTION PLAN, 109
STEP 5: EVALUATING THE POLICY-MAKING EFFORT, 110
SUMMARY, 111
DISCUSSION QUESTIONS, 111
SUGGESTED PROJECTS, 111
IMPORTANT TERMS AND CONCEPTS, 112

7 **Policy Evaluation, Research, and Analysis**   **113**

PROGRAM EVALUATION, 114
  The Purpose of Evaluating Programs, 114
  Preevaluation Activities, 115
  Identifying Program Goals, 118
  Identifying Variables for Evaluation, 118
  Collecting and Analyzing Data, 119
  Reporting Evaluation Results, 121
POLICY RESEARCH, 121
  The Scientific Method and Policy Research, 122
  Approaches to Policy Research, 125
THE ANALYSIS MODEL, 126
  A (Approach), 127
  N (Need), 127
  A (Assessment), 128
  L (Logic), 129
  Y (Your Reaction as a Practitioner), 130
  S (Support), 130
  I (Innovation), 131
  S (Social Justice), 131
  Summarizing the ANALYSIS, 131
SUMMARY, 131
DISCUSSION QUESTIONS, 133
SUGGESTED PROJECTS, 133
IMPORTANT TERMS AND CONCEPTS, 133

8 **The Practitioner's Role in Influencing Public Policy Change**   **134**

FINDING OUT ABOUT SOCIAL WELFARE POLICY, 135
  Local Governmental Policies, 135
  State-Level Policies, 138
  Federal Policies, 139
USING LIBRARY RESOURCES, 140
INFLUENCING THE POLITICAL PROCESS, 141
  The Hatch Act, 142
  Written and Verbal Communication with Legislators, 142
  Lobbying, 143
  Public Hearings, 144
  Using the Media, 144
  Supporting a Political Candidate, 145

Voting, 146
Going to Court to Change Policy, 147
SUMMARY, 147
DISCUSSION QUESTIONS, 148
SUGGESTED PROJECTS, 148
IMPORTANT TERMS AND CONCEPTS, 148

9 **The Practitioner's Role in
Changing Agency-Level Policy**   **149**
FINDING OUT ABOUT AGENCY-LEVEL POLICIES, 150
ORGANIZATIONAL-LEVEL CHANGE, 151
    The Practitioner's Responsibility for Organizational Change, 151
    *Changing Individuals' Attitudes and Behavior within
        the Organization,* 152
    Why Is There Resistance to Change? 154
    Force or Persuasion? 155
    Changing Organizational Goals, Structure, or Procedures, 155
THE PROBLEM-SOLVING MODEL AND
    ORGANIZATIONAL CHANGE, 157
    Assessing the Need for Organizational Change, 157
    Developing an Action Plan, 160
    Implementing the Action Plan, 160
    Evaluating the Organizational Change, 160
SUMMARY, 161
DISCUSSION QUESTIONS, 161
SUGGESTED PROJECTS, 161
IMPORTANT TERMS AND CONCEPTS, 162

APPENDIX A. CODE OF ETHICS, NATIONAL ASSOCIATION
    OF SOCIAL WORKERS, 163
GLOSSARY OF TERMS AND CONCEPTS, 170
REFERENCES, 177
INDEX, 181

Preface

IN THE 1990s, SOCIAL WORK as a profession is enjoying renewed interest; this is evident from the swelling numbers of undergraduate majors and increasingly competitive entry into graduate programs. It would be ideal if this renewed interest were the result of a sensitized collective consciousness of hunger, poverty, and discrimination. Alas, it is not, and we know it. Most likely, an overwhelming interest in private clinical practice accounts for much of this professional revival. This interest is indicative of the profession's shift from issues in social change and social justice to a focus on counseling and therapy. It also indicates the political neglect suffered by the people social work has long sought to help.

Like other educators, I have seen students merely *tolerate* studying social welfare policy as a requirement of accredited programs in social work. Rarely have they expressed either an interest in or an appreciation of policy as an integral part of our profession. It has been difficult to convince students that social welfare policy and social work practice are not two distinct entities. When the social welfare policy sequence is taught by faculty who have little or no practice experience, even the best and brightest students can have difficulty figuring out how dealing with these policies can legitimately be called social work. Such students are content to leave social welfare policy considerations to politicians, researchers, and whoever else makes policy.

Years later the same students bemoan the pitfalls of life in an organization. "It is all so political" and "I'd be fine if I didn't work in such a messy bureaucracy" are familiar comments. Former students have become painfully aware of the complex political system, in which change takes time. Too often we work with clients only to see them return to environments in which it is difficult, if not impossible, to sustain the effects of the interventive effort. This book is for every student who wants to work in direct services but who doubts that social welfare policy is relevant to his or her career. It is also for every instructor who has struggled to present an integrated model of social welfare policy and social work practice.

Unlike many other texts on social welfare policy, this book examines social welfare policy through the eyes of the social work practitioner, not the political scientist or economist. The practitioner's perspective goes beyond a description of the policies and programs that make up the social welfare system in this country to a broader view that includes the influence of the social service agency as well as the political environment within which the direct services professional practices.

The book is intended as a text for a social welfare policy course, an advanced practice course, or a concurrent field practicum seminar. If the social welfare policy sequence is taught by faculty with extensive practice experience, it is appropriate for that course. If social welfare policy is taught by non–social work faculty, a practice course is an excellent forum for helping the student make the connection between policy and practice. For some programs, the field practicum is the best location for this material as students struggle with the day-to-day reality of policy and practice.

The Plan of the Book

Chapter One addresses the policy resistance of many direct service–oriented students as it examines how the social service agency and social welfare policy define the context for direct practice. The combination of society's ambivalence about helping those in need and the political nature of social work practice presents an exciting challenge to every social worker.

The internal and external environments of the social service agency are discussed in Chapters Two and Three, respectively, using the example of a fictitious mental health center. The difficulty of establishing organizational goals, the uncertain nature of social work technology, and the constant scramble for resources are discussed as they directly affect the work of the direct services practitioner. Chapter Four broadens the student's perspective from the individual social service agency to the patchwork of programs and services we know as social welfare policy and programs.

Chapter Five examines the three primary means by which policy is developed: the legislative process, the media, and the court system. Chapter Six presents an in-depth example of a community's struggle to develop a policy to address teenage parenthood. This example illustrates the use of the problem-solving model, a familiar tool for the direct services student.

Program evaluation and policy research are the focus of Chapter Seven. This chapter is an introduction to the ANALYSIS model, a framework for assessing programs and policies specifically useful to the social work practitioner. Using the word *ANALYSIS* as a mnemonic device gives students an easy-to-remember, practical tool for evaluating programs. The ANALYSIS model includes the assessment of policies and programs within the framework of social justice—still the most important value underlying our profession.

Once students have learned to identify the roles of agency and social welfare policy and to assess policy strengths and weaknesses, they are ready to discuss the means by which both kinds of policies can be changed. This is the focus of Chapters Eight and Nine.

Learning Aids

Each chapter contains several examples of direct service practice for each concept or idea presented. By discussing the relevance of agency and social welfare policy, using examples of direct service, the student is more likely to begin to think of social welfare policy and social work practice as integrated. Each chapter contains a list of important terms and concepts, discussion questions, and suggested projects to help the student apply new ideas to current experiences in either volunteer work or their field placements.

Acknowledgments

I would like to thank those who reviewed early drafts of the book, including Lynn Atkinson, Oklahoma State University; Norman H. Cobb, University of Texas at Arlington; Kevin Marett, Brigham Young University; Lois M. Miranda, University of Wisconsin at Oshkosh; Tom Roy, University of Montana; and Margaret Tacardon, Skidmore College. Their frank comments and suggestions helped me keep my focus narrow enough to be specific and broad enough to be useful. I am deeply indebted to Peggy Adams, who gave me the early encouragement I needed to turn an idea into a book. Claire Verduin, Gay Bond, and Laurel Jackson at Brooks/Cole have been incredibly helpful and supportive through the complexities of production. But I am most appreciative of their energy, enthusiasm, and senses of humor—the three best things I can say about anyone!

Yet, it is the clients I worked with during my years as a direct service practitioner and the students I work with every day who have been and will always be *my* best teachers. Chapter Eight, "The Practitioner's Role in Influencing Public Policy Change," was written for the social work graduates of the Class of 1992 at Marquette University. This amazing group of students reminded me every day of the words attributed to Margaret Mead: "Never doubt that a small group of thoughtful and committed citizens can change the world." I have no doubt they will.

—KATHLEEN McINNIS-DITTRICH
Marquette University

The Social Work Practitioner and Social Welfare Policy

*I got into social work 20 years ago because I wanted to
spend my life helping people. My clients with disabilities are
so appreciative of anything I can do for them. It touches my
heart when I see people start believing in themselves for the first
time! But I also get very discouraged when I see them struggle
with the bureaucracy at the rehab center. Paperwork, forms, and
more forms! Everybody wants a report in writing. I wish the
agency cared as much about the client as they do about all the
forms. Clients cannot get help until they meet all kinds of
bureaucratic requirements. The center will not touch a client
until they are sure they will get their money. Accountants run
this agency, not service providers!*

—TWENTY-YEAR VETERAN SOCIAL WORKER
IN A REHABILITATION CENTER

*The Wilson family is really a pretty normal family that has
come on some hard times. I can find housing for a few nights
and get emergency medical care for the children, but I can't seem
to do anything about the loss of jobs when the plant closed or
persuade the city to build more low-income housing. And how
can clients keep everything straight? Application for this
program is made at the County. For another program, it is the
Social Security Administration. A public agency handles the
AFDC-UP payments, but a private agency handles the counseling
for this family. Sometimes we trust low-income people with*

cash—other times they are forced to use vouchers. I wonder how clients manage! If it was up to me, I would dump the whole system and start over!

—NEW B.S.W. STUDENT WORKING AT
A SHELTER FOR THE HOMELESS

I love working with teenagers! At least I get the feeling that I can do something that will really make a difference in their lives. Maybe if we can help them soon enough, they won't have to live the same kinds of lives as their parents. And it makes me feel so good when kids turn their lives around. But sometimes I find it hard to do my job as a social worker. I can get these kids to think about their future, but I cannot make jobs appear magically or stop the violence in their schools or get the gangs out of their neighborhoods. If society wants kids to have a fighting chance, big things will have to change.

—SENIOR SOCIAL WORK FIELD STUDENT
IN A COMMUNITY CENTER

The frustrations voiced by the social workers in the opening quotations are common to all of us who work with clients. The satisfaction of working with people, watching them overcome the obstacles of poverty, discrimination, and personal discouragement, draw people to the profession of social work. Unfortunately, the tangled web of social service bureaucracy and the punitive values by which we judge those in need of help make all social workers stop and wonder about their career choice. Seeing bright, young, single mothers drop out of school due to lack of day care, or older people place their spouses in nursing homes because they cannot find home health care seem to defeat our professional efforts. Our wide-eyed idealism about helping people clashes head on with the reality of the system of laws and services we know as social welfare policies and programs.

Blindly accepting the system as simply the way it is betrays the very foundation of our profession. Too often social work practitioners walk away from the challenges of working with agency, local, state, and federal policies out of fear and ignorance. Under the guise of "I just want to help people," practitioners leave policy considerations to agency administrators whom they hope will become more humane, and to politicians whom they hope will miraculously stop ignoring the plight of their constituents. Without the input of front line workers, like those quoted in the opening statements, neither is likely to happen.

This book is intended to help you, the social work practitioner, understand the impact of social welfare and agency policy on the client as the consumer of services and on the practitioner as the provider of services. Competence in the area of social welfare policy is much more than knowing what programs exist to meet what needs. It requires you to expand your perspective in the assessment process to include identifying issues that are the result of agency or social welfare policy. This book explores social work's context for practice, which includes both the agency setting in which most social workers practice and the greater external environment. Direct services and social welfare policy are not separate and distinct areas of professional education.

DIRECT SERVICES AND SOCIAL WELFARE POLICY: AN UNNATURAL DIVISION

If you are like most students, you see practice and the field experience as separate from, and unrelated to, the policy sequence in social work education. If so, you might be eager to master direct practice skills but fail to share the same enthusiasm for understanding the importance of policy.

The structure of social work education contributes to this division. Separate courses might be offered on casework, group work, community organization, administration, and social welfare policy. Attempts to integrate these various components of your education are often limited. Graduate programs usually give you an opportunity to specialize in either direct services (also called clinical or treatment specialties) or macro-level practice such as administration, middle management, and social welfare policy. This separation gives you the impression that these professional areas are distinct from each other.

Clinical or direct services courses are most frequently taught by faculty with extensive clinical experience, which may include a current private practice. The macro-practice sequence, on the other hand, might be taught by faculty with an interest not only in social work, but in economics or political science. As a result, you get the impression that real social work involves direct services, and the study of social welfare policy belongs to administrators, community organizers, and researchers. You may enter the field with the erroneous notion that these two aspects of the profession are only tangentially related to one another. This division is an unnatural one. Effective direct services requires a strong knowledge of social welfare policies and programs. Developing effective social welfare policy requires a strong understanding of direct services. Professional social work practice means *integrating* social welfare policy and social work practice.

THE SOCIAL SERVICE AGENCY AS THE CONTEXT FOR PRACTICE

Let's return to the first of this chapter's opening quotations. In the social worker's exact words,

I also get very discouraged when I see [my clients] struggle with the bureaucracy at the rehab center. Paperwork, forms, and more forms! Everybody wants a report in writing. I wish the agency cared as much about the client as they do about all the forms. Clients cannot get help until they meet all kinds of bureaucratic requirements. The center will not touch a client until they are sure they will get their money. Accountants run this agency, not service providers!

If you have felt the same way in a field placement, you know how frustrating it is to be bogged down with recording and assessments when you want to work more closely with clients. Aren't social workers supposed to be independent professionals who retain the major decisions, along with the client, about what is best for the case? In reality, this is not so.

The Myth of Autonomous Practice

With the exception of a few independent clinical social workers in private practice, most social workers provide service within a social service agency setting. Independent professional practice, unaffected by the trials and tribulations of the bureaucratic setting, is what Jansson (1990) calls the **mythology of autonomous practice.** Autonomous practice implies social workers have complete control over the nature of their work with clients. The practitioner may mistakenly believe that, through the process of identifying problem areas and possible courses of action, the worker and client have almost complete freedom to choose a course of action.

Social work practice is not autonomous. Workers rarely have complete freedom to determine what intervention they will use with clients. The social service agency has its own set of operational procedures for running the day-to-day operation, maintaining agency accountability, and providing the framework within which social welfare policy (developed outside the agency) is implemented. These operational procedures are known as **agency policy.** The frustrations of cumbersome reports and strict eligibility requirements are examples of agency policy at the rehabilitation center mentioned at the beginning of this chapter. The center is both constrained and enabled by the philosophy of the agency and who pays for the service.

The Philosophy of the Agency.   The philosophy of the agency providing the service places limits on the nature of social work practice. For example, many rehabilitation centers provide services only to people who have been determined to have a reasonable chance of recovering some level of independent functioning. If an older person suffers a completely debilitating stroke or a young person becomes a quadriplegic, the rehabilitation center might consider them inappropriate clients. The agency has defined its philosophy as that of rehabilitation, not maintenance care for individuals with limited potential for habilitation. The philosophy of the agency may or may not coincide with the worker's personal philosophy. It is a logical, compassionate response to want to provide service to all who request help. However, the constraints of the agency might not allow us to do that. Agency policy effectively curtails our professional autonomy.

Who Pays for the Service. Who pays for the service to be provided is perhaps the most common example of social work practice's lack of autonomy. Take, for instance, the rehabilitation social worker's complaints about the endless reports needed on each client. Likely, many of these reports are required by the insurance company or health care program that is paying for the patient's treatment at the rehabilitation center. Who may provide the service, for how long, and where the services are offered are clearly stipulated for both private insurance patients and Medical Assistance and Medicare recipients. If the social worker fails to follow the insurance company's regulations, the rehabilitation center might not get paid nor the client served. What appears to be an annoying nuisance and an obstacle to service provision is the very thing that enables the service to be provided in the first place. You must know how services are being paid for and use intervention techniques that are practical within those restraints.

Social service agencies exist primarily to provide services for persons in need. This objective would lead one to believe these agencies would be efficient and compassionate. However, agencies operate like all other bureaucracies. Organization goals become displaced as agencies seek to survive in an atmosphere of intense competition for limited resources. Surviving as an agency might become more important than the original organizational goal of providing services. Social work practitioners who are promoted to administrative positions may appear to leave their professional concern behind them to be suddenly transformed into petty bureaucrats.

The social service agency is a critical player in the process of integrating social welfare policy and social work practice, for it is within the agency that social welfare policy is implemented. Agency goals, technology, authority and power, and the dynamics of decision making are directly connected to how a policy becomes a program of client services.

As a social work practitioner, you must learn not only to survive in the sometimes frustrating internal environment, but also to use your knowledge of how organizations operate to make that environment more humane for both workers and clients. Chapters Two and Three explore the internal and external environments of the social service agency. Being able to recognize how organizations take on a life of their own can help you avoid participating in goal displacement, in which surviving the challenges of organizational life becomes more important than helping clients. Knowing what to expect within the agency and assessing external pressures that affect the daily operation of the agency can make you far less apprehensive about organizational survival and allow you to provide more effective services to clients.

A PATCHWORK SYSTEM OF
SOCIAL SERVICES AS THE CONTEXT FOR PRACTICE

The second quotation presented at the beginning of this chapter identifies the second major component in the context for social work practice, a complicated and disparate system of social and financial services. In the words of the new B.S.W. student working with the homeless family:

> . . . how can clients keep everything straight? Application for this program is made at the County. For another program, it is the Social Security Administration. A public agency handles the AFDC-UP payments, but a private agency handles the counseling for this family. Sometimes we trust low-income people with cash—other times they are forced to use vouchers. I wonder how clients manage!

You might also wonder how we have ended up with a fragmented and poorly coordinated system of cash and in-kind benefits, universal and means-tested programs, and public and private agencies. It is not surprising that social welfare's critics suggest scrapping the entire program and starting over. Yet, when we examine the vast array of means of providing assistance to persons in need, we see that the way the United States organizes its social welfare system reflects basic societal values that may or may not coincide with our values as social workers.

Institutional Social Welfare Services

The American welfare system is, in many respects, unique among Western nations. Most other industrialized nations employ an **institutional model of social welfare.** By institutional, we mean a system in which the welfare system has a first-line function in people's lives and is designed specifically to aid individuals in attaining satisfying standards of life. Such a system is dedicated to helping individuals reach the fullest development of their capacities (Wilensky & Lebeaux, 1965, p. 138). Rather than carrying the stigma that accompanies welfare receipt in the United States, social welfare services in an institutional system are seen as a legitimate function of modern industrial society. Individuals are *not expected* to be able to meet their needs without assistance because of the complex nature of industrial society. Services are provided based on the philosophy that the task of meeting the social, medical, and emotional needs of citizens falls appropriately within the role and function of government.

In the United States, public education and fire and police protection are examples of institutional services. Public education is considered important enough to be provided on a free, universal basis to all children in the country without regard to the income of their parents. Education is considered necessary for both the individual's and the nation's basic welfare.

Fire and police protection are provided for the basic good of the community. We would never think of denying fire protection to a low-income family because they could not afford to pay for the cost of the service. Police do not ask for payment before they answer a call reporting a robbery. Education and personal protection from both fire and physical danger are so important to us that the services are offered through and regulated by the local, state, or federal government. The government's commitment to the well-being of citizens in countries with institutional social welfare services goes beyond education, fire protection, and police protection. It includes any service which helps an individual to cope with the pressure and problems of industrialized life.

For example, in Sweden, the government provides day care, health care, higher education, and retirement benefits to all of its citizens, regardless of their incomes, as illustrated in Table 1.1. Low-income and upper-income families place their children in the same day care centers with no more stigma attached to using public day care services than we feel toward attending a public university. The Swedish government and citizens do not expect people to be able to find quality day care without some difficulty, so day care is provided on a public basis. This makes it more cost efficient and easier to regulate and control. Institutionalized services are seen as an investment in the well-being of the individual, part of the effort to encourage healthy and productive citizens. These services are funded through high tax rates. Scandinavians may pay between 60 and 70% of their incomes after deductions to support social and public expenditures (Einhorn & Logue, 1989).

A Residual System of Social Welfare

The United States employs a **residual model of social welfare services.** Residual services are created or used only when the normal structures of the family and the marketplace break down. Our economic and social welfare system is based on the assumption that the family and the marketplace (that is, employment) should be expected to meet our individual needs before we expect help from others or from the government. The residual model expects social welfare institutions to come into play only when people cannot make use of family or market resources.

For example, if families find themselves homeless due to financial difficulties, society expects that they will first exhaust all possibilities for assistance from their families. Securing housing and employment is not seen as a front-line function of the government. It is only when such help is unavailable that services will be provided through public and private agencies.

Residual programs are reactive. Reactive programs are developed and funded only when the demand for services exceeds the ability of society to meet those needs in the private sector. In the United States, we react when problems develop rather than anticipating that services will be needed. A network of homeless shelters for individuals and families was developed only

TABLE 1.1

The United States and Sweden:
Social Welfare Systems Compared

BENEFIT	UNITED STATES	SWEDEN
Old Age, Disability, and Survivors' Benefits	Known as Social Security. Employers and employees pay into an annuity fund. Covers employees and their dependents.	Government and employers pay all costs—no contributions from employees. Covers employees and their dependents.
Sickness and Maternity Benefits	Medical Assistance covers all medical costs for low-income families. Medicare pays for part of the cost of medical care for the elderly and disabled. All others must provide for their own medical insurance; 17% of population has no coverage. No government maternity benefits.	Government and employer pay for cash benefits to sick workers or parents caring for a sick child. Minimum cost for physician services. Free hospitalization. Low-cost medication. Pregnancy and childbirth are considered short-term disabilities and are covered like a disability.
Work-Related Injury	Workers' Compensation covers part of medical costs and small cash benefit for limited time. Worker is responsible for all other costs. Government- and employer-provided.	Free medical care for work-related injuries. Benefits extend for entire time of temporary or permanent disability. Government- and employer-provided.
Unemployment Benefits	Time is limited—usually maximum is 26 weeks. Payment levels vary by state. Financed by tax on employers and state funding. No means test.	Daily subsidy up to 300 days a year. Connected to labor union membership but available to all citizens. Liberal means test.
Family Allowances	No family allowance. Federal income tax system allows deductions for each child.	Government pays parent for each child regardless of income and assets. Covers child under 16, or up to 20 if a student.

SOURCE: Adapted from *Social Security Programs Throughout the World 1989*, Research Report #62, by the Office of Research and Statistics, U.S. Department of Health and Human Services. Washington, DC: Government Printing Office.

after the country had gone through several major recessions, a massive de-institutionalization effort in the 1960s, and record unemployment levels. We reacted to the problem well after it developed.

Residual systems can legitimately be accused of attempting to exert social control over the recipients of government-sponsored services. For example, Aid to Families with Dependent Children (AFDC) was designed to help single parents provide for the economic well-being of their children. That aid is provided to people who meet the categorical eligibility requirements, but in exchange for those benefits, recipients are expected to seek employment. Some states penalize families for having more children while on public assistance by providing less generous increases in welfare benefits after the first three children. Others make benefit levels so low that it is a better economic decision for poor families to work at low-paying jobs than to try to survive on minimal public assistance benefits.

Reconciling Value Differences

Social workers believe that all individuals should be treated with respect and dignity and are entitled to be active participants in deciding how best to solve their own problems. Social workers also support the idea that members of society should recognize their mutual obligations to help each other when problems arise. Societal values, however, do not always mesh with those ideas. Our residual form of social welfare provides assistance to others only as a last resort when other social mechanisms, such as the family and employment efforts, fail—not as a first line of service. Demands are placed on people as a condition of receiving assistance. In essence, a residual system says "We'll help you, but you will do it our way." This conflict between societal and professional social work values is the crux of understanding how social welfare policy and social work practice conflict with each other. If this connection is so crucial, how is it the social work profession so frequently fails to recognize that many of the frustrations of direct services are the shortcomings of policy?

Chapter Four examines the broad array of programs that constitute the social welfare system in the United States. This system reflects the translation of American social values into an array of programs and policies. These disparate programs exist because they have been developed, not as a coherent set of programs and policies, but as reactions to needs that have become apparent in our society. Understanding the current system also helps you begin to identify how policy is developed, from the straightforward legislative process to the complicated policy-making function of the court system.

EVALUATING POLICY AND CHANGING IT

The purpose of this book is not to encourage you simply to accept the complexities of integrating policy and practice and to learn to live with the frustrations. As the student pointed out in the third quotation that begins this chapter, "I can get these kids to think about their future, but I cannot make jobs appear magically or stop the violence in their schools or get the gangs out of their neighborhoods. If society wants kids to have a fighting chance, big things will have to change." Something does have to change in current social welfare policy. And the profession of social work has a long and admirable tradition of being an active part of bringing about change.

Social Work as a Political Profession

Social workers often resist anything that appears to be political. The term political has become associated with manipulating and deceiving people rather than serving their best interest in government. Within the last 20 years government has often been seen as the profession's adversary rather than the close ally we would like it to be. However, the bottom line is that the government funds, regulates, plans, and executes most of the major service programs we rely on to serve clients. If we look at the term *political* in a more favorable light, that is, as a mechanism for improving the current social welfare system, we see that social work by its very nature is a political profession. As it is used in the following discussion, **political** refers to seeking and using power over the allocation and distribution of resources; this can require compromise, negotiation, and, at times, conflict. Political activity implies working to maintain or change the current allocation and distribution of resources.

Social Work's Political Role in the Allocation of Resources. Historically, people have relied on their families and friends to help them in times of need. Families have provided resources. However, when families cannot or will not help, people come to the social welfare institution for help. When available services are deemed inadequate, social workers often advocate for more services. In other words, they work to change the allocation and distribution of resources. Any social worker who has attempted to cut through the red tape for clients or who has advised clients on how to do so has engaged in political activity.

To Change or Accept the Status Quo: A Political Decision. Social work is often seen as a profession that seeks social change as a way to improve the lives of the people we work with. Yet as social workers we continually "judge, assess and intervene in ways which maintain the status quo." (Adams, 1982, p. 55). How much do we really encourage each other to change a system we see as unjust? How much of what we do is simply helping people to adjust to the status quo? In *The Politics of Therapy,* Seymour Halleck (1971) contends that what we do as therapists is primarily to help people adjust to the way things are with minimal real effort to encourage change outside of individual personal changes. Halleck and others such as Galper (1975) contend that social work, along with other helping professions, is a very conservative profession, rather than the liberal, change-oriented profession we consider it![1]

If we are not active participants in that change or encourage our clients to make changes, we run the risk of what Ryan (1976) calls "blaming the victim." **Blaming the victim** means that we attribute fault for the development and maintenance of social problems to the individuals who are victims of circumstances, rather than actors in their own lives.

For example, the teenage pregnancy rate in the United States is the highest among civilized countries in the world (Jones, 1986). It is easy to blame teenagers for being irresponsible and not using contraception or for keeping their babies when they themselves are still children. It is also easy to find fault with teenagers' parents for providing poor supervision of their adolescents or for failing to warn them about the hazards of early sexual activity. It is convenient to accuse the young mother of being too lazy or poorly motivated to finish high school while trying to raise a baby. But many teenage mothers are actually victims of forces beyond their control. Many teenagers do not see that they have options. Contraceptives can be difficult to use or even obtain. Peer pressure both to become sexually active and to keep their babies in case of pregnancy is as powerful to many low-income teens as the peer pressure to wear certain clothes is to middle-income suburban teens. It is difficult to convince any teenager of the importance of doing things with an eye to the future. A sense of immediacy is part of the developmental stage of adolescence. Middle-income teens may believe their parents can afford to send them to college, so it makes sense to them to complete high school and delay parenthood. But what vision can we give to low-income teenage girls who do not know their options and have trouble believing that their lives can be any better than those of their parents? A minimum-wage job waiting after graduation is not a very strong incentive to complete high school.

Our Clients' Lack of Political Power

Historically, social work developed as a profession whose major focus was the poor. The poor included disproportionate numbers of minorities, women with children, and persons with disabilities. These groups have traditionally not received the economic benefits of our capitalist, democratic system because they could not access our political system. Running for office costs money. Testifying at legislative hearings requires strong public speaking skills and transportation to the hearing site. Voting requires access to the polls, the conviction that your vote matters, and someone to watch your children.

Every day as social workers we are confronted with the consequences of unequal access to the resources of capitalism. Poor single mothers live in poor-quality housing because there is not enough political pressure to force federal governments to construct more low-income housing. The children of the working poor go without medical care because their parents' jobs do not provide health insurance benefits. Teen mothers drop out of school because they cannot afford private day care and no universal system of child care exists in the United States. Our efforts to encourage the development of these programs on the local, state, or federal level are political. Our purpose is to influence the allocation of these resources to reach the people who need them most.

Social Work Ethics Are Political

The National Association of Social Workers adopted a Professional Code of Ethics in 1979 that is intended to guide social workers in making sound ethical choices regarding their professional activities and their relationships with clients, colleagues, their employing agency, and society. Section VI, "The Social Worker's Ethical Responsibility to Society," confirms the political nature of the social work profession:

> P. *Promoting the general welfare.* The social worker should promote the general welfare of society.
>
> 1. The social worker should act to prevent and eliminate discrimination against any person or group on the basis of race, color, sex, sexual orientation, age, religion, national origin, marital status, political belief, mental or physical handicap, or any other preference or personal characteristic, condition, or status.
> 2. The social worker should act to ensure that all persons have access to the resources, services, and opportunities which they require.
> 3. The social worker should act to expand choice and opportunity for all persons, with special regard for disadvantaged or oppressed groups and persons.
> 4. The social worker should promote conditions that encourage respect for the diversity of cultures which constitute American society.
> 5. The social worker should provide appropriate professional services in public emergencies.
> 6. The social worker should advocate changes in policy and legislation to improve social conditions and to promote social justice.
> 7. The social worker should encourage informed participation by the public in shaping social policies and institutions. (Compton & Galaway, 1989, pp. 201–207)

Clearly, these ethical responsibilities confirm the political nature of the social work profession. "Changes in policy," "improving social conditions," and "shaping social policies and institutions" imply political activity.

Chapter Six helps you to develop a basic set of skills in evaluating both social welfare and social service agency policy. Although large-scale, empirical analysis of current social welfare policy is usually conducted by professional researchers, *evaluating* the policies that affect our practice with clients falls legitimately within the activities and responsibilities of every social work practitioner. The ANALYSIS model has been developed specifically for prac-titioners who might not be involved in the everyday activity of making policy, but who must live by the decisions of policy makers. A solid understanding of the policy in question is the first step in identifying the ways in which a governmental or agency policy must be changed. Chapters Seven and Eight discuss the means by which you can apply your knowledge of policy to a con-crete plan to change it.

SUMMARY

Good direct practice work involves what Briar and Briar (1982) call a "dual awareness." A dual awareness requires that social workers understand how policy affects practice and how practice can inform policy decisions. This chapter's opening quotations are vivid examples of the restrictions agency and social welfare policy can place on the social work practitioner. An agency's philosophy and payment mechanisms can limit the practitioner's autonomy. A patchwork of social welfare programs can confuse worker and client alike. We are drawn to a helping profession out of a deep commitment to people and to working directly with them, yet the system seems to present more obstacles than solutions.

These quotations also offer the most important hope for both clients and workers: if we know how policy is made and can offer an insightful and competent evaluation of that policy, we have taken the first step to changing it. A policy change affects the quality of life for many more clients than just those we serve. Social work is a political profession, meaning that in the pro-cess of helping clients both directly and indirectly through social welfare policy changes, our profession plays an important role in the allocation of resources and the decision to accept or change the conditions in which our clients live. Advocating on behalf of clients and working toward social change are important aspects of social work practice. Ultimately the student of social welfare policy and the student of direct practice will have much more in com-mon than they initially suspected.

Chapter Two examines the first context in which most social welfare policies are translated into programs that affect both client and practitioner—the social service agency. It is within the social service agency that most of you will work during your professional lives.

DISCUSSION QUESTIONS

1. *What are* social values? *Give examples of what you consider to be American social values. How do social values affect society's willingness to provide services to clients?*

2. *What is meant by* agency policy? *How does agency policy affect what social workers can do for and with their clients?*

3. *Do you agree that social work is a political profession? Does this appeal to you if you have chosen social work as a career? If not, what do you find unattractive about the political aspects of the profession?*

4. *How do you see "blaming the victim" operating in the provision of social services to the following client populations:*
   a. *Persons with AIDS*
   b. *Battered women and their children*
   c. *Alcohol and drug users*
   d. *Corrections*

SUGGESTED PROJECTS

1. Interview several social workers in your community. Ask them the following questions:
   a. What do you find most frustrating about your job?
   b. How does social welfare policy influence what you can and cannot do with your clients?
   c. Is your agency involved in changing the policies that make your work with clients most difficult?
2. Find out what political organizations in your community were started by social welfare clients. For example, some communities have an active group of AFDC recipients who work toward change in the public assistance system. Other communities have politically active groups of persons with AIDS or of older adults.
3. Invite a guest speaker from the local office of the National Association of Social Workers to discuss how social workers have been politically active in your state.

Notes

1. Jeffrey Galper's main assertion is that although social work as a profession appears to have taken a progressive point of view on social reform in the short term, in the long run its actual operation as a profession strengthens the basic repressive characteristics of society. Social work reinforces conservative values and ideologies that are destructive to human well-being (Galper, 1975).

IMPORTANT TERMS AND CONCEPTS

agency policy

blaming the victim

institutional model of social welfare

political

residual model of social welfare

the myth of autonomous practice

Implementing Social Welfare Policy: The Internal Environment of the Social Service Agency

*It is next to impossible to be a healthy fish in badly
polluted waters.*

—JAMES A. WILSON, 1979, p. 125

Unlike other professionals, such as physicians and lawyers, only a few social workers practice independently. *Agencies are the context in which the vital connection between social work practice and social welfare policy takes place.* They serve as "the intermediary between individuals [and] nation-states," as policies instituted by units of government become actual services to clients (Blumberg, 1987, p. 222). An understanding of social welfare policy's connection to social work practice is incomplete without an understanding of the forces that operate within and outside the agency setting in the process of implementing these policies. The operating procedures used to control the functioning of the agency and to implement social welfare policy are known as *agency policy.* The internal and external environments of an agency contribute both to the functioning of the agency and to our understanding of the agency as the context for implementation of social welfare policies and programs.

The **external environment** consists of all the elements *outside* the agency's organizational environment that influence the type of service provided by the agency and characteristics of clients and agency staff. The external environment is discussed in Chapter Three.

The **internal environment** of an agency consists of the elements *within* the agency, known as the elements of bureaucracy, that determine what happens to clients and staff inside the agency. Agency goals, technology, authority and power, and the dynamics of decision making directly affect how a policy becomes a service program. This chapter explores the internal environment of the social service agency—the bureaucracy, or the "polluted waters" Wilson refers to in the opening quotation. When social workers express their frustration about their jobs, it is often in terms of complaints about endless red tape and petty bureaucrats. The complexities of life within the organization are probably more responsible for professional burnout than the challenges of working with clients.

This chapter includes the following:

✦ A discussion of the differences between social work's role in primary and secondary settings for social services
✦ An analysis of the importance of well-defined goals for the operation of social service agencies
✦ A definition of *organizational technology* and the difficulties technologies pose for organizations
✦ A discussion of the importance of authority and control in determining how the agency operates
✦ An examination of the organizational elements that affect decision making

PRIMARY AND SECONDARY SETTINGS FOR SOCIAL WORK PRACTICE

Social workers are found in a variety of settings, including child welfare agencies, departments of social services, hospitals, schools, and rehabilitation centers. Settings in which social work is the primary purpose of the organization and social workers the dominant professional category are known as **primary social work settings.** Direct services to clients with identified social service needs is the main activity of the organization. Child welfare agencies are an example of a primary social work setting. Most staff are social workers, and working with children and their families is the agency's main task.

In a primary setting, social workers maintain some level of control over how policies are implemented. As policies lead to the development of programs, social workers can be more effective in ensuring that clients are treated with dignity and that every effort is made to maintain confidentiality—issues central to the values of the profession. Social work is committed to client **self-determination,** the belief that clients should be active participants in determining how they will work with professionals to solve their problems. Therefore, when a program is developed, clients should be given every possible opportunity to be involved in decisions that affect their well-being.

Schools and hospitals are examples of **secondary social work settings.** In secondary social work settings, social workers work in conjunction with another profession that dominates the staff and whose work is seen as primary to the purpose of the organization. In a hospital, social workers might help a patient learn to live with a debilitating illness, but the physician and other medical staff are the first-line professionals working with the patient. The final decisions about a patient's treatment are under the authority of the physician, not the social worker. School social workers work only with students who have been referred by teachers or administrators. The educational function of the school is the primary focus, and the social worker's counseling and supportive work with children, although considered very important, is secondary. Examples of primary and secondary social work settings are given in the following lists.

PRIMARY SOCIAL WORK SETTINGS

    Child welfare agencies
    County departments of social services
    Family service associations
    Sectarian social services (for example, Catholic Social Services, Lutheran Social Services, Jewish Social Services)
    Adoption agencies
    Family counseling agencies
    Battered women's shelters
    Homeless shelters
    Child abuse prevention agencies
    Runaway shelters

SECONDARY SOCIAL WORK SETTINGS

    Hospitals
    Public and private schools
    Day care centers
    Alcohol and drug rehabilitation centers
    Nursing homes
    Rehabilitation centers
    Business and industry
    Legal Aid offices
    Employment counseling agencies
    Planned Parenthood agencies
    Developmental disabilities agencies
    Community centers
    Senior centers
    Social development commissions
    Fair housing councils
    Hot-lines and helping lines
    Councils on alcoholism
    Independent living agencies

Social Work Values versus Other Professional Values

According to Dane and Simon (1991), four predictable problems face social workers in secondary settings. The first is the discrepancy between the values of the social work profession and the dominant profession of the organization. In the correctional setting, for example, wardens and guards (members of the primary profession) see confinement and punishment as the primary goal of their work with offenders, whereas social workers (members of the secondary profession) see their role as rehabilitation and treatment. These goals contradict each other. If most financial resources within the correctional setting are committed to the goal of punishment, it is unlikely that a prison social worker will make much progress toward treatment goals. Social welfare funds allocated to the correctional system might be designated for the rehabilitation of offenders, but the agency (in this case, the prison) might determine that rehabilitation is best accomplished by confinement and punishment. Social workers might not see confinement as treatment, but they have little bargaining power on behalf of the clients because they work within a secondary setting for social work practice.

The Marginality of Token Status

A second problem identified by Dane and Simon (1991) is the marginality of token status. This means that, in a given secondary setting, social workers are few and their visibility is high. Therefore, their decisions are scrutinized and constantly evaluated to determine whether the decisions are in line with the organizational norms of the secondary setting. In a hospital, physicians and nurses might continually be on their guard to ensure that social workers do not overstep their bounds. A physician might recommend that a patient be placed on life-support equipment and be very persuasive with the family. If the social worker knows from working with the family that they have mixed feelings about using extraordinary means to prolong their relative's life and communicates this to the physician, conflict is inevitable. The social worker is compelled to protect the best interests of the patient and his or her family; the physician's job is to provide the best possible medical care. The social worker's concerns will most likely take second place to the physician's orders.

The Devaluation of Social Work

In secondary settings, social work may be "devalued as women's work in settings that are predominantly male in inspiration and composition" (Dane & Simon, 1991, p. 208). Social work is a profession dominated by women in direct services, the most frequent kind of service performed by social workers in a secondary setting (Leiby, 1978; Lubove, 1975). In a hospital setting, most physicians and administrators, the primary sources of power, are usually male. Most social workers and nurses are female. Social work and nursing professions are designated as women's work because of their nurturing functions. Like nursing, social work might not be considered an integral part of the case planning for the patient and is thus devalued.

Role Ambiguity

Role ambiguity is the fourth problem identified by Dane and Simon (1991). Role ambiguity occurs when the social worker is responsible for developing a helping relationship with the client in an effort to solve problems and must also perform in a role that reinforces the norms of the organizational setting. For example, a student might be referred to a school social worker for chronic absenteeism. After working with the child, the social worker might conclude that excessive absences are due to the child's intense dislike of the teacher. This places the social worker in a particularly difficult position. If the social worker advocates for the client by suggesting a change of teachers, the school system might be resistant. Advocating for the client might not be seen as the appropriate role for the social worker. Rather, the school system might see the social worker as a truant officer whose job it is to force the child to attend classes. Because the social worker is in a secondary setting, most likely the school system will enforce the norms of attendance and pay little attention to the plight of the child in a classroom where the child does not like the teacher. The policy of the school, mandated by law, is compulsory attendance. The school social worker, on the other hand, might see beyond the attendance problem to other issues in the child's life.

In primary social work settings, social workers have a greater influence on implementing policies in a way consistent with the values and philosophy of social work. In secondary settings, social workers find themselves subject to the professional practices and philosophies of another profession, which at times may conflict with the values of the social work profession. The setting in which social workers practice plays a critical role in how social welfare policy is translated into actual programs.

ELEMENTS OF THE
INTERNAL ORGANIZATIONAL ENVIRONMENT

Whether social workers practice in a primary or secondary setting, much of what they do is influenced by forces and factors within the organizational environment. Agency and program goals, organizational technology, the people served by the agency, authority and control, and the nature of decision making limit as well as expand the choices of the worker in determining the best course of action for the client.

THE DAVIS COUNTY
MENTAL HEALTH CENTER (DCMHC)

The rest of this chapter uses the example of a fictional social service agency (DCMHC) to illustrate the influence of the internal elements of the social service agency on the practitioner's functioning within the agency setting. DCMHC is located in Walton, a rural area of a sparsely populated state. Walton, the county seat of Davis County, has a population of 10,000 persons, which is 50% of the population of the entire county. Because the county is so sparsely populated, DCMHC is the only major provider of mental health and substance abuse services to county residents. A private nonprofit child welfare agency and the Davis County Department of Social Services are also located in Walton.

One of the most serious social problems in the county is alcohol abuse. Long, hard winters, social isolation, and the abundance of alcohol at local functions appear to have contributed to escalating alcohol use among all age groups of the population. Due in part to the alcohol use, the incidence of domestic violence continues to rise dramatically, not only in Davis County but throughout the state.

In response to this alarming increase, the state legislature has just passed the Alcohol and Domestic Violence Awareness Act, which requires that if alcohol use is determined to be a factor in a case of domestic violence, the abuser must participate in an alcohol and drug abuse assessment and evaluation. This policy is extremely unpopular throughout the state and became law only by a very narrow margin after the governor's veto was overturned.

Based on estimates by the police and local social service providers, the Alcohol and Domestic Violence Act is expected to generate approximately 300 cases for evaluation and assessment from Davis County alone and over 7,000 cases statewide. It is difficult to be more precise because of the hidden nature of domestic violence. Social workers, physicians, attorneys, and teachers are required to report individuals if they suspect alcohol use has contributed to domestic violence, even if the incident was not reported to the police. Police officers called to the scene of a domestic dispute are also charged with the responsibility of determining whether or not alcohol contributed to the domestic violence incident. Referring agents report the suspected use to DCMHC who may provide the assessment or refer clients to other agencies of their choice. Brian is one of the social workers at DCMHC who will be arranging assessment and providing treatment for individuals who are referred for evaluation. He is an experienced B.S.W. with Alcohol and other Drug Abuse Certification (AODA). He has been a lifelong resident of Walton and is himself a recovering alcoholic.

Social Service Agency Goals

One of the most important parts of working with individual clients in direct services is identifying goals for the intervention effort, the desired results of any planned activity. Organizations have goals also. It is important for agencies to identify and articulate their goals so most agency activity can be directed toward them. Goals are also important because they are a means of evaluating whether the agency is accomplishing its purpose.

The goals of an agency are usually directly connected to social welfare policy, either as a direct translation of policy into programs or as an agency effort to provide services that policy fails to address. The Alcohol and Domestic Violence Awareness Act requires that the public substance abuse treatment agency, DCMHC, provide treatment for persons who are identified as perpetrators of domestic violence due in part to alcohol abuse. That is the direct translation of a policy into a program with services to be provided by a direct services practitioner. The two major types of organizational goals include the general goals of the agency and specific goals of the programs operated by the agency.

The Agency Mission Statement.   The general goals of an agency are often listed in a **mission statement.** A mission statement is a broad statement about the scope of social problems addressed by the agency and a general description of how the agency intends to address them. Figure 2.1 presents the mission statement of DCMHC. The mission statement makes the scope of the agency's services clear to clients and the community. From the mission statement, it is obvious that DCMHC concentrates on services primarily in the areas of mental and alcohol abuse. It does not specialize in child welfare or services to older adults or persons with developmental disability except in cases directly connected to mental health or substance abuse issues. A mission statement defines the boundaries of service for the agency within the external environment.

Program Goals.   Programs within the agency also have **program goals,** those ends that individual programs within the agency hope to accomplish. Figure 2.1 shows the program goals for both the Inpatient Adult Alcohol Treatment Program and the new Alcohol and Domestic Violence Awareness Program. These are only two of the programs within DCMHC and are most germane to our discussion. Program goals are geared to the specific desired outcomes of each program but are based on the general mission statement of the agency.

For example, both the Inpatient and Domestic Violence Awareness programs have identified the number of patients they intend to treat and have projected a reduced incidence of alcohol use and domestic violence. Goals for the programs are measurable and specific in terms of how many units of service can and will be provided. These types of goals are referred to as **output goals.** Output goals describe the quantity of goods and services the organization provides for its clients, in this case specific services for inpatient treatment and domestic violence reduction. At the end of a fiscal year, it will be possible to determine whether each of these programs has achieved its goals. Have 175 adults been treated in the inpatient unit? Are

MISSION STATEMENT

Davis County Mental Health Center sees as its mission the provision of mental health and substance abuse prevention and intervention services to all residents of Davis County regardless of age, gender, race, color, creed, handicap, veteran status, or sexual orientation. DCMHC's aim is to prevent the development of mental illness and substance abuse through an aggressive program of community education and services to individuals and families. In those cases where mental illness or substance abuse are identified through self-referral or through family, court, or physician referral, DCMHC will provide a comprehensive range of inpatient and outpatient services designed to maintain the dignity of the individual and maximize self-determination in the course of treatment.

PROGRAM GOALS

Inpatient Adult Alcohol Treatment Program

A. Provide inpatient treatment services to 175 persons with alcohol dependency problems, supplemented with services to their families. This figure is estimated to be one-fourth of the active alcohol population in Davis County. Of those 175 persons targeted for treatment, the program aims to achieve sobriety in 75 of those cases.

B. Increase the number of Alcoholics Anonymous and Al-Anon groups in Davis County by 25% (from 10 to 13) during the coming year in recognition of the need for community and family support for those in recovery.

C. Develop a special unit for female alcoholics, increasing service from 30 patients a year to 50 a year.

Alcohol and Domestic Violence Awareness Program

A. Reduce the number of alcohol-related incidents of domestic violence by one-third (that is, by 200 incidents).

B. Develop a specialty program, in conjunction with the Inpatient and Outpatient programs, that recognizes the unique problems associated with alcohol use and domestic violence and serves 40 families the first year, and 60 and 80 families in the next two years, respectively.

C. Initiate a community-awareness training program for police officers, teachers, and social workers that addresses identification and treatment of alcohol-related domestic violence.

Figure 2.1   DCMHC mission statement and program goals.

half of those treated sober after one year? Are there three new Alcoholics Anonymous groups? Has domestic violence related to excessive use of alcohol been reduced by one-third? Goals are most meaningful when they serve as actual measures of the service provided and can show concrete progress to-ward reducing the incidence or severity of the social problem identified.

Unfortunately, organizational goals are rarely this specific and measurable. Practitioners know from their own work with clients that goals are most useful when they state clearly and concisely what is hoped to be accomplished in an effort with a client. For example, Mr. A. will attend four Alcoholics Anonymous meetings and one family counseling session a week and reduce the number of verbal arguments with his wife by 50% within the first six months of treatment. Mr. A. and his social worker both know whether these goals have been accomplished. Vague treatment and organizational goals, such as "help the client to feel better" and "meet the needs of the community," make it difficult to hold clients and social workers accountable for their achievements. If we do not know what we are trying to accomplish, how will we know when we have accomplished it? It is difficult, if not impossible, to decide when the patient no longer needs services or when the organization has completed a successful program if the original aim of intervention is unclear.

Goal Displacement

Neugeboren (1985) identifies the difficulty of articulating goals and the ambiguous nature of social service goals as among the most serious problems facing social service agencies and other human service organizations. He attributes the lack of concise goals to the tendency of social service agencies to emphasize the means of service (counseling, community education, inpatient services) rather than the end they hope to accomplish. This is called **goal displacement.** Goal displacement occurs when the means becomes the end. What an agency does becomes more important than what it accomplishes. For the Domestic Violence Awareness Program, simply engaging in a broad series of community education programs, holding training sessions with police officers and other referral agents, and running as many people as possible through residential treatment becomes a classic case of goal displacement *if* there is no documented evidence that alcohol-related incidents of domestic violence have been reduced as a result.

Goal displacement can also occur when an agency's goals conflict with one another. DCMHC has had a much smaller program to serve women with substance abuse problems than the program that exists to treat men. Some of this difference centers around the unique problems of women, such as the need for child care while receiving treatment and the misperception in Davis County that women do not have a problem with alcohol. Staff at DCMHC know this misperception is incorrect and have included in the Inpatient unit's program goals a plan to expand the services to women. However, DCMHC also intends to develop the Domestic Violence Awareness Program, which is aimed at men. As funds become available to DCMHC through new grants and expanding programming, where will the expansion of services take place? Can DCMHC increase services to both, or will services to women be sacrificed for the opportunity to increase services to men? The potential exists for a conflict between these two goals.

How Do Goal Ambiguity and Conflict Affect the Practitioner?

The problems of ambiguous and conflicting goals in social service agencies affect the practitioner in several ways. First, ambiguous or conflicting goals make organizational life confusing for the practitioner. Working in an atmosphere in which staff are never clear about the agency's goals can make one's job dissatisfying. Is the agency accomplishing what it wants to? Are staff performing successfully? Does the staff's work make a difference in the lives of the clients? These are all questions that might remain unanswered. It is difficult to feel good about your job if you are not clear about whether or not you are even doing it. The goal displacement that occurs on an organizational level can translate itself to the individual case level. Emphasis might be displaced onto the hours of service provided to a client over a given period instead of being placed on a clear statement about how the intervention will change the client's behavior or life situation.

Second, goal conflict can perpetuate conflict among staff members within an agency. The gender issue illustrated earlier is a good example. Staff working in the women's treatment unit might feel they are being shortchanged when they consider the expansion funds available to staff in the male treatment unit. In arguing about resources and "turf," staff might find it hard to remember that the enemy is alcohol abuse, not each other.

Finally, because social service agencies find establishing goals so difficult, they also have trouble achieving respect within the communities and populations they serve. If an agency provides substantial hours of service but cannot clearly determine when it has accomplished its goals, how does it justify its existence to outside funding services and to its clients? Much of the social work process is hard to observe or measure. The difficulty of articulating, implementing, and measuring goals in the social services is a constant obstacle to the development of new social welfare policies. It is exasperating to attempt to convince lawmakers and taxpayers to support programs that have ambiguous goals or that display no evidence of their effectiveness.

Self-Determination and Organizational Goals.   Self-determination is defined as the right of clients to have maximum input into the decisions that affect their lives. Self-determination is strongly supported by the NASW Code of Ethics as a crucial element in competent professional practice. Theoretically, it would be ideal if clients had significant input into courses of action to be taken on their cases. However, in reality, many of the clients enter the social service system as **involuntary clients.** That is, they seek social services because the court has required that they do so. Not only do these clients have little input into what happens, they have no real choice about being at the agency in the first place. We can give clients some range of choice, but not much. You might find yourself enforcing the agency's regulations rather than advocating on behalf of the clients.

ORGANIZATIONAL TECHNOLOGY

Much of the difficulty in establishing concrete and measurable goals in an agency setting derives from the **organizational technology** of human service agencies. Organizational technology is "a set of systematic procedures used by the organization to bring about predetermined changes in its raw material (clients)" (Hasenfeld & English, 1974, p. 279). In human services, the technology includes the various roles that social workers play in working with clients, such as broker, advocate, mediator, resource coordinator, or therapist (Neugeboren, 1985). For example, counseling agencies focus on using a therapeutic relationship to empower the client to identify and solve problems through behavioral, task-centered, or family systems techniques. These techniques are within the confines of the organizational technology. Juvenile probation officers, on the other hand, are officers of the court and are more likely to take on roles such as enforcer of social norms, resource coordinator, and mediator in addition to that of therapist. Within the social service agency, social workers assume roles that reflect the organizational technology.

Hickson, Pugh, and Pheysey (1969) identify specific components of organizational technology: the knowledge base of the technology, the nature of the raw material to be worked upon, and the sequence of activities and equipment used in the technology. In examining these components in greater detail, we will see why organizational technology is so problematic in social service agencies.

The Knowledge Base of Social Work

Social work is an excellent example of an **eclectic profession,** in which knowledge is borrowed from a wide range of disciplines, such as psychology, sociology, anthropology, economics, and political science. It is only quite recently that the profession has begun to develop its own knowledge base through its adaptation of systems theory as a way to analyze problems and select interventive methods (Compton & Galaway, 1989). However, there is much about human behavior that social work does not know; this makes our attempts to change that behavior difficult. Human behavior does not always manifest a clear cause-and-effect relationship. For example, victims of domestic abuse handle their experiences in different ways. Some develop mild symptoms of depression; others become seriously emotionally disturbed. Some abused individuals never leave the abuser, whereas others leave early in the progression of domestic violence. The same stimulus provokes different responses in people.

Unlike business and industry, the technology of human services is highly indeterminate because our knowledge base is so variable. There is tension within the profession between the focus on the individual and the focus on the environment. The focus for social work intervention suggests the technology to be employed (Neugeboren, 1985). Depending on the case, we may aim to change a person's behavior, or we may look at changing the situation in which the client lives. Each requires different techniques and skills.

For example, Jim is a 35-year-old accountant who recently became unemployed when a factory in Walton went out of business. Occasionally, Jim would have a beer with friends, but he has never been considered a heavy drinker. However, after losing his job he went on a heavy drinking binge that ended in his abusing his wife and child. The police referred Jim to the Domestic Violence Awareness Program at DCMHC. If the goal of the interventive effort is to change the situation, the social worker at DCMHC will use the roles of broker, mediator, and advocate to help Jim find another job. The social worker will do this because unemployment seems to have been the precipitating factor in the domestic violence incident. Another social worker, although aware of the effect of unemployment on Jim's behavior, would use an approach with a more intense focus on Jim's gaining insight into his own behavior and exploring other factors that might have precipitated the behavior. Both workers would adamantly defend their approach to Jim's case even though they each used different technology.

People: The Raw Material of Social Work Technology

Manufacturers can control the output of their factories by controlling the quality of the raw materials used in production. Social work's raw material is people. For ethical and practical reasons, social service agencies cannot control the "quality" of the people who receive services. The success of the social worker depends greatly on the type of client who comes to the agency for services. When clients are highly motivated and bring a number of personal strengths with them to the helping effort, the social worker is more successful in helping clients identify goals and develop action plans to meet them. However, if the client is mandated by an outside authority to seek services, as often happens in a corrections setting, the social worker's experience is much different.

Clients are what Hasenfeld and English (1974) call "self activating," meaning that they can neutralize the technology of the social worker. Counseling never changes anyone who does not want to be changed. In alcohol treatment settings, social workers have long known that if someone is determined to continue drinking, no amount of intervention will stop them until they decide they want to stop. Despite all the sophistication we would like to attribute to our professional techniques, the client retains control of their ultimate effectiveness.

The Sequence of Activities in Social Work Technology

Working with people is not a series of rational, predetermined steps. Social work will never approximate the precise nature of the assembly line, where raw material is fed into a process and comes out a certain way. The work we do with people is not conducive to the development of a predictable routine.

Certain therapeutic approaches, such as behavior modification and hypnosis, have a prescribed set of steps, but for the most part the progress of social work practice is indeterminate. That is why evaluation of the treatment effort and the social worker's individual role is so critical in the process. We cannot predict what will happen for clients and the course of our work with them because we have no control over most of the other factors in a client's life. For example, recovering alcoholics may remain sober for many months, then a particularly bad day or a crisis can send them back to alcohol. This incidence of relapse is not a reflection on the skill of the worker or the value of the treatment technique. Rather, it is an inevitable part of working with clients on whose lives many other factors exert an influence far more powerful than our work with them.

AUTHORITY AND POWER

As discussed earlier, all social service agencies have goals that prioritize and guide their activities. The staff carries out the activities necessary to achieve these goals. Monitoring the work of the staff, mandating compliance with agency goals, and coordinating the work of the agency are the jobs of the executive director, the person who is recognized as the agent of authority and control within the agency.

Authority can be defined as the position in which an individual's right to exert power over others is recognized and supported by those who grant that power and those over whom the power is exerted. Authority is granted to an executive director in an agency by the board of directors in private agencies or by a unit of government in public agencies. *Power*, the ability to influence people to do things (Daft, 1989), is usually associated with authority. However, persons who are not in recognized positions of authority can exert considerable power in a social service agency.

The Functions of Authority and Power

According to Perrow (1979), there are three primary functions of authority and power. The first function is "to structure the agency environment to maximize goal attainment" (Perrow, 1979, p. 145). That is, authority within the human service organization sets priorities for the organization and then structures the environment of the agency to promote the realization of those priorities. Second, authority is required to monitor the work performance of organization members to ensure compliance with agency goals. Authority figures are responsible for assessing whether current agency programs and personnel are moving toward the accomplishment of agency goals. Third, authority coordinates all the agency work activities, maximizing efficiency and effectiveness and minimizing conflict.

Manifestations of Authority and Power

Unfortunately, the words *authority* and *power* have negative connotations for many. Authorities are often thought of as those who make us do things we do not want to do. Power is seen as a personal characteristic of greedy bureaucrats rather than as a necessary element in getting the work of human service agencies done. Authority and power can be observed in social service agencies in several ways.

The Organizational Chart.   The most obvious way to determine who has authority in an agency is to review the agency's organizational chart. Organizational charts depict how an agency is structured into various departments and programs and indicate who has formal authority over whom. From these charts, we can see the organization of **vertical authority.** Vertical authority is the formal position of any person in the hierarchy of formal authority from those with the greatest power to those with the least. For example, the board of directors is at the top of the organizational chart of a private social service agency, directly above the executive director (see Figure 2.2). Under the executive director are unit supervisors for each of the agency programs. The

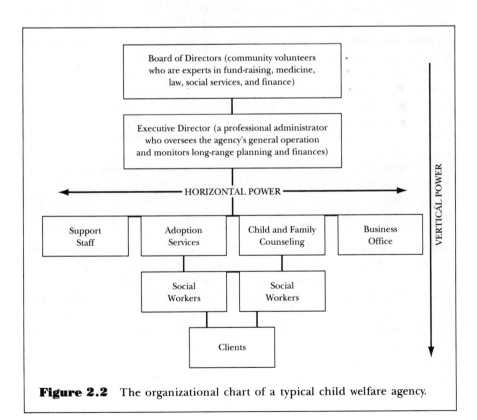

Figure 2.2   The organizational chart of a typical child welfare agency.

organizational chart is helpful in identifying formal lines of authority but tells us little about the power structures of an agency. Those in formal authority positions do not necessarily have power over those in lower positions.

Power over Resources.   The person who controls or has access to the financial resources of an agency is often the most powerful member of an organization (Marcus, 1988). An entire school of organizational theorists, the school of political economy, states that an organization is simply "an arena in which groups with different access to resources compete with each other to optimize interests" (Marcus, 1988, p. 93). In this context, *political* refers to the process by which power is acquired, and *economy* refers to tangible and intangible organizational resources (Marcus, 1988). Although this text approaches organization in a broader context than do more traditional political economy approaches, it illustrates that access to resources (that is, power) may be a more important organizational element than authority. Different elements—that is, programs within an organization—have different levels of power, based on their access to resources. The Alcohol and Domestic Violence Awareness Program at DCMHC will increasingly gain power within the agency structure as it secures resources from both the state government and private insurance companies. The money will create a substantial increase in the **horizontal power** of the Alcohol and Domestic Violence Awareness Program. Horizontal power refers to power in relationship to others in the same tier of the organizational structure. The program will now have access to additional tangible resources (in this case, money and staff) unavailable to other programs within the agency.

Resources can also be intangible. The attention paid to the Alcohol and Domestic Violence Awareness Program by the state legislature will bring prestige and recognition to the staff. Prestige and publicity are intangible resources that give the program a different kind of horizontal power.

The System of Rewards and Sanctions.   Access to raises, promotions, and choice work assignments are all examples of agency rewards and sanctions, the ways in which the organization controls the behavior of its members. Staff who do a good job and contribute to meeting organizational goals are more likely to get salary raises or be promoted. Those who do not make a positive contribution to meeting the agency's goals are likely to remain with low salaries or eventually be asked to leave the agency. Authority and power manifest themselves in the ability to reward workers or punish them. Early in our first jobs we learn who has what kind of power and authority over us, and power becomes an effective way to shape our behavior. Although you might not agree with what your boss or supervisor tells you to do, most likely you will do it anyway to avoid being reprimanded or fired. Workers who play the organizational game are those most likely to be promoted within the agency and eventually move into positions of power themselves. This text does not judge whether playing the organizational game is good or bad. It simply points out that the organizational game is a reality you might face in agencies in which you work.

Informal Authority and Power.   Persons who have direct authority over workers are not always the ones who have power over those workers. Informal authority and power may not be reflected in organizational charts, but they play an important role in the organizational life of a social worker. Examples of informal sources of authority and power are secretaries, typists, receptionists, maintenance, and housekeeping staff. Respecting staff members in the lower levels of the organization chart is a wise investment in a positive working environment. Support staff are critical to the smooth functioning of an agency; this is clear from the crucial role of legible recordkeeping, phone messages, and correspondence in our professional work. If treated with lack of respect and consideration, support staff are likely to respond in kind.

Support staff can also control access to others in positions of authority and control. We can all think of instances when we could not get past the secretary in our efforts to contact someone. Although support staff people might have relatively low standing in the organizational chart, they can exert significant power in the daily operation of the agency.

Authority and Power Issues Unique to Social Service Agencies

Several authority and power issues present unique challenges to social service agencies. These problems reflect the conflict between the independent nature of professional social work practice and the organizational restraints of the social service organization.

Lack of Autonomy.   Most social workers practice within an agency setting, subject to the organizational structure and goals set by the agency board of directors. Social workers are considered professionals who are recognized as having the ability to engage in autonomous, self-regulated practice, although from Chapter One, we know this is not entirely the way they work. Autonomous practice is granted to professions with strict, structured educational requirements set by an accreditation body (in the case of social work, the Council on Social Work Education) to ensure competency. However, only social workers engaged in private practice have authentic autonomy. Other professions, such as medicine and law, have much more control over their own professional activity. Physicians and attorneys decide what they will do for their clients, rarely having to check with a supervisor or make sure their actions fall in line with agency goals and programs.

Although social work has fought for increasing recognition as a profession, it is experiencing less, rather than more, professional autonomy. Hartman (1991) has identified four factors contributing to an erosion of autonomy in the social work profession:

1. Increased bureaucratization of social welfare agencies, which encourages fragmentation of services to clients.
2. Hierarchical organizational styles borrowed from the business world, which treat professionals as components of an organization aimed primarily at efficient, rather than effective, delivery of services.
3. Employment of business-trained bureaucrats, rather than social workers, to administer social service agencies, which distances agencies from the value base of the social work profession.
4. Increasing control by funding sources (or lack of funding sources) over the nature of practice, which results in increasing pressure on workers to do more for their clients with fewer resources.

These issues create a bureaucratic bind for social workers that conflicts with the purpose and mission of the social work profession. Hartman (1991) suggests that the burnout frequently associated with the social work profession is more often due to working within a rigid, inflexible bureaucratic structure than to the intensity of close work with multiproblem clients. Although social workers learn to work independently and make choices based on their own professional judgment, they may have many restrictions placed on them in the organization environment that are incompatible with the model of autonomous practice associated with a profession.

Discrepancy between Professional and Organizational Goals.   The inability to engage in truly autonomous practice leads to the development of a discrepancy between the professional goals of the social worker and the goals of the organization. Social work in the correctional setting is a common example of this phenomenon. Social work values state that each individual should be treated with respect and dignity and that social workers should make every effort to foster clients' maximum self-determination (NASW Code of Ethics, 1979, Section G). From a professional perspective, the social worker in corrections sees rehabilitation of the client as the primary goal of intervention. However, the corrections system as it has evolved focuses primarily on confinement and punishment rather than on rehabilitation. The professional goal of the social worker (rehabilitation) conflicts with the organizational goal of the corrections agency (confinement and punishment). It is easy to see how frustrating it would be for a social worker in this setting to maintain a strong sense of professional commitment to the client. The organizational restraints make it very difficult to adhere to professional goals.

The Dual Role of Supervision in Social Work.   In most organizations, supervisors are primarily authority figures who make work assignments, coordinate work activities, and observe and evaluate a worker's performance in a specific unit of the organization. However, in social work, supervisors take on the role of teacher and educator.

Social work relies heavily on the transmission of knowledge between supervisor and worker. University- and college-based programs provide students with a basic level of knowledge and information, but it is in the field placement setting that knowledge is applied to actual cases. The supervisor helps the student with the transition from knowing to doing (Kadushin, 1976) while helping the student to internalize the values of the social work profession. Field instructors help students to apply knowledge appropriately and offer insight and advice based on their own professional experience. Professional social workers continue to rely on supervision to help them with professional development and growth.

Professional supervision involves providing emotional support for those supervised. Clients with many problems can be difficult to work with. Constant exposure to social problems such as family violence, substance abuse, and criminal activity take an emotional toll on a worker. Being able to ventilate these frustrations and receive encouragement from a supervisor can help a worker to survive emotionally.

What makes this difficult is that while supervisors in social service settings may serve as a source of emotional support, they also maintain their supervisory functions. As figures of authority and control, supervisors find themselves caught between their role as a source of support for a social worker and their role as an administrator in the agency. Workers and supervisors may become confused about each other's roles in this complicated process.

DECISION MAKING

The final element of the internal environment of the social service agency discussed in this chapter is decision making. Decisions vital to agency survival are made every day in the organizational setting. Although members of the organization might question the wisdom of the decisions made by boards of directors, executive directors, and supervisors, they have little choice but to abide by them. Let's take a closer look at the decision-making process to discover how decisions (even those that do not make sense to us) are made.

Bounded Rationality

Bounded rationality is a term coined by March and Simon (1958) to describe the process within which decisions are made. If individuals were completely rational and had access to all possible choices in making a decision *and* to the consequences of those decisions, they would make the same decision. The best course of action would be readily apparent.

However, decision making is not a completely rational process. Decision makers are limited in their capabilities to know all possible choices and their consequences, much as our clients are limited in their knowledge of all the possible consequences of their actions. The range of real alternatives is limited, and decision makers attempt to be as rational as possible within those boundaries. Some decisions are smart choices for the organization or the client, and other decisions have negative consequences that simply could not be foreseen by the decision maker.

When the state legislature passed the Alcohol and Domestic Violence Awareness Act, it assumed that the statewide system of public mental health centers was the logical location for the program. Mental health centers already employed substance abuse workers and had the physical facilities to treat the medical and social aspects of alcohol addiction. Within the boundaries of the legislators' knowledge, this seemed like the right decision. However, they did not anticipate the stigma attached to these mental health centers in rural areas and how that stigma would present an obstacle to participation of persons referred for treatment. Individuals referred to the program were highly resistant to what they had always known as "the old county insane asylum." In addition, in rural areas people knew who was hospitalized and why, so they were embarrassed to go to the county mental health center for treatment. Despite every effort on the part of the mental health center, people either failed to participate in treatment or never even showed up. Legislators could not have anticipated this within the confines of their bounded rationality.

The Organization as the Decision Environment

Decision making within an organization is strongly affected by what Perrow (1979) calls the decision environment. The decision environment includes the demands of the external environment on the agency, professional demands on the decision maker, time constraints surrounding the decision, and the role of the decision in the survival of the organization. Let's return to the state legislators' decision to locate the Alcohol and Domestic Violence Awareness Program in the county mental health system. Executive directors of county mental health agencies had input into the decision to locate the programs within their agencies. Some of those directors were acutely aware of the problems with their agencies' reputations in the community. However, in view of declining numbers of patients and shrinking allocations from county units of government, taking on the program made good financial sense. Payment would be assured through private and public insurance, and the program would be a natural way to work toward improving relationships with the community. The organizational decision-making environment at the time of the decision exerted enough pressure on the county mental health system to prompt the recommendation that the county system house the program.

The Importance of Decision Making to Job Satisfaction

As practitioners, we all know that helping clients to be active participants in making decisions about their lives is crucial to the success of any intervention.

If clients believe they can make good decisions, they begin to believe they also have some control over their environment. This lessens their feelings of power-lessness and despair. The same phenomenon exists within the agency context. Members of the organization are most satisfied with their jobs and more pro-ductive in their work when they feel they have access to decision making as it affects their jobs (Arches, 1991). Agencies that employ a model of joint de-cision making and a broad delegation of decision-making models are more likely to attract and keep satisfied, competent, professional social workers. In return, more satisfied workers deliver more effective services to their clients. In the long run, the organizational context directly affects the agency's clients.

MENTAL HEALTH AND SURVIVING IN THE ORGANIZATION

At this point, you are probably wondering how anyone survives all the com-plexities of life within the social service organization plus the challenges of working with clients. The mental health of the employees of any organiza-tion is a legitimate concern of responsible social service agencies. It seems ironic that agencies express such deep concern for clients and sometimes ignore the welfare of their own employees. The social work profession has been negligent in helping students to address the effects of the organization on conditions of work (Arches, 1991). Identifying those conditions helps the practitioner anticipate and recognize when bureaucratic elements, rather than client demands, are responsible for pressures within the agency. Knowing the source of the stress can help us address it.

THE PRACTITIONER'S VIEW

In this chapter, we have seen how elements of the social service agency's in-ternal environment shape the context in which the social worker translates policy (such as the Alcohol and Domestic Violence Awareness Act) into ser-vices to clients (an education, awareness, and treatment program housed at DCMHC). Figure 2.3 illustrates elements the practitioner must consider, in-cluding the goals of the agency and the specific program, the technology sanc-tioned by the agency, the amount of authority and power granted to the worker, and the factors influencing the decision-making environment. All of these elements affect what and how much workers can do as professional helpers.

SUMMARY

This chapter explores the internal environment, the first of two important contexts in which the social service agency must operate in order to turn social

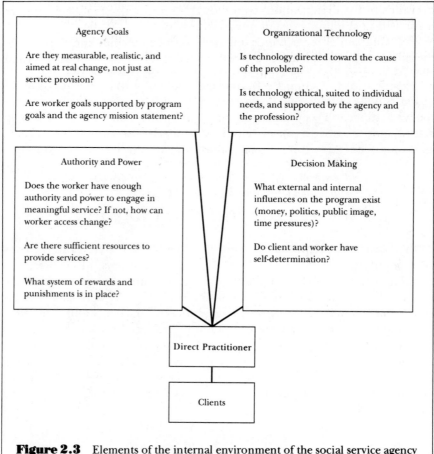

Figure 2.3 Elements of the internal environment of the social service agency from the worker's perspective.

welfare policy into services to clients. Whether you operate in a primary or secondary setting, you will be challenged by the difficulty of articulating goals for your work and the inevitability of either goal conflict or goal displacement. Much of our difficulty with identifying goals reflects on the esoteric nature of social work technology. How do we quantify services to clients and measure our success?

Although social workers are theoretically autonomous professionals, in the organizational setting all workers are subject to several kinds of authority and control. Access to rewards, finances, and other resources determines who will have power over whom in the organizational setting. Those in positions of power are also those who will have responsibility for making most decisions in the organization, even though we recognize that decisions are made within the limits of bounded rationality.

Chapter Three expands our perspective to include the elements in the external environment of the social service agency. Like their workers and clients, agencies operate within a greater context.

DISCUSSION QUESTIONS

1. *What is the difference between a primary and a secondary social work setting? How does social work's professional role differ in these two settings?*
2. *Why is social work devalued in some secondary settings?*
3. *Define goal displacement. How can an agency develop a problem with goal displacement?*
4. *What constitutes social work technology? Give examples of specific technological approaches the social work professionals use and examples of vague technology.*
5. *Give examples of vertical and horizontal authority. How do they differ in their effect on the social work practitioner?*
6. *What is meant by bounded rationality? Discuss how clients also operate within bounded rationality when they are trying to decide what to do to solve their problems.*

SUGGESTED PROJECTS

1. Contact a local social service agency in your community, and ask to see their mission and other goals statements. Are these goals statements specific enough to allow achievement of goals to be measured? Find out how the agency measures these goals.
2. Interview social workers who work in secondary social work settings. What kinds of problems have they had with the dominant profession in those agencies? How have they coped with the four issues identified in the first part of this chapter?
3. Compare a goal statement from a local business or industry with a goal statement from a social service agency. How are they different? How are they the same?
4. Interview a social worker from a local community service agency regarding the use of power in his or her agency. Compare the official organizational chart with the real distribution of power in the agency. How do they differ? What is the source of power of those in official positions of authority?

IMPORTANT TERMS AND CONCEPTS

authority ✓
bounded rationality
eclectic profession
external environment
goal displacement ✓
horizontal power ✓
internal environment
involuntary clients ✓
mission statement ✓

organizational technology
output goals ✓
power ✓
primary social work setting ✓
program goals ✓
secondary social work ✓
   setting
self-determination
vertical authority ✓

The External Environment of Social Service Agencies

We can best understand a particular organization, if that is our interest, if we understand the network it has to play in.

—CHARLES PERROW, 1979, p. 225

ocial service agencies exist in a network (Perrow, 1979). This network is a complex array of social, political, and economic influences that constrain or enable agency functioning. Much of what an agency can or cannot do depends on the environment in which it functions. For example, community attitudes and funding sources determine whether an abortion clinic survives in a small city. The availability of professional staff determines whether an alcohol and drug rehabilitation center locates in a rural community. The ability of a low-income neighborhood association to meet rigid, expensive standards for handicapped accessibility determines whether a federally subsidized day care center is built in that area. Attitudes, resources, and government regulations are all part of an agency's external environment. These elements, combined with the internal elements of the social service agency, can result in the implementation of a social welfare policy that only vaguely resembles the original intent of the policy legislation.

This chapter discusses the agency network or external environment, which consists of all the elements *outside* the agency's immediate organizational environment that influence the type of service the agency provides and the characteristics of clients and agency staff (see Figure 3.1).

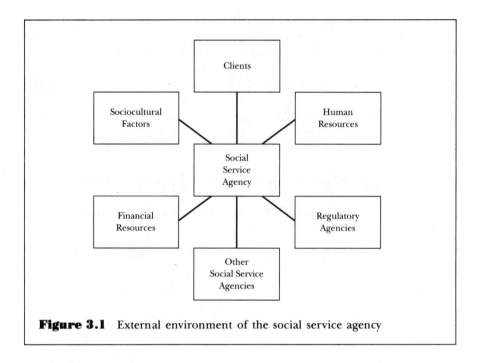

Figure 3.1 External environment of the social service agency

Specifically, this chapter discusses the following:

+ Elements of the social service agency's external environment
+ How access to and competition for clients determines the types and quality of programs agencies offer
+ How the availability of human resources and the public's perception of the agency affect the agency's effectiveness in carrying out social welfare policy
+ The influence of the agency's financial and economic environment on its ability to meet mandated social welfare policies and develop nonmandated services
+ The roles government and regulatory bodies play in restricting an agency from implementing policy
+ The importance of interorganizational relationships to an agency's ability to deliver social services and to survive
+ The influence of the sociocultural environment on the agency's translation of policy into programs

This chapter continues the discussion of the Davis County Mental Health Center begun in Chapter Two, shifting the perspective from that agency's internal environment to its external environment. Most residents of Walton are employed by a local lumber company or by small businesses that serve the entire county. The rest of the county's residents own small farms or drive to Walton for work. Davis County residents are a good example of **the working poor,** people who hold full-time jobs but who work at such low wages that they rarely earn much above the poverty line (Levitan & Shapiro, 1987). Davis County residents and elected officials take a dim view of public assistance recipients. People who receive aid from AFDC or from other public assistance programs often find themselves socially isolated and scorned.

Immediately after the Alcohol and Domestic Violence Awareness Act became law, Community Rehabilitation, a private for-profit counseling service, expanded into rural areas of the state in anticipation of the need for additional alcohol counseling services. Community Rehabilitation is owned by an out-of-state company.

Let's examine how the elements of the external environments of Community Rehabilitation and Davis County Mental Health Center affect how policy is implemented within the agencies and the effect those factors have on social workers' ability to provide services to clients.

THE POTENTIAL CLIENT POPULATION

Much as business relies on raw materials to produce products and on retailers and wholesalers to purchase those products, social service agencies rely on a supply of potential clients to turn a policy into a program. In this case, the policy has created a new group of potential clients that did not exist before the legislation passed. Passage of the new law does not guarantee that clients will be referred for or provided the service. For example, the state may mandate alcohol treatment services under the Alcohol and Domestic Violence Awareness Act, but if the referral agents who investigate a case of domestic violence do not cite alcohol as a factor in the domestic violence incident, no clients are referred to the program. Although domestic violence occurs throughout all socioeconomic strata, low-income and minority individuals are more likely to be referred for prosecution or treatment. These are also the clients most likely to be served by DCMHC as the public agency.

The opposite may occur as well. If police officers and other human service workers in the community have been frustrated by the amount of domestic violence and their inability to do anything concrete to stop it, they might refer every case of domestic violence for treatment even if the role of alcohol in the incident is in question. In that case, the supply of clients may far exceed the services available to meet their needs. In reality, the social welfare policy may require a level of services that cannot possibly be provided without a significant expansion of the service delivery system.

Before the arrival of Community Rehabilitation, DCMHC as the sole provider and public agency had no competition for clients referred for evaluation and treatment of substance abuse problems in Davis County. All clients referred for evaluation were forced to seek services from DCMHC, regardless of their socioeconomic status or the kind and quality of their private health insurance coverage. However, with Community Rehabilitation now operating in Walton, we might expect some competition between the two agencies. Like businesses, social service agencies compete for clients. If several agencies provide the same necessary service, each agency will actively seek clients by soliciting referrals or by advertising.

Referrals

In the past, social service agencies have relied on referrals from other agencies within the community or on "word of mouth" about the agency. In Davis County, referral sources for mandated services under the Alcohol and Domestic Violence Awareness Act include arresting police officers, workers from the county department of social services, private physicians, and even workers at the local child welfare agency. Brian, the social worker, no doubt has developed professional connections in each of these sources, so it is likely that the referring agent will refer an individual directly to Brian at DCMHC. In this respect, DCMHC has a distinct advantage in its competition for clients. However, it has the disadvantage of also being the public service provider in the community; therefore, it is subject to stereotypes about service that may or may not be true. In small towns, everyone seems to know everyone else's business, and clients may be resistant to receiving services from someone they know as well as Brian. Anonymity is a precious commodity in a small community.

Community Rehabilitation may not have built up referral sources in the community to the extent Brian has. They may find police officers, county social workers, and physicians hesitant to refer clients to them when so little is known about the agency. On the other hand, they may find that people who are resistant to receiving services from DCMHC are more willing to receive services from a private agency, even without knowing the quality of its services. Individuals with comprehensive benefits from private health insurance may seek services from Community Rehabilitation primarily because they feel they will receive higher quality service from a private agency.

Hence, the situation for competition for clients emerges. If clients seek services based on their perception that private agencies are better and in line with their private insurance coverage, it is likely that those who can afford private services will receive them. Those who cannot (the working poor and public assistance recipients) will be forced to use the services at DCMHC. Although there is no evidence of qualitative differences between alcohol services in the public and the private sectors, low-income families sometimes believe they receive substandard services from a public agency.

Advertising

With the advent of private for-profit agencies, referrals may not be sufficient, especially if the agency is new to the community. In many communities, advertising for social service clients has increased. The cost of advertising is included in the cost of services in for-profit agencies. Therefore, in many ways, advertising increases the price of the service. Advertisements in the local newspaper, posters, and mailings to both prospective clients and referral agents can effectively increase the awareness of the availability of a service in a community. Community Rehabilitation need not be in Walton long before it discovers the stereotypes the community holds about DCMHC and, through its advertisements, appeals to those perceptions. One need only look through professional practice journals such as *Social Work* to see advertisements like the ad shown in Figure 3.2. Like commercial product advertising, this advertisement is intended to appeal to the reader on both professional and personal levels in the interest of generating referrals.

Public agencies like DCMHC are far less likely to engage in an aggressive advertising campaign to secure clients. Most public agencies have as many clients as they can effectively serve already and need not recruit clients. The type of advertising in which public agencies are more likely to engage centers around public information campaigns designed to inform the public that a service exists, not to entice them to choose one service over another. These public information advertisements are most likely to take the form of public service announcements, which are discussed in another chapter.

Thus, clients are the first element in the external environment of the social service agency. Clients' perceptions of the agency, how clients are referred to the agency, and the real or potential demand for service have a strong effect on the agency's implementation of a social welfare policy. Policies like the Alcohol and Domestic Violence Awareness Act frequently create a client population where none existed before. However, service will not be provided to those clients unless adequate professional staff are available.

HUMAN RESOURCES

A second element in the external environment of the social service agency that affects how social welfare policy is carried out is the availability of **human resources,** staff who provide the services to clients. First-rate, professional staff can improve the quality of services provided and eliminate some of the hostility in the organizational environment. If community members perceive agency staff as competent and professional, the agency is more likely to be seen as providing a worthwhile service in the community, and hostility toward the agency is reduced. If potential clients feel agency staff can help them, they are more likely to seek services without coercion and to commit themselves to being active participants in the change effort.

Individuals drawn to the social services field are motivated by their desire to help people and by their interest in a work setting that allows some level of independent functioning. Social workers' commitment to their profession, rather than to the organization, makes them different from employees

Some children need help to overcome life's transitions.

To emotionally disturbed children and adolescents, life is confusing and frightening. Their true potential is often hidden under rage, withdrawal and even chemical abuse. That's why young people need an environment designed exclusively to respond to their young needs.

At Cedar Crest, we offer quality residential care for children and adolescents nationwide. Through specialized programming we serve as an emotional bridge back to a productive, healthy lifestyle for kids ages 4-17. Our multi-disciplinary team works with residents and their families through programs for dual diagnosis, young latency, and adolescent males and females. We also offer special issue groups for sexual and physical abuse, adoption, and step-family adjustments.

Our timely admissions format makes the referral process easy on patients and professionals. We offer a 48 hour approval or denial turnaround time that expedites discharge planning while focusing on clinical appropriateness.

See how we're helping young people across America. Call 1-800-888-4071 for a **free video** that can also be viewed by your clients.

Cedar Crest
Residential Treatment Center
1-800-888-4071

Figure 3.2 Advertisement for a for-profit social service agency
SOURCE: Reprinted by permission of HCA Cedar Crest Residential Treatment Center.

of traditional business organizations (Mason, 1984) in much the same way that business and social service agencies differ. Therefore, efforts to recruit and retain human resources needed to provide social services are more likely to emphasize the opportunities to meet interests rather than simply to offer lucrative salaries.

In planning for implementation of the Alcohol and Domestic Violence Awareness Act, agency administrators must assess many factors. First,

---

WANTED:
Highly motivated self-starter with BSW and extensive experience in alcohol rehabilitation to develop and provide treatment services to alcohol-involved perpetrators of domestic violence. Must have personal familiarity with Davis County, its people, resources, and sociocultural environment. Willing to work long hours for modest salary in hostile organizational environment with clients who resist social intervention in their personal lives. Despite prejudiced environment and lack of social support, minorities are encouraged to apply. Sense of humor imperative. Contact Davis County Mental Health Center.

Figure 3.3   Fictitious job advertisement for a social worker, listing realistic working conditions.

---

they must find the balance between anticipated demand for services under the new law and the availability of staff to provide those services. Is 300 new cases of alcohol evaluation and assessment too large a number, or can existing resources provide these services? If the number of current staff is too small, what limitations or opportunities affect hiring new staff members? Figure 3.3 is a sample job advertisement that reflects realistic working conditions.

In an ideal world, agencies would hire only workers who have the most extensive experience and the best credentials suited for the job to be done. However, despite an agency's best intentions, staff rarely meet that ideal. Legislative mandates, availability of professional staff in the community, labor union requirements, and the agency's reputation influence the composition of agency staff.

Legislative Mandates

New social welfare policies usually imply that present staff will have to be supplemented in order to turn a policy into a program of services. The process of hiring necessary staff may be subject to two legislative mandates: procedures for ensuring nondiscrimination in hiring and minimum qualification requirements.

Nondiscrimination. Since the mid-1960s, strong legislative efforts have counteracted the forces of discrimination against women and minorities. The Equal Pay Act of 1963 and Title VII of the Civil Rights Act of 1964 were passed to prevent discrimination on the basis of gender and race, respectively. In 1968, Executive Order 11246 (later revised as Executive Order 11375) moved beyond simple prohibition of discrimination to what has become known as **affirmative action.** Affirmative action is an active effort on the part of an organization to address existing inequities in racial and gender composition of an agency staff. Affirmative action plans are required of all organizations that have federal sources of funds, including all public and most private non-profit social service agencies. Plans must identify the steps an agency will take to give preferential treatment to the hiring of women and minorities. The philosophy of affirmative action is that short-term discrimination against white males is justified to correct the underrepresentation of women and minorities in organizations (Weinbach, 1990, p. 102).

In the example of Walton and the DCMHC, state funds pay for mandated services under the Alcohol and Domestic Violence Awareness Act, so hiring decisions are subject to the state requirements for affirmative action. These requirements and the amount of effort DCMHC must show to satisfy them have serious implications. Finding qualified women for social service positions is rarely difficult because women dominate direct service positions in the profession. However, finding qualified minority professionals who are willing to practice outside an urban area or one in which their own ethnic group resides can be very difficult.

Staff Qualifications. If the Alcohol and Domestic Violence Awareness Act requires staff providing services under the legislation to be certified Alcohol and Other Drug Abuse (AODA) counselors, the policy has dictated the qualifications of the staff. Even the most experienced social workers cannot be hired unless they meet the minimum requirements for AODA certification.

Theoretically, few agency directors would object to stringent staff qualifications in an area as specialized as AODA. Even fewer directors would have trouble recognizing the importance of providing special employment opportunities for women and minorities. However, the well-meaning stipulations of affirmative action and the qualifications portion of the enabling legislation can place agencies such as DCMHC, or even Community Rehabilitation, in a difficult position if they cannot find applicants who possess these qualifications.

Availability of Staff

Walton is a small rural area that most likely has few qualified, competent social workers like Brian. Lower salaries, the isolation of rural areas, limited opportunities for job advancement, and personal preference can make attracting qualified staff to rural areas extremely difficult. Rural communities may have to make a substantial financial commitment to attract qualified professionals.

Recruiting staff can also present a problem for Community Rehabilitation. If they bring their own staff with them when they locate in Walton, staffing might not be a problem. If they rely on local recruiting efforts, they will find they are in competition with DCMHC for staff as well as for clients. Because private for-profit agencies traditionally are able to pay higher salaries, they may skim off the professional talent in the community as well. If they are simply unable to find qualified staff to provide the services, Community Rehabilitation may be forced to terminate service delivery and leave Walton. Therefore, the quality and availability of a service is directly related to the availability of staff within the community.

Unionization of Professional Staff

Unionization of the professional staff is another component of the social service agency's human resources environment. Many social workers in public, government agencies are members of organized labor unions such as the American Federation of State, County and Municipal Employees (AFSCME). The union may require that new positions be filled on the basis of seniority of existing employees or on the basis of written examinations, creating additional obstacles to securing staff. Union requirements may limit the agency's discretion in hiring the employee who most closely meets the job requirements.

The Agency's Reputation

The agency's philosophy of operation affects the way it operates and the nature and quality of services it provides to clients. Likewise, an agency's reputation affects the kind of staff who will be interested in working there. According to Mason (1984), "free spirits," those who seek flexibility, innovation, and creativity, abound in nonprofits but may not survive well in either the private for-profit or government sector. For example, Brian is a lifelong resident of Walton. He has deep roots in the community and is strongly committed to improving life for the residents of Davis County. He might be frustrated by some aspects of working in a public agency, such as extensive paperwork, cumbersome rules and regulations, and a conservative county board, but working for DCMHC is his professional choice. He may enjoy the security of civil service employment and have little interest in seeking major changes in the public system.

Other social workers, however, avoid social work practice in the public sector because the cumbersome bureaucracy and rigid system discourage them. They are more likely to be drawn to the private nonprofit sector. Less estrangement from management, more flexible benefits, and room for creativity are more important to these workers than the security the public system offers. Still other social workers avoid both the public and private nonprofit sectors for the private for-profit sector, which might offer the highest salary.

The trend toward moving away from public sector social work practice to the private sector is a continuing concern of the profession (Abramovitz, 1986; Lewis, 1988; Stoecz, 1988). In many respects, this trend is synonymous with moving away from the profession's original commitment to working with the poor toward an increasingly middle-class focus. Whether those who continue in the public sector are more committed to working with low-income people than those who choose to seek employment in the private sector is not clear, but level of commitment may be a factor in determining the character of the social service staff in an agency.

The elements of human resources, legislative mandates for staff, unions, and the agency's reputation are either opportunities or obstacles in securing the staff necessary to turn a social welfare policy into social service programs.

THE AGENCY'S ECONOMIC AND FINANCIAL ENVIRONMENT

The agency's external economic or financial environment is probably the most familiar element of the external environment to the novice social worker. Social work practitioners are acutely aware of the way the availability of funds for services directly affects their ability to provide services to their clients.

Securing sufficient financial resources to survive occupies much of an agency's effort and time. Administrators of agencies must be sensitive to the national and local economy and their effect on the amount of money available through taxes and voluntary giving for human services. Agency administrators must follow proposed legislation relevant to their agency's domain and monitor budget allocations once legislation becomes law. Finally, they must advocate on behalf of the agency and its clients to secure funds through local fund-raising organizations.

The Local Economy

The economy of the community in which an agency is located is a powerful influence on the agency's operation. For public agencies relying on tax dollars, there is a direct connection between the taxes collected and the budget for the coming year. In a thriving local economy, businesses pay taxes and create jobs so others also work and pay taxes. Revenues available for human services are more abundant in such communities than in those in which businesses are not thriving and unemployment rates are high.

The health of the local economy also determines voluntary giving through organizations such as United Way. When individuals are unsure about their own financial situations and fearful of their employment security, they are less likely to contribute to charitable causes. When unemployment rates are high, United Way has less access to planned giving campaigns organized through employers, and people have less extra money. In Walton, the health of the local lumber company and small businesses will directly affect tax revenues and charitable giving.

The state of the local economy will in many ways increase or decrease the demand for services from public and private agencies in Walton. Alcohol consumption and domestic violence are often related to the condition of the local economy. When individuals are working and can support their families, they are less likely than the unemployed to drink for relief from depression and frustration. We can assume that less relief drinking results in at least some decrease in the amount of domestic violence, which is also a symptom of depression and frustration. That is why low-income areas often have a combination of both alcohol abuse and domestic violence problems. Ironically, communities with the greatest need often have the smallest amount of resources available for services.

Budget Allocations

A budget allocation is the amount of money allocated for developing and implementing the proposed social welfare policy. In the case of the Alcohol and Domestic Violence Awareness Act, let's assume that the budget provisions of the act are twofold. First, a set amount is allocated to all public mental health agencies, such as DCMHC, to cover the cost of services for individuals in public medical insurance programs (such as Medicaid or Medicare) or for those who do not have private insurance. Medical Assistance and Medicare do not pay for the alcohol dependency evaluation. In other words, DCMHC has a set amount of funds available to implement the program based on a projection of the demand for services during the program's first year. If the demand for service exceeds the amount available, DCMHC can either petition the state for more money or reallocate its funds internally from other programs.

Second, the state provides a portion of the cost of the service for individuals who seek services outside the public sector from agencies such as Community Rehabilitation or the private child welfare agency in Walton. These agencies, however, must bill the private insurance carrier for the remainder of the cost of service. Private insurance companies may determine how much they will contribute to the cost of the service. This will work out nicely as long as the demand for service does not exceed the amount of money allocated for it.

The budget allocation for a specific social welfare program, however, is only a small part of the social service agency's economic environment. In the interest of survival, most social service agencies do not rely exclusively on a single source of financial support even for mandated programs.

Diversification of Resources

Relying on a single source of income for all agency activities is a dangerous practice for social service agencies, particularly private nonprofit and for-profit agencies. Rarely does traditional business rely on the income from a single product for survival. Most businesses, and more recently social service agencies as well, rely on a **diversification of resources.** That is, organizations seek income from several sources to minimize the damage should one of the sources no longer be available to an agency. Diversification of resources not only minimizes financial risks but can help the agency develop a wider range of constituencies in the community, earn community goodwill, and reinforce the agency's identity in the community (Kramer, 1981).

DCMHC relies on its fiscal allocation from both state and county units of government. Because it is a public agency, it is prohibited from seeking income from sources other than tax revenues. This constraint is unique to the public sector. If the funds allocated to the Alcohol and Domestic Violence Program are not sufficient to provide the amount of service demanded, DCMHC is restricted to operating at a loss, refusing potential clients service, or petitioning the state for additional resources. The inability to diversify resources limits DCMHC's funding possibilities and may put their clients in a precarious position.

Private agencies have access to more sources of funds, but their funding sources may be less predictable than tax revenues. Private agencies may seek resources from purchase of service contracts, fees for service, insurance coverage of clients, allocations from community fund-raising groups such as United Way, intra-agency proprietary units, agency fund-raising activities, contributions, and memberships. The broader the base of funds for agency operation, the less likely it is for an agency to dissolve when one of the funding sources disappears. Private for-profit agencies may likewise secure purchase of service contracts, use fees for service, and insurance payments. For-profit agencies are not eligible for community funds provided through United Way. Table 3.1 is an example of how the child welfare agency in Walton diversifies its resources.

Local Fund-Raising.   Private nonprofit agencies, such as the child welfare agency in Walton, may actively engage in fund-raising in addition to receiving fees for service or government grants. These efforts can take several forms; the most common include engaging in a separate fund-raising campaign or seeking funds from the local United Way.

Due to declining government resources for social services, private nonprofit agencies have had to resort to more fund-raising than ever before. According to Kramer (1981), fund-raising is the number-one activity of volunteers in nonprofit agencies and has become so institutionalized that at times it displaces the service goals of the agency. If a private agency launches a fund-raising campaign, it is likely to consume almost as much in staff and agency resources as it generates (Mason, 1984). When the local economy is weak, citizens are not likely to make significant contributions.

TABLE 3.1

Example of Diversification of
Resources for a Nonprofit Social Service Agency

SOURCES OF INCOME FOR CHILD WELFARE OF DAVIS COUNTY

SOURCE	AMOUNT
United Way of Davis County	$100,000
Davis County Purchase of Service Contracts	150,000
Alcohol and Domestic Violence Awareness Program ($50,000)	
Treatment Foster Care ($25,000)	
Teen Parent Program ($75,000)	
Fees for Service	25,000
Private pay ($6,250)	
Private insurance ($6,250)	
Medical Assistance ($12,500)	
Membership Drive	5,000
Foundation Grant	10,000
Charitable Contributions by Individuals	5,000
Children's Walk-a-Thon	5,000
TOTAL AGENCY INCOME	$300,000

The United Way, like other **federated fund-raising organizations,** was developed to consolidate the fund-raising efforts of a large number of community agencies. United Way organizes and executes a fund-raising campaign for a specified list of member agencies. Member agencies receive an allocation of the funds raised. The allocation is based on the priorities United Way has identified. In theory, consolidating fund-raising minimizes the number of independent fund-raising campaigns that take place in a community and promotes more efficient fund-raising.

Redistribution of Funds.   It is not uncommon for public and private agencies to use excess funds from one program to subsidize another; this is another way to diversify resources. For example, let's say Community Rehabilitation has recently secured a purchase of service contract with the local lumber company to provide occupational social work services to employees of that company. If providing those counseling services does not cost as much as Community Rehabilitation is being paid by the lumber company, Community Rehabilitation's management may decide to use the extra funds to subsidize the cost of providing services under the Alcohol and Domestic Violence Awareness Act. Neither the occupational social work services nor the alcohol assessment program may be profitable for the agency, but they are not losing money. This is a concession Community Rehabilitation may be willing to make as it develops its own niche in the community.

An internal redistribution of funds offers both for-profit and private nonprofit agencies a degree of flexibility unavailable to the public sector. The drawback, however, is that they cannot petition the state for additional funds should they begin to operate in debt.

INTERORGANIZATIONAL RELATIONSHIPS

Walton's agencies have been discussed as though they are in competition with each other. However, the scarcity of resources allocated to services under the Alcohol and Domestic Violence Awareness Act may require that DCMHC, the child welfare agency, and Community Rehabilitation find ways to work together. Agencies coordinate their activities in the best interest of all involved through **interorganizational relationships.**

Conditions for Interorganizational Cooperation

Neugeboren (1985) and Reid (1965) cite the following four conditions necessary for organizations to coordinate their efforts successfully to maximize the amount of service and minimize duplication of services:

1. *Voluntary participation.* Agencies in a community must want to work together and feel that working together is in each of their best interests. If the state forces DCMHC, the child welfare agency, and Community Rehabilitation to forge a cooperative agreement against their wishes, coordination will be difficult, if not impossible.

2. *Agency autonomy.* All agencies involved in interorganizational agreements must believe that they will be allowed the autonomy to provide services consistent with their operating policies and philosophy. Public agencies are accountable to units of government and may be required to keep detailed records to justify expenditures. The private child welfare agency may be most interested in families with children and less interested in childless couples, an attitude consistent with the agency's goals. Community Rehabilitation may resent interference in the setting of rates for services, consistent with its profit motive.

3. *Shared goals.* Neugeboren (1985) and Reid (1965) contend that interorganizational cooperation is possible only when cooperating agencies have similar goals so the possibility of conflict is minimized. The public and private sectors have different goals. DCMHC, a public agency, exists to meet the public mandate for services to people in the community. Community Rehabilitation may have service goals as well, but the profit motive will direct the quality and quantity of services it provides.

4. *Complementary resources.* The term *complementary resources* refers to an exchange of resources among agencies that agencies perceive

to be to their mutual benefit. Interorganizational cooperation is doomed to failure if one agency perceives the arrangement as more beneficial to other agencies than to themselves.

Developing Coalitions

At first glance, the preceding conditions may seem impossible to meet. The agencies might be too different to cooperate in the case of the Alcohol and Domestic Violence Awareness Act. Competition for clients is not necessarily negative, but agencies must anticipate competition and design strategies for getting the number of clients they want. As already suggested, DCMHC may be perfectly content to have Community Rehabilitation provide as much of the alcohol assessment services as possible, freeing up their own staff to provide other mental health services. Or all three agencies may decide that the limited budget allocation can be most effectively used if they develop a coalition. A **coalition** of agencies is a relatively short-term agreement between agencies to work together on specific issues. In forming a coalition, agencies neither give up their specified domains nor trade their services to another agency (Reisch, 1990). They simply agree among themselves how they will divide the responsibilities of handling a specific social problem, such as alcohol assessment mandated under the Alcohol and Domestic Violence Awareness Act.

Let's see how this might work. Agency executives meet and decide that DCMHC is best suited to handle low-income and elderly clients referred for evaluation because it is a public agency with access to state funds designated specifically for that population. The child welfare agency might agree to provide services to both low-income and middle-income families with children, specifically domestic violence cases that involve child abuse or neglect. This client population is consistent with the agency's mission to serve families with children from all economic groups. They can secure funds to provide services by billing private or public insurance and the state for the service subsidy. Community Rehabilitation might agree to serve childless couples or individuals with comprehensive private health insurance. Private insurance and the state subsidy will provide the funds for service in the agency. In this case, each agency agrees to focus its efforts on the client population most consistent with its goals and domain.

This arrangement is a three-tier approach to providing services. The quality of service among the three agencies may differ under this arrangement, and clients are denied the opportunity to select services. The quality of services at all three facilities might decline without competition among themselves, or all three agencies might focus their energies on providing service rather than on competing for clients. Competition in social services can encourage agencies to provide high-quality service at a reasonable cost. However, scrambling for clients and resources can also consume energy better spent providing services.

Every social service agency is involved in interorganizational relation-ships in the process of turning social welfare policies into social service programs. Having limited resources to devote to any social problem requires agencies to work together even when they do not meet the four conditions essential for successful coordination. In other instances, conflicting goals, a fear of losing agency autonomy, and an inequitable distribution of resources make interorganizational cooperation impossible.

RELATIONSHIPS WITH REGULATORY AGENCIES

The fifth element in the external environment of the social service agency is relationships with regulatory agencies. Regulatory agencies are government organizations that influence the methods by which policy is implemented. The implementation of social welfare policy by both public and private agen-cies, for-profit and nonprofit, is affected by a complex array of procedural requirements known as **administrative regulations.** The administrative rule-making process requires almost as many compromises as the policy-making process. Shifting the focus on policy from the political sphere to the agency sphere clarifies why this is so.

The Delegation Doctrine

Federal and state legislative bodies provide only general guidelines for social policy. Few pieces of social policy would ever become law if legislative bodies were forced to identify all the conditions necessary for the implementation of the policy. Therefore, both federal and state legislatures operate under the **delegation doctrine**. The delegation doctrine allows laws to be only broad frameworks of intended policies. Formulation of the specific rules and pro-cedures for implementing the program is delegated to administrative agen-cies. On the federal level, this administrative agency is the Department of Health and Human Services (DHHS). On the state level, administrative ac-tivities are delegated to the state equivalent of DHHS or in some states to a department of administration.

Prospective and Retrospective Rule Making

Administrative rule making is intended to be prospective; that is, it guides future agency action regarding a policy's relationship to clients (Helms, Henkin, & Singleton, 1989). Most state administrative agencies use expert staff to identify a tentative set of rules and regulations and then seek public input from hearings and written communications from agencies, clients, and service providers. The preliminary rules are then modified before they are officially adopted.

At times, a state regulatory agency may create policy by adjudication. Adjudication creates policy by the accumulation of legal or administrative precedents that guide future action. The local, state, and federal court systems are the most obvious examples of adjudicative organizations. The specific rules and regulations for implementation of the Alcohol and Domestic Violence Awareness Act are set by the state's Department of Health and Social Services. These rules authorize police officers, social workers, teachers, and other referral agents to require offenders to seek evaluation and treatment at one of the community service agencies. The rules require that individuals be informed of their rights to choose an agency at which to receive the treatment and to be informed of all agency findings and recommendations. These administrative rules allow for voluntary cooperation in seeking evaluation and provide referral agencies with support from local police and DCMHC in seeking services for involuntary clients. These administrative rules are prospective—they anticipate how programs will be implemented and furnish guidelines to the agencies providing the services.

However, if clients claim that administrative rules have been violated, the state Department of Health and Social Services may function as an adjudicatory agency. The state DHSS will have to judge the appropriateness of an agency's or client's activities against the standards of administrative rules. For example, if Brian at DCMHC fails to inform a client of his or her right to seek services at Community Rehabilitation if he or she can afford it, the client may seek an **administrative hearing** at which he or she may redress this grievance. An administrative hearing is a meeting between a representative of the regulatory agency and the client or agency, at which the area of disagreement is discussed. An administrative hearing is not a court hearing but an opportunity for a client or agency to settle differences without formal legal action. The decisions reached at an administrative hearing are legally binding but may be reviewed in a court of law.

Box 3.1 is an excerpt from the program brochure for Medical Assistance in the state of Wisconsin. It is typical of the state's efforts to recognize the client's right to appeal the decision regarding program benefits through the process of an administrative hearing.

DCMHC is an arm of the state Department of Health and Social Services, although it must abide by the administrative rules and regulations established by the agency. Community Rehabilitation and the child welfare agency must observe the rules and regulations of the state agency when working with clients referred under the provisions of the Alcohol and Domestic Violence Awareness Act because the state agency is paying for part of those services. They must also observe the rules and regulations of any private health insurance company providing payment for services. If agencies fail to observe the rules, payment for services can stop, putting the agency out of business.

Administrative rules frequently conflict with the agency's policies and procedures or the values and ethics of the social work profession. The requirements of the Alcohol and Domestic Violence Awareness Act are a good example. The social work profession places a high value on client self-determination, the right of clients to make choices about the course of their lives and any intervention by a social service agency. Evaluation and

BOX 3.1

Example of Client's Right to Appeal

You may appeal to the state Department of Health and Social Services for a Fair Hearing if you believe your application for Medical Assistance was unfairly denied, or was not acted upon promptly, or if you believe your benefits are unfairly discontinued, terminated, suspended, or reduced.

You may request a Fair Hearing if a Prior Authorization request is denied.

Appeal for a Fair Hearing should be made to your local county or tribal social or human services department. If you file an appeal of a discontinuation, termination, suspension, or reduction of benefits prior to the effective date of the action, coverage will be continued pending the hearing decision. The appeal should include the pertinent facts of the matter and your Medical Assistance identification number.

An appeal must be made no later than 45 days after the date of the action being appealed. The hearing will be held in the county where you live.

SOURCE: State of Wisconsin Department of Health and Social Services. (January, 1991). *The Wisconsin Medical Assistance (Medicaid) Program: Eligibility and Benefits* (pp. 17–18).

---

assessment under the Alcohol and Domestic Violence Awareness Act is mandatory. Abusive treatment of oneself or others is not condoned under the principle of client self-determination, but what happens after alcohol is determined to be the precipitating cause of domestic violence in a family? If a person does not want treatment and no criminal charges are filed by the adult victim of the abuse, can social service agencies, or even the state, require persons identified as having an alcohol problem to seek treatment? Can a state law require a professional to treat individuals against their will?

Regulatory agencies serve an important function in providing the parameters within which an agency turns a policy into services to clients. Yet social service agencies are often faced with ethical dilemmas created when laws and regulations come into conflict with professional ethics or with the reality of working with uncooperative clients.

THE SOCIOCULTURAL ENVIRONMENT

The ethnic, economic, social, and cultural characteristics of the community in which an agency is located comprise the sociocultural environment. The survival of an agency is contingent on the agency's ability to understand that environment and to maximize the opportunities presented by that environment. An appreciation for the sociocultural environment is at the heart of social work's person-in-environment perspective. People are the product of, and active participants in, the world around them.

Three aspects of the sociocultural environment affect not only how policies become programs but also how the agency survives in the community. These aspects are the influence of community values on the goals of the agency, the influence of sociocultural values on the clients who receive services, and the dependency of the agency on the financial and social support of its host community (Hasenfeld & English, 1977).

Community Values and Agency Goals

Brian at DCMHC knows from experience that Davis County residents are fiercely independent, in part due to their heritage, and in part due to their own personal commitment to taking care of their own. Frequent, unregulated underage drinking and excessive recreational use of alcohol, combined with the attitude that "men need to discipline their wives occasionally," has led to the acceptance of domestic violence as a way of life for some residents. Most people mistrust professional busybodies standing in judgment of what they consider to be family business—unless they are receiving public assistance. Many Davis County residents believe that if they accept welfare, the taxpayers have the right to tell them what to do; if they do not accept it, no one has any business telling them how to run their lives. A social atmosphere that condones alcohol use as part of life, attitudes of self-sufficiency and independence, and a resistance to professional intervention in people's lives are all components of the sociocultural atmosphere in Davis County. All these elements must be recognized before services can reach those who need them most.

A strong educational program will be needed to prepare the residents of Davis County for the provisions of the Alcohol and Domestic Violence Awareness Act. Appealing to the qualities of self-reliance and the importance of family are more likely to produce a cooperative client population than the law-enforcement approach. Strong assurances of privacy and confidentiality will have to be made before clients will participate in the service. In many ways, the residents of Davis County will have to reexamine their own sociocultural values to accept the new law. Although agencies in urban areas might succeed using aggressive techniques and requiring clients to receive services, Davis County may have to take a more calculated approach, focusing first on education and then on voluntary evaluation and assessment. In essence, community values will shape the goals of DCMHC, Community Rehabilitation, and the private child welfare agency in implementing the program. The values of the community will limit agency actions (Hasenfeld & English, 1977).

Client Values

Clients are the agency's raw material. A policy may exist, but without clients, it cannot be implemented nor services provided. "An organization's success is tied to its ability to provide client satisfaction—the client is the consumer" (Wallendorf, 1979, p. 116). If DCMHC and Community Rehabilitation are insensitive to Davis County's sociocultural environment and proceed as though the law is the law and it does not matter what the residents think, they are headed for trouble. The clients referred for evaluation and assessment are the products of their environment; their ties to the community cannot be neutralized. The values of self-sufficiency and independence that are characteristic of the community are also characteristic of the individual clients who come for service.

Resource Dependency

If an agency antagonizes the community, it will have difficulty generating clients and resources from the community, and its survival will be difficult, if not impossible. The social service agency needs the funds and patronage of clients in the host community, but the community may not necessarily patronize the agency. In many respects, the agency exists at the will of the host community. The main aim of any organization is survival. Financial support and client participation are crucial to the survival of the social service agency.

THE PRACTITIONER'S VIEW

The elements of the internal and external environments of the social service agency are illustrated in Figure 3.4. These combined elements determine social service agency policy, the way the agency operates on a day-to-day basis. No matter how competent and thorough a practitioner's assessment of the individual client, all decisions made and services offered to the client are contingent on the opportunities and restrictions determined by these elements. Services cannot be offered if potential clients are not aware of their existence or are not referred to the agency that will accept them. Competent and effective services cannot be offered if the agency has insufficient or inadequately trained staff. And if the demand for services exceeds allocated resources, practitioners and the agency cannot serve the clients for which the program was intended.

SUMMARY

The study of social welfare policy and programs involves more than identifying how and where policies are made. It involves understanding the context in which policies are implemented—that is, transformed from general

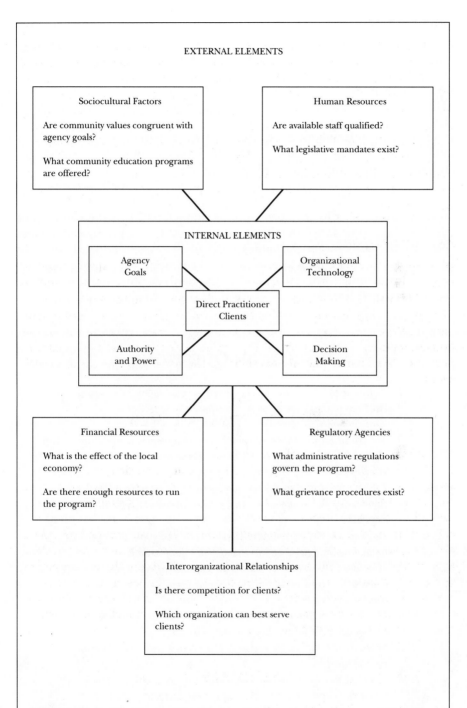

Figure 3.4   The internal and external environments of the social service agency: the worker's perspective

statements of purpose into specific services to clients. That context is the social service agency. With minor exceptions, all social workers will practice within organizational settings, and most of these settings are social service agencies. Agencies exist in complicated systems composed of client and staff, as well as fiscal, governmental, interorganizational, and sociocultural elements. These elements determine an agency's capabilities for the clients it serves. Directly and indirectly, these elements affect what social workers can do for their clients. Understanding the external environment of an agency explains why even the best-intentioned social welfare policy can undergo significant transformation before it is finally carried out.

The variety of services provided by the American social welfare system is described in Chapter Four. As Davis County Mental Health Center is strongly influenced by the sociocultural characteristics of the community, the broad social welfare system in this country is likewise influenced by competing and conflicting social values. Our current system is clearly the product of continuing conflict between our recognition that government has a role in providing for its citizens and this country's philosophical commitment to rugged individualism, as we shall see in Chapter Four.

DISCUSSION QUESTIONS

1. *Define what is meant by the social service agency's external environment. What elements compose the external environment?*
2. *We traditionally think of social service agencies controlling clients. Describe how clients as an element in the external environment exert control over an agency.*
3. *Private for-profit social service agencies frequently advertise their services. To whom do these advertisements typically appeal?*
4. *Do you see any incompatibility between the goals of organized labor and the goals of the social work profession?*
5. *How does the health of the local economy affect the demand for and availability of social services in a community?*
6. *Discuss when interorganizational relationships can benefit an agency and when they are detrimental.*
7. *What is the difference between prospective and retrospective rule making?*
8. *What is meant by the sociocultural environment of a social service agency? Describe the important sociocultural factors in your community.*

SUGGESTED PROJECTS

1. If your state has a policy similar to the Alcohol and Domestic Violence Awareness Act (or a mandatory arrest policy in cases of domestic violence), find out how the program operates. Who refers clients for services? Do public or private agencies provide most services? What external elements in the environment affect how the agency provides services?
2. Collect examples of advertising done by public and private social service agencies in your community. To whom do you think the advertisements are intended to appeal? Are they effective?
3. Interview the executive director or personnel director of a large social service agency in your community. How does the agency recruit workers? What are their affirmative action mandates? What problems do they have in securing qualified staff to provide agency services?
4. Interview the head of United Way in your community. Find out how funds are allocated after they are raised. How is United Way affected by changes in the local or national economy?

IMPORTANT TERMS AND CONCEPTS

administrative hearing ✓
administrative regulations ✓
affirmative action ✓
coalition
delegation doctrine
diversification of resources ✓

federated fund-raising
  organizations
human resources
interorganizational
  relationships
working poor ✓

block grants =

The Current Social Welfare System: A Patchwork of Programs

Criticizing the social services has become so popular an activity in the United States that it sometimes seems a national pastime. As with some other national pastimes, the participants represent a broad spectrum of races, creeds, and ideologies. Among the frequent players are conservative politicians, who use the attacks on services as a way to demonstrate their commitment to traditional values; clients, who speak of the services' failure to meet their needs; social service workers, who are sometimes concerned about the limitations of what they can do to help clients and are often frustrated by their working conditions; and ideologues of all sorts, those who argue that the social services are destructive because they undermine our basic values and those who argue that they are destructive because they support our basic values.

—JEFFREY GALPER, 1975, p. 1

A s Jeffrey Galper points out, no one seems happy with the social welfare system in this country. Perhaps no topic generates a more emotional response from both its critics and its supporters than the welfare system. Much of the hostility toward the current system results from society's ambivalence about government's role in social services. Some citizens feel the government is too involved in people's lives and too expensive; others feel government programs are inadequate to meet even the basic needs of the nation's poor. Some taxpayers insist social welfare programs instill the traditional American values of hard work, strong family life, and independence. Still others remind us that depending on who is criticizing the system, current programs either destroy or preserve basic values.

It is characteristic of a residual form of social welfare to see such services as income maintenance and social services as temporary, a means to help the individual for a short time until the normal mechanisms of the family and the marketplace are once again able to help people meet their needs. This attitude accounts for the emphasis on employment and job training as part of the social welfare system in the United States. If we can help people find jobs and generate their own money, social welfare services can be discontinued. As long as the role of social welfare services is seen as temporary, stigma is attached to the receipt of those services. The stigma stems from the fear that if people become comfortable receiving public welfare services, they might not be motivated to become independent.

The United States moved from the concentration of service delivery in the private sector before the Depression to the public sector's assumption of most service delivery between 1930 and 1970. As this chapter demonstrates, the highly industrialized nature of the American economy suggests that an institutional approach to providing social welfare services would be a more effective, efficient way to meet the needs of citizens. However, the enduring influence of rugged individualism and a continuing resistance to government influence make conversion from a residual to an institutional system highly unlikely in the near future. The United States appears to be moving toward the privatization of its social service system, which means a more residual approach.

Specifically, this chapter includes the following:

+ A comparison of public and private social service agencies, the two largest providers of service in the United States
+ A discussion of the emergence of for-profit social service agencies and their role in contemporary social welfare
+ Characteristics of the American social welfare system that contribute to a fragmented system of social and financial services

PUBLIC AND PRIVATE SOCIAL SERVICE AGENCIES

The United States' residual system of social welfare maintains that the government does not provide all social services; therefore, both public and private agencies exist in this country. Private agencies include both nonprofit and for-profit agencies, which are described in this chapter. The social service providers in the United States are defined in Box 4.1.

BOX 4.1

Social Service Providers in the United States

Social service agencies: Public or private organizations that provide social or financial services to people in need. Public agencies are part of the governmental structure; private agencies are separate from the government and are nonprofit organizations.

Private for-profit social service agencies: Providers of social and health care services that are organized and run as profit-making businesses, usually with a paid board of directors and stockholders who hold a financial interest in the organization.

U.S. Department of Health and Human Services: A federal cabinet department that administers all federal income and public health care programs. The Secretary of Health and Human Services reports directly to the President and the U.S. Congress. The DHHS administers all state departments of social services.

Social Security Administration: The federal government agency that distributes all social insurance benefits. The agency maintains the records of workers' contributions to the social insurance fund and distributes the money to them when they retire, become disabled, or lose a family breadwinner.

County departments of social services: The county-level public welfare agency that provides financial and social services to people living within the county.

Public Agencies

Public social service agencies are primarily local public welfare offices or state- and county-run hospitals and institutions. These agencies are part of state and local government. Instead of a board of directors, elected and appointed state and local officials make the administrative decisions that determine policy within these agencies.

As illustrated in Figure 4.1, the administrative structure of public agencies is complicated. It is not surprising that social workers and clients complain about the cumbersome bureaucracy of public agencies.

The Department of Health and Human Services (DHHS) is a cabinet department directly accountable to the President of the United States. The United States is divided into regional offices of DHHS, each responsible for a different number of states. Each state is accountable to the regional office of DHHS and to the governor and legislature of the state. This is why public agencies are considered a federal-state partnership. Public agencies are funded in part by state money and in part by federal funds. Because both levels of government contribute tax dollars to the operation of public agencies, they both have some input into how the public agency is run.

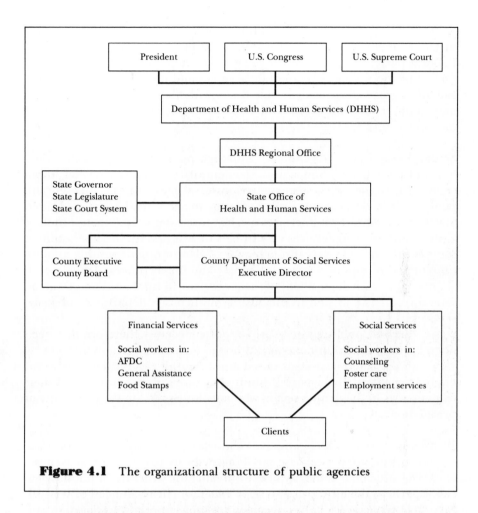

Figure 4.1   The organizational structure of public agencies

Most states divide their counties into regions, much the same way that DHHS divides the country into regions. Each county has its own department of social services headed by an executive director. In public agencies, the real "boss" is the immediate county unit of government and the corresponding office of DHHS.

By law, public agencies are required to provide the following services (Compton, 1980, p. 501):

1. Financial Assistance Programs, which include AFDC, General Assistance (GA), and Refugee Assistance.
2. Medical Assistance, a health insurance program for low-income individuals and families.
3. Social Services, such as counseling and foster care.
4. Child Welfare services, such as protective services, foster care, adoption, and services for pregnant teenagers.

The quality and quantity of these services is affected by the amount of money these agencies receive from local or state units of government. Public agencies are completely dependent on money from the taxpayers for their operation. That is why public agencies and the services they provide can differ greatly from state to state. States with high income taxes may have more funds to devote to social services. Poorer states have less money available for human services.

Strengths of Public Agencies. Although public welfare agencies often have unfavorable reputations in the community, they do have several advantages. First, public welfare agencies are universal, meaning that, theoretically, public social services are available to anyone in need anywhere in the United States. However, receiving services can be more complicated than it sounds. Criteria for receiving services vary from county to county. In some counties, services are available only through court order. In other counties, application for and receipt of services is a simple and timely process. Usually, each county has its own department of social services. In rural and isolated areas, several counties may join to establish a multicounty department of social services.

Second, public agencies are supported by taxes; therefore, they need not rely on voluntary fund-raising. Although the public agency's budget may vary with the amount of taxes raised and the priorities of the county unit of government, public agencies' funds are more stable than those of their counterparts in the private sector, who must often rely on the generosity of private donors.

Weaknesses of Public Agencies. Unfortunately, despite their universality and tax-supported fiscal base, public agencies are plagued with many problems. The size and complexity of the bureaucratic structure of public agencies is perhaps the most frustrating problem for clients in need of services. Like all bureaucracies, public agencies are subject to rigid sets of rules and hierarchical structures that do not allow for a flexible approach to individual problems. Application forms that clients must complete before receiving assistance are often lengthy and complex, creating a serious obstacle to receiving help for applicants who cannot read or write. Furthermore, social workers in a public agency are bound by these complex sets of rules and regulations, which makes their jobs more difficult.

Another weakness of public agencies is their inability to consider cases individually. Financial assistance payments are made on the basis of the size of the family and the urban or rural location of their residence. The amount of money received is based on a formula that determines how much it should cost a family for food and shelter. This impersonal approach makes no provision for the special circumstances that face individual families, such as the special dietary needs of a family member, needs for child care, or the costs of transportation clients incur while looking for employment.

A final weakness of public agencies, and the public welfare system in general, is the stigma society attaches to those who seek services from them (Johnson & Schwartz, 1991, p. 11). By stereotyping public assistance recipients as "living off the public dole" and as "welfare bums," society has become insensitive to the very real needs of people who must rely on public assistance to survive. These stereotypes operate as prejudices against all recipients of public assistance.

Private Nonprofit Social Service Agencies

In the United States, there are more than 800,000 **nonprofit agencies,** which serve the low- and moderate-income population, the mentally and physically disabled, ex-offenders, the elderly, and children (Corman, 1987, p. 101). Other private nonprofits may provide social and recreational services to groups of clients or communities rather than to individual clients.

Private nonprofit agencies can be sectarian (that is, affiliated with an organized church) or nondenominational (that is, run by nongovernmental groups that have no religious affiliation). Organized religion has a history of helping people in need. In fact, in the early history of social welfare, churches were the only service providers. Concern for the well-being of orphans, widows, the disabled, and the elderly is an important part of the Judeo-Christian tradition. Nondenominational, private nonprofit (but not church-related) agencies developed out of a shared concern for the poor. Most private agencies provide services such as counseling, adoption, specialized foster care, and single-parent services but do not provide financial assistance. Financial assistance is the responsibility of public agencies.

Regardless of affiliation, most private nonprofit agencies have a voluntary board of directors that serves as a policy maker and advisor to the executive director. The board of directors is composed of volunteers who are active in the community. They are often people who are experts in social services, medicine, law, or business. These board members have professional and personal knowledge helpful to staff social workers and the executive director in designing the best possible services for clients. Private nonprofits try to include among board members individuals who are representative of clients or client concerns. These people may be parents of clients, in the case of children, or former clients, in the case of mental health or corrections agencies.

The board of directors hires a paid executive director who is responsible for the day-to-day operation of the agency. The executive director supervises the various departments within the agency, such as adoption, counseling, foster care, the business office, and support staff. Depending on the size of the agency, these separate units may have their own supervisors.

Private agencies rely on funds from private donations, charity events, support from community fund-raising organizations such as United Way, and fees for service. Some private agencies, such as Catholic Charities, are organized nationwide. Others, such as Children's Service Society of Wisconsin, are statewide agencies. Still others exist as separate organizations only in the communities they serve. Examples include shelters for abused women and children, centers for the homeless, and local telephone help lines.

How Do Public and Private Agencies Differ?

We have already seen that public and private agencies differ in terms of who runs the agency and how the agency is funded. However, public and private agencies differ in several other ways. These differences shape the working environment of the social work practitioner. Differences include service eligibility requirements, philosophy of care, and the scope of services.

Service Eligibility Requirements.   **Service eligibility requirements** determine who may receive services from an agency. To become a client, you must be eligible for services. To be eligible, you must meet criteria that differ among public and private agencies. Public agencies must serve all citizens who live in their area. Although only people who have financial need may receive financial assistance, counseling and foster care services are available to people of all income levels.

Private agencies, on the other hand, need not provide services to everyone who comes to the agency. They may establish a special set of eligibility requirements, such as residence, type of problem, age, family, income, and family composition. Unlike public agencies, private agencies may restrict who receives services. Few private agencies deny services based on such strict requirements, but in certain circumstances they have the right to do so.

Let's look at this difference in practice. Mrs. Kelly has just decided that her 4-year-old son, Sean, must see a doctor. He has a fever of 102 and has been ill for a few days. Now Sean has developed a strange rash on his legs, and Mrs. Kelly is concerned about him. She takes him to the emergency room at Mercy Medical Center, a private hospital in the neighborhood. The emergency room nurse discovers that the Kelly family has no health insurance, and therefore, she cannot admit Sean until the family has been seen by the emergency room social worker, Fran.

Fran checks with administrators in the hospital and discovers that the hospital will not admit the child without an assured method of payment. The hospital has provided a significant level of free care already this year and cannot survive financially if it continues to do so. Fran must turn the Kellys away and refer them to the emergency room at Bellwood County Medical Center, a large public medical center. Bellwood County Medical Center must provide medical services to Sean, regardless of the Kellys' health insurance status.

Fran knows that the Kellys will have to wait a very long time at Bellwood to be seen by a physician, but if the Kellys cannot pay for Sean's care, the county will assume the costs as a part of their public obligation.

Fran may be moved by the case and see the need for medical services, but the private hospital cannot provide them. The hospital's eligibility requirements simply do not allow her to help admit the child.

Philosophy of Service.   A second difference between public and private agencies is their **philosophy of service.** Philosophy of service refers to the agency's value orientation and its approach to the care of its clients, which are reflected in the kind and quantity of services the agency offers. Agencies' decisions are based on their values. The following example shows how a philosophy of service affects what social workers can or cannot do for their clients.

Sandy is a 16-year-old girl who has just found out she is pregnant. She and the child's father have no intention of marrying, even if they could obtain their parents' permission. Sandy has not decided whether to have and keep the baby, consider adoption, or obtain an abortion. Right now she needs to talk through all the possibilities with someone who can help her decide what to do. Sandy has made appointments with two social workers. One of the appointments is with Mary Kate, who works for the State Department of Health and Human Services, the public agency that handles all teen pregnancy cases in the state. The other appointment is with Kristin, who works for Catholic Social Services. This agency also handles single-parent services. Sandy is Catholic and was referred to that agency by her parish priest.

Mary Kate, the public agency worker, discusses all possible alternatives with Sandy. Sandy can continue her pregnancy and have the child. If Sandy decides to keep the child, Mary Kate can help her in several ways. First, Mary Kate can help Sandy apply for and receive financial assistance. Second, special child care can be arranged so Sandy can remain in school. Third, Mary Kate can help Sandy secure financial help from the baby's father. On the other hand, if Sandy decides to have the child and release it for adoption, Mary Kate will work with the adoption worker to find good parents for Sandy's child, although she cannot guarantee that the child will be placed in a Catholic home. If Sandy decides to terminate the pregnancy, Mary Kate can help Sandy find an agency that will perform a safe abortion. Mary Kate has discussed all legal options with Sandy; now Sandy must decide what to do.

The state agency's philosophy of service is that the client, in this case Sandy, should be offered all possible legal alternatives. It is Sandy's responsibility to choose what she intends to do. Regardless of the social worker's feelings regarding adoption, abortion, or keeping a child, all alternatives must be discussed with the client.

When Sandy talks with Kristin at Catholic Social Services, a private agency under the auspices of the Roman Catholic Church, she has a much different experience. Kristin cannot discuss with Sandy the pros and cons of an abortion because the Catholic Church opposes elective abortions. If Kristin is caught discussing abortion, she might lose her job. In her meetings with Sandy, Kristin talks more about adoption, emphasizing the number of good Catholic families who are willing to adopt infants. Keeping the baby after birth is also discussed, although with much less emphasis than adoption.[1]

In this example, the philosophy of service of Catholic Social Services does not allow Kristin to discuss abortion with Sandy, regardless of how Kristin personally feels about it. It is obvious that the agency's philosophy of service is heavily weighted toward adoption. Kristin's work with Sandy reflects that orientation. It is the right of private agencies to have philosophies of care that differ from public agencies. If individuals do not agree with the agency's philosophy of service, they have the right to go elsewhere for services. Clients may choose another agency that offers services more in line with their own personal philosophy.

Services to single mothers is only one example of how different philosophies of service affect the type of services clients receive. In this instance, public agencies can provide more choices than private agencies. In other instances, public agencies may be more restricted than private agencies because of public funding and state law. County social service boards may intentionally shape public agencies' philosophies to be the least controversial to the taxpayers or at least to reflect the prevailing social values.

Scope of Services.   The scope of services is another way public and private agencies differ. The **scope of services** of an agency refers to the kind of service the agency offers. Most likely this is determined both by sources of funding for services and by the designated purpose of the agency (Pierce, 1984). For example, most private child welfare agencies provide adoption, family and individual counseling, specialized foster care, and services to unmarried parents. Foster care, substance abuse, financial assistance, and protective services traditionally fall within the realm of the public agencies. Families who have a broad range of needs may have to go to both public and private agencies for the services they need.

Purchase of Service Contracts.   Since the early 1960s, public agencies have increasingly turned to the private sector to purchase services instead of providing services directly. In **purchase of service agreements,** state and county agencies buy the services of social workers employed by private agencies. Although clients are served by a private agency, they remain clients of the government agency.

For example, treatment foster care is a service frequently contracted out under a purchase of service agreement. Usually, treatment foster care children are severely disabled or have serious emotional problems that require intensive work with a social worker. These children are placed in special foster homes where the parents have extensive experience caring for physical, emotional, or intellectual disabilities. The social worker may see the child and foster parents weekly rather than once a month or once every three months. The social worker may have to schedule regular therapy weekly with these children or provide extra emotional support for their foster parents.

Private agencies can usually provide these services at less cost than public agencies (Demone & Gibelman, 1987). Let's say, for example, that Green County allocated $15,000 for treatment foster care services. If the social workers at Green County Department of Social Services provide the service, it will cost $150 an hour, including the worker's salary and administrative costs. Administrative costs are very high in public agencies because of all the administrative levels. These levels range from the county right up through the Department of Health and Human Services. However, if Green County contracts for the same services with the local Children's Friend Society, a private agency, the cost per hour of service drops to $75. Lower administrative costs may make the private agency more cost-efficient. At $150 an hour, Green County workers can provide 100 hours of service. At $75 an hour, a worker at Children's Friend Society can provide 200 hours of service, twice as many hours of service for the same amount of money.

This policy arrangement affects the workers in public and private agencies in several ways. On the positive side, purchase of service arrangements generates more services for the same amount of money—an important issue in times of reduced funding for social services. These arrangements allow clients who might otherwise not receive a special service the opportunity for the kind of care they need. They also broaden the scope of services for private agencies, which might otherwise be unable to provide such a diverse array of services.

On the negative side, purchase of service contracts further fragments the social service system. Clients may receive some services from the public agency and others from the private agency. An additional social worker and supervisor may become involved in a child's case, a situation that often confuses and irritates parents. An even more frustrating situation for social workers occurs when both public and private agency social workers must learn to deal with each other's agencies. Recording forms, case notes, and administrative accountability may differ dramatically between the agencies. With the renewed emphasis on federalism and an increasing disenchantment with government involvement in the provision of services, Demone and Gibelman (1988) predict that more, rather than fewer, services will be transferred from government agencies to private agencies through purchase of service contracts. Lower costs and the flexibility and creativity of the private sector are cited as the main reasons for an increase in purchase of service contracts. Demone and Gibelman (1988) also predict that once the private sector becomes heavily involved in providing services previously provided by the public agencies, the same disenchantment that plagues the public sector will affect the private sector (Kettner & Martin, 1987).

Private For-Profit Agencies

Private nonprofit social service agencies do not expect to earn a profit. If they do, the profits must be reinvested in the agency. A relatively new development in social service agencies is the growth of the private for-profit social service agencies. **Private for-profit agencies** are private agencies owned by private investors who expect a financial return on their investment. Private for-profit agencies actively seek clients who can either afford to pay for the services they offer or who have health insurance that covers the cost.

The biggest pressure on private nonprofit social service agencies is financial survival. Most agencies cannot generate enough funds through community funding sources and donations to survive without actively seeking purchase of service contracts and other public funds. The retrenchment of the Reagan years has affected the private sector both directly and indirectly. The private sector is expected to provide more of the services typically provided by public agencies. However, because of the weak economy, since the 1980s agencies have received fewer voluntary contributions, compounding their financial pressures.

For-Profit Structures within Nonprofit Agencies

Some private nonprofit agencies have developed for-profit enterprises within the agency structure. These for-profit ventures supply money for agency programs that do not pay for themselves. For example, Community Living is an agency that helps the mentally ill make the transition from psychiatric institutions to independent living in the community through a system of supervised living arrangements and financial and social support. These services are very expensive and are not paid for by any of the financial assistance programs that serve the chronically mentally ill. Therefore, the program does not generate sufficient funds to pay for itself. Community Living decides to open a counseling clinic staffed by therapists who are qualified to bill both public and private insurance companies for their services. The counseling clinic makes a profit, which is transferred to the supervised living program. Technically, Community Living remains a nonprofit agency because the profits are not distributed to stockholders or members of the board of directors. This is one scenario of the for-profit movement in human services.

The For-Profit Agency.   The other, more common approach involves setting up an agency that provides social services, usually mental or physical health services, exactly the same way a private business operates. Large, nationwide for-profit agencies, such as Community Psychiatric Corporation, sell stock to investors just as IBM and Xerox do. Profit generated by the organization is returned to investors as stock dividends. As the business grows, the value of stock increases, generating a profit when the stock is sold. Other for-profit agencies may be owned and operated locally by a small group of investors who serve on the agency's board of directors. Profits generated by the agency are returned to these investors.

Corman (1987) cites three reasons why the for-profit sector of social services has grown so quickly since 1985:

1. Historically, the private sector has been able to offer expertise in solving problems the government has failed to solve. For example, many of the advances in the space program and in medical research have come from research and development operations within private business. Access to profits for research, incentives for creativity, and organizational flexibility contribute to this development.

2. For-profit social service agencies may be seen as a good way to diversify the investment portfolios of private individuals or businesses. Private and public insurance are stable financial sources of income and may be less susceptible to the uncertainties of the economy than other consumer products.

3. Opportunities for for-profit ventures exist outside of public health insurance benefits, including child care and educational services. The potential is unlimited for private enterprise.

Criticisms of For-Profit Agencies.   Private for-profit agencies have strong critics and equally strong defenders. The critics point to philosophical difficulties in making a profit at the expense of people with problems and gouging insurance companies for the maximum amount of benefits they will pay for social and psychological services. For-profit psychiatric hospitals have been accused of providing more services than are necessary (that is, inpatient rather than outpatient services) as long as private insurance companies pay for the services. When insurance benefits are depleted, patients are discharged from the psychiatric hospital whether or not they are well enough to leave.

Private for-profit agencies are accused of using deceptive advertising to entice consumers to use them and then cutting the quality of the services to increase profits (Demone & Gibelman, 1987). Even supporters of the for-profit movement in the United States admit that the private for-profit social service agencies may provide more efficient services, but the private sector is not necessarily better at solving the problems for which they provide services.

Critics accuse the for-profit sector of skimming the best clients away from the public sector, leaving public institutions as the last resort for low-income clients (Demone & Gibelman, 1987). If for-profit agencies serve only clients who can afford to pay for services directly or through private insurance, low-income uninsured (or underinsured) clients may be relegated to crowded public facilities. High-quality services may be available from for-profit agencies, whereas low-income clients must accept whatever services they can obtain from public agencies, regardless of quality.

Critics also question whether the profit motive is incompatible with the values of the social work profession. If workers know that their salaries are tied to the amount of profit they generate from working with clients, do they lose the incentive to provide quality care and substitute quantity care instead? Are their professional ethics compromised when their commitment to providing quality service to the client conflicts with the mechanics of paying for the service? For example, a serious ethical dilemma may develop when a family's private insurance benefits are exhausted, but the family still needs treatment. Whose best interest is served by terminating the client's services—the agency's or the family's?

The Case for For-Profit Agencies.   The defenders of the private for-profit agencies contend that "the private market enhances the efficiency of human services while promoting the responsiveness of services to the needs of consumers" (Jansson, 1990, p. 80). Eikin (1987) reminds critics of the for-profit structure that our current system of public welfare and public agencies was originally set up in the 1930s, when most citizens were desperate for assistance from the government. A universal, public system was the only system feasible under the circumstances, and the desperate nature of the times allowed citizens to tolerate an intense level of government intervention in their lives. Government has long since lost its ability to address the needs of its citizens, so the time is right for a wide-scale intervention of the private sector in the business of human services. Eikin (1987) also believes that the "avenues for critical thinking are stunted in the public sector" (Eikin, 1987, p. 175). The "monopoly of authority" traditionally evidenced by government's involvement in the provision of services is an obstacle, rather than an opportunity, for creative solutions to the people's problems.

Another case for the for-profit agency is that the government is not as sensitive as business to the constant shifts in individual preferences and local conditions. Let's return to the example of Walton in Davis County. Funds allocated to Walton for chemical dependency intervention programs are woefully inadequate. A group of investors sees a brilliant opportunity to develop additional chemical dependency services that will not only serve the community but provide employment for some of the community's residents. These private investors can be flexible and sensitive to Walton's unique characteristics in ways the government cannot—thus, Community Rehabilitation comes into being.

A FRAGMENTED SYSTEM

Up to this point, we have seen how the residual nature of the American social welfare system has led to and perpetuates the coexistence of private and public agencies. Looking closer at the social welfare system, we see that within the public and private sector are additional factors that contribute to a fragmented and confusing system of services, as shown in Table 4.1. Among these factors are universal versus means-tested programs, cash versus in-kind as the form of services, and state versus federal in the administration of those services.

TABLE 4.1

The American Income Security System

PROGRAM	FORM OF BENEFIT	MEANS TEST?	FINANCING	ADMINISTRATION
Public Assistance				
Aid to Families with Dependent Children	Cash—varies by state	Yes—varies by state	Federal-state partnership	Federal, state, and county governments
Food stamps	Coupons	Yes—varies by state	U.S. Department of Agriculture	Federal, state, and county governments
Medical Assistance	In-kind	Yes—varies by state	Federal-state partnership	Federal, state, and county governments
Supplemental Security Income	Cash—varies with state supplement	Yes	Federal-state partnership	Social Security Administration
General Assistance	Cash—varies by county	Yes—varies by county	County	County department of social services
Social Insurance				
Medicare	In-kind	No—but must be receiving Social Security	Premiums paid by recipients	Social Security Administration
Social Security, Retirement, Disability, and Survivors' Benefits	Cash	No—if covered by certain number of work quarters	Social Security taxes paid by employee and employer	Social Security Administration

Universal versus Means-Tested Programs

Universal Programs.   As already discussed, countries with institutional forms of social welfare have **universal programs.** That is, anyone can receive services from the government without having to prove a financial need. Universal programs in the United States include public education, fire and police protection, Social Security benefits, and other public services. The services are not free but are paid for indirectly through taxes or, in the case of Social Security, through payroll taxes throughout a person's working life.

One of the advantages of a universal program is that it is easy to administer because no verification of a person's personal financial assets is required. If individuals meet the basic requirements, which usually include residency, they can receive services. The National Health Care System in Canada is a good example of a universal program. People need only show that they are Canadian citizens to receive no-cost health care paid for by the Canadian government. Patients are not billed for services they receive from physicians employed by the Canadian government. The program is supported by income taxes and high taxes on alcohol and cigarettes.

Another advantage of universal programs is that they reduce the stigma attached to receiving services. One's income and personal circumstances are not taken into consideration when services are provided, so no one knows who is poor and who is not.

Finally, universal services provide some assurance that people who need a service will receive it and not be deterred either by cost or by the stigma of receiving services. For example, if everyone had to pay for elementary education in the United States, it is likely that most poor families would not be able to send their children to school. This would widen the gap in the quality of life even more between upper- and middle-income and low-income populations. Low-income children would have no opportunity to improve their lives through education.

The biggest disadvantage of universal services is the cost. Universal services are prohibitively expensive. Taxpayers must be willing to pay for the services indirectly through taxes. The philosophy in the United States is that, with few exceptions, people should pay for services as they use them, or the government should pay only for services of those who can prove they cannot pay for services themselves.

Means-Tested Programs.   Other services are **means-tested programs.** In means-tested programs, people must prove financial need to receive the service. They may have to show proof of income, specify the number of members in their family, and indicate the value of their home and savings accounts to qualify for services. Examples of means-tested programs include AFDC, food stamps, subsidized housing, college financial aid, and Medical Assistance. Applicants for these services must be screened to ensure that only those people who need a service receive it. Means-tested programs are characteristic of our residual social welfare system.

One advantage of means-tested services is that only people who need the service are eligible for it. People who have sufficient incomes pay for services as they use them. This allows some control over the amount of public funds allocated for public assistance programs. It is also consistent with the American value that society has obligations to help the poor, but people must be able to prove they need help.

A second advantage is that, by not universalizing services, individuals retain freedom of choice in deciding where they receive services and what kind of services they want to receive. For example, medical services in the United States are primarily controlled by the private sector. Individuals can choose to go to the physician of their choice and arrange payment through their own funds or private insurance. Freedom of choice is important to Americans, especially in the area of health care.

A third advantage is that, at least superficially, programs can be tailored to meet the needs of special populations. For example, AFDC is designed for individuals and families with dependent children. Assuming that the heads of these households are young enough to work, employment requirements can be built into the program. Supplementary Security Income, on the other hand, is designed for older adults and for persons with disabilities who are not expected to work, so work requirements do not apply. Each public assistance program is specifically geared to the needs and expectations of the population it serves.

The disadvantages of means-tested programs are the opposite of the advantages of universal programs: administration is complex, stigma becomes attached to receiving services, and some people never receive the services they need because of the stigma and the complex application process.

The coexistence of universal and means-tested programs in the United States is a strong example of this society's unresolved questions about how much the government should provide for its citizens and why people need help in the first place. This ambivalence is rooted in the continuing tensions between institutional and residual approaches to social welfare.

Cash and In-Kind Programs

The social welfare system in the United States uses both cash and in-kind methods of providing services. **In-kind programs** are those in which people receive a service, such as medical care, subsidized housing, or food stamps, rather than the cash to purchase the service for themselves.

Cash Assistance.   AFDC, General Assistance, and Supplementary Security Income are all examples of cash public assistance programs. If applicants meet the criteria, they receive a check each month that they may spend as they choose. Cash assistance programs assume that recipients will spend their public assistance checks on shelter, utilities, transportation, and clothes. Some recipients spend their money wisely; others do not.

One of the most controversial aspects of cash assistance programs is that society cannot control how public assistance recipients spend their money. We determine people are in financial need, and they can receive assistance, but we cannot determine how they spend the money they receive. Those who spend their money on alcohol, drugs, cigarettes, and expensive clothes are often cited as examples of why we should not give people money directly. However, the importance of freedom of choice has remained a more powerful influence in this aspect of public assistance than the value of social control.

In support of cash programs, it can also be said that giving public assistance recipients cash and letting them decide how to spend the money is important because it fosters responsibility among recipients. If the long-term goal of public assistance is to encourage self-sufficiency among recipients, then we must give them the freedom to make choices, even if we do not agree with the choices they make.

In-Kind Services.   Services such as medical care may be more efficiently handled as in-kind services because of what is called *target efficiency;* that is, the money allocated for the service can be spent only on the service, ensuring that even if clients cannot always be relied on to spend their money for basic needs, the service will be available. For example, if we asked public assistance recipients to use part of their cash benefits to purchase health insurance for their families, we have no guarantee that they would actually do it. In the case of a medical emergency, could we ethically deny a family medical care because they did not buy health insurance? Health care is so important that our social welfare system provides it as an in-kind service to low-income families receiving public assistance.

A second advantage of in-kind services is that, because of centralized administration and payment for certain services, some consistency in quality can be guaranteed. To receive reimbursement under Medical Assistance, providers must meet certain federal criteria that are constantly monitored by the federal government. This ensures that Medical Assistance patients are not treated inequitably in the medical system.

In-kind services are more expensive to provide than cash services because of the additional administrative responsibilities. Instead of simply providing cash and allowing recipients to purchase their own services, another level of administration is needed to reimburse providers for the service and monitor in-kind programs. However, taxpayers may be more tolerant of expenses for in-kind programs than for cash programs because they know exactly where their money is going (Compton, 1980, p. 550).

Federal, State, and Local Administration

As indicated in Table 4.1, public assistance programs are administered on one of the three levels of government: local, state, or federal. It is important to understand at which level potential recipients must apply for programs.

Although most public assistance programs are applied for and regulated by county departments of social services, federal, state, and local governments may all be involved in funding and administering those programs. This explains why public assistance benefits vary from state to state. For programs such as AFDC, the federal government provides a certain level of benefits that may or may not be supplemented by state funds.

The result of this administrative fragmentation is general confusion among applicants, social workers, and taxpayers. The sharing of administrative authority is another characteristic of a residual social welfare system. In countries with institutional systems, one central administration handles all income maintenance programs. This centralized system eliminates much of the confusion and fragmentation characteristic of the U.S. system.

Implications for the Social Work Practitioner

Understanding the maze of social welfare agencies and the various kinds of services available to clients is important to the social work practitioner for several reasons.

First, the social worker plays an important educational role in the process of working with clients. Clients may have little or no understanding of where to go to receive certain services and which services are cash or in kind. In public agencies, a major concern of workers is the administration of financial assistance, but in private agencies workers may have little day-to-day contact with the details of financial assistance programs. A better-informed worker will be infinitely more helpful to clients who ask questions or who are current or potential recipients of programs they do not understand.

Second, the complex system of public and private services is often a source of frustration for both workers and clients. Understanding where to direct clients for financial or social services can make our work as direct practitioners more efficient and effective. Our proficiency is directly related to our knowledge of the resources we need to serve clients.

Instead of bemoaning the red tape of the social welfare system, it is more productive to learn as much as possible about it both to cope with it and to identify areas in which change is needed. This is the third reason knowledge of the system is critical. Knowledge of how the current system developed, how it works, and what is wrong with it are prerequisites to determining what changes are needed. In many respects, a solid knowledge of the complex social welfare system is analogous to the individual assessment of a client before we identify the intervention methods to employ. We need to know where we are before we can ascertain where we should be.

SUMMARY

Americans' general ambivalence about the government's role in providing help to those in need and the enduring influence of rugged individualism have contributed to the existence of a fragmented, residual system of social welfare. Social welfare services exist as a last resort for people for whom the mechanisms of the family and the marketplace have failed. The underlying expectation of our social welfare system is that the need for services is temporary. Once people can find employment and take care of themselves, help from the government will no longer be necessary.

This perception that help is temporary, not a basic function of government, has led to the development of a fragmented system of services. Some services are provided on a universal basis; others require a means test. Some services are cash; others are in kind. State and local governments are responsible for some income maintenance programs; the federal government administers and regulates others.

The next chapter examines how social welfare policy develops within this fragmented system through the democratic political structure. The interplay among political voices in this country further contributes to social welfare policies that may more accurately reflect the choices of the taxpayers than of those for whom the service is intended.

DISCUSSION QUESTIONS

1. *What are the two unresolved questions the United States has struggled with throughout history regarding social welfare services? Why do these questions remain unresolved?*
2. *Compare and contrast public and private social service agencies.*
3. *Discuss the case for and against private for-profit social service agencies. Do you think the profit motive is incompatible with the ethics of the social work profession?*
4. *How is the American social welfare system fragmented? Is there a way to eliminate some of the fragmentation in the system without changing to an institutional system of social welfare services?*

SUGGESTED PROJECTS

1. Interview executive directors at the public and private agencies in your community. What do they consider the advantages and disadvantages of each of their agencies? Find out what services the public agency provides directly and what services are contracted out under a purchase of service agreement.
2. Obtain copies of the application forms for public assistance services at the local county department of social services and review them with your class. Are separate forms required for each service, or is there only one

form to fill out? What obstacles do you see in the application process for people who do not speak English, are aged, or have physical disabilities?

3. Most communities have at least one private for-profit social service agency. Interview the executive director about the arguments presented in this chapter for and against the idea of for-profit social services. Then interview social workers at that agency to see if they feel there is an inconsistency between their professional motivations to help people and the profit motive.

Notes

1. Catholic Charities and Catholic Social Services agencies throughout the United States differ on whether they allow their workers to discuss abortion as an option in an unplanned pregnancy.

This example is included primarily because Catholic agencies have been the most resistant to including abortion as an alternative because of Roman Catholic Church doctrine.

IMPORTANT TERMS AND CONCEPTS

in-kind program
means-tested program
nonprofit agency
philosophy of service
private for-profit agency
private social service agency

public social service agency
purchase of service agreement
scope of services
service eligibility
    requirements
universal programs

Developing Social Welfare Policy: A Political Process

The examination of almost 100 years of social work history
suggests that over the years the profession has used a variety of
political action strategies and activities. Playing roles that range
from social worker as informed citizen to active lobbyist to
federal or state administrator to politician, social workers have
been engaged in political activity. Whether or not it is part of
their formal role or training, political action has been part of
social work history and will be part of its future.

—KAREN HAYNES & JAMES S. MICKELSON, 1991, p. 14

D eveloping social policies to help solve social problems would be
relatively easy if we could assume that making social welfare policy
were a **rational process.** DiNitto (1991) describes a policy as rational
if "the ratio between the values it achieves and the values it sacrifices is positive
and higher than any other policy alternative. . . . Rationalism involves the
calculation of all social, political and economic values sacrificed or achieved
by a public policy, not just those that can be measured in dollars" (p. 4). In
a rational policy-making process, problems would be identified, solutions
proposed, and policies adopted and implemented with minimal conflict or
negotiation. We would know all the possible alternatives for solving social
problems and would select the most efficient, effective solution.

Social welfare policy making, however, is *not* a rational process. It is
the most political component of the social work profession because it is

neither made nor funded exclusively within the social work community, but involves external forces and funds. Social work has a long history of political involvement because of the political processes that influence the policies under which we practice. Although social workers and their clients may be most acutely affected by the ramifications of social welfare policy, they are a very small part of the broad range of forces that contribute to policy making.

Specifically, this chapter includes the following:

- ✦ A discussion of the role of personal and public values in defining and solving problems
- ✦ A review of the process by which a bill becomes a law in the U.S. Congress—the most common way social welfare policy is developed and funded
- ✦ A discussion of the influence of the media (newspapers, magazines, radio, and television) on identifying issues as social problems that then become the focus of policy making
- ✦ A discussion of the court system's role in determining policy on the basis of legal decisions

WHAT MAKES THE POLICY-MAKING PROCESS POLITICAL?

The definition of *political* in Chapter One includes negotiation and conflict as components in the political nature of social welfare policy. Nowhere is this more evident than in the process of making policy. Four major factors contribute to the politics of policymaking: values, the legislative process, the role of the media, and the power of the courts to change existing policies.

Values Determine Problem Definition and Intervention

Social welfare policy directly reflects prevailing social values. If children are an important resource to our society, social welfare policy should reflect that commitment. The commitment might be in the form of a strong medical care program for children of all ages or a national system of child care, structured similarly to public education. Likewise, if our society values defense against unfriendly nations, that value will be reflected in a strong military.

Social values also determine what society *defines* as a social problem, which then becomes a focus for policy making. This does not mean what *causes* a problem but why a certain set of behaviors are defined as a problem. For example, teenage pregnancy is considered a social problem for a number of reasons, but teenage pregnancy is not unique to the 20th century. In the 19th century, most girls were mothers in their teenage years because they married early. If teenage pregnancy was not defined as a problem then, why is it defined as a problem now? Society has changed dramatically since the pioneer days, when girls married at 14 years of age, bore as many children as they could because infant mortality rates were so high, were considered old at 35, and usually died very young. Girls at that time rarely had the opportunity for an education beyond grade school. Divorce was extremely rare. Couples stayed together because they needed each other to survive.

Today, most teenage pregnancies occur out of wedlock (Vinovskis, 1988). Teen fathers are rarely in a position to support their children, so often young mothers must obtain welfare to support their children (Moore & Burt, 1982). The opportunities available to women of all ages are much different now, and few women can afford to stay home and raise their children, regardless of their marital status. American values have changed. The social context in which teenage pregnancy occurs and the consequences of early parenthood have changed along with values.

Teenage Pregnancy and Social Values.   Let us examine five problem statements about teenage pregnancy.[1] These statements reflect different values, and each defines teenage pregnancy in a slightly different light.

1. *"Many teenage mothers drop out of school, limiting their career choices in the future. This results in disproportionate numbers of lifelong poor."* This perspective reflects the value of education and the importance of economic well-being for mothers and their children. Teenage pregnancy is considered a problem because interrupting one's education increases the risk of lifelong poverty, which affects the physical and psychological health of both mothers and their children.

2. *"Teenage mothers often rely on welfare to support their children because of failure on the part of the child's father to provide support. The welfare system makes it too easy for teens to keep having babies for the welfare."* Connecting teen pregnancy with public dependency reflects a concern over the value of self-sufficiency and people taking care of their own children. The problem then becomes one of taxpayers supporting someone else's family. Unfortunately, some situations are not defined as problems until they start to cost the taxpayer.

3. *"Teenage pregnancy is a problem because teenagers are not mature enough to be sexually active in the first place."* A concern over moral values underlies this statement. From this view, what happens to the teen mother and her child is not as significant as the fact that the young woman was sexually active. Some people think sexual activity is inappropriate or morally wrong for anyone outside of marriage, especially for teenagers.

4. *"Teenage pregnancy occurs because teens do not have access to reliable, affordable means of contraception."* This view makes no judgment about the morality of teenage sexual behavior but implies that most teenage pregnancies result from lack of access to means of preventing the pregnancy.

5. *"Teenage pregnancy reflects the general problem in society of deteriorating family values. Parents do not supervise their children or cannot raise them with the correct ideas about having and raising children."* This view of the cause of teenage pregnancy places the blame on the family, which seems to be blamed for every social problem. In this view, the problem is not that teenagers have children but that teenage pregnancy reflects the deterioration of the American family.

These are just five of the common reasons people feel teenage pregnancy is a problem in this country. Some of the statements view the consequences of the pregnancy as the problem (welfare dependency or a life of poverty), whereas other statements view the sexual behavior as the problem (teens
are too young; they do not use contraception; they are not being supervised).

What we believe causes a problem guides what we think is the best
policy solution to the problem. Finding a solution to a problem usually relies
on understanding the cause of that problem. For example, if we believe that
the consequences of teen pregnancy are the most serious problem, it makes
sense to focus our efforts on preventing teen pregnancy in the first place
or on providing services to prevent lifelong dependency, the second component of the problem. The policy intervention we select depends on the values
underlying our definition of the problem.

If we assume that sexual activity rather than teen pregnancy is the
problem, we will select a different approach. This perspective suggests an
educational or parental effort to discourage teens from sexual activity. If teens
are sexually active despite our protestations, they must have access to and
know how to use contraceptives.

Causes of a Problem Imply Methods of Intervention.   Each of the statements about teenage pregnancy also implicates a different group as the focus
of the intervention effort. Welfare dependency issues and lifelong dependency
imply the involvement of state and federal governments, which are responsible for income maintenance programs. The behavioral problem approach
implies that the schools and parents are responsible for preventing teenage
pregnancy. How we see the problem will determine *what* needs to be done,
who is going to do it, and *where* it is going to be done.

The example of teenage pregnancy has been simplified to illustrate
how values can determine the intervention effort for a social problem. Few
professionals working with teenage pregnancy would agree with such simple
statements. In some respects, teenage pregnancy is a problem for all the
reasons given. Its complexity is the reason it has become such a challenging
issue. The last section of Chapter Six explores how developing a social welfare
policy to address teenage pregnancy involves careful negotiation among these
different perspectives.

Most Policy Is Made in the Legislative Arena

The second reason policy making is political is that many of the laws and
legislative mandates that determine social welfare policy must pass the U.S.
Congress or state legislatures. This chapter does not address the differences
among state legislatures. Instead, we review how a bill becomes a law in the
U.S. Congress and where political influence might be felt in the process.

How a Bill Becomes a Law.   For the purposes of this discussion, the process required for a bill to become a law has been condensed to five basic
steps, which are depicted in Figure 5.1.

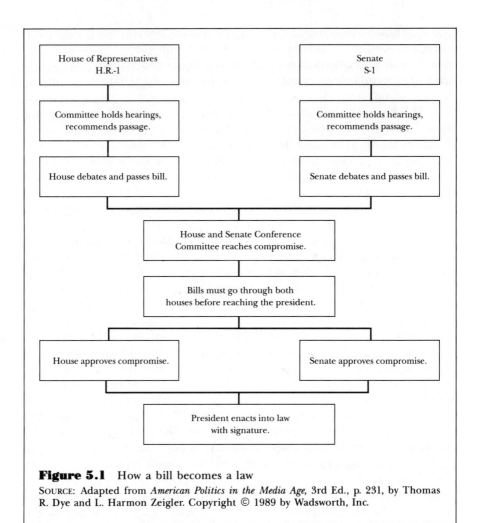

Figure 5.1 How a bill becomes a law

SOURCE: Adapted from *American Politics in the Media Age,* 3rd Ed., p. 231, by Thomas R. Dye and L. Harmon Zeigler. Copyright © 1989 by Wadsworth, Inc.

1. *Introduction.* A bill is introduced by a legislator in either the House of Representatives or the Senate. When a bill is introduced, it is assigned a number. The initials *H.R.* plus a number designates a bill introduced in the House of Representatives by a congressional representative. The letter *S.* plus a number indicates a bill introduced in the Senate by a senator. A bill does not carry over between the two-year sessions of Congress. If no action is taken on a bill, it must be reintroduced by the same procedure in a future session of Congress.

The personal and political agendas of lawmakers determine which bills are introduced. Although lawmakers are elected to represent the political views of their constituents, no legislator goes to Congress without a clear idea of what he or she wants to accomplish. The bills introduced by a congress-person or senator may or may not accurately represent his or her constituents' views.

2. *Committee assignment.* Bills are assigned to committees that have expert knowledge in the subject matter covered by the bill. For example, in the House of Representatives, social welfare bills are usually assigned to the House Social Security Subcommittee. Bills that deal with health coverage are usually referred to the Subcommittee on Health, a subcommittee of the House Ways and Means Committee. Committees consist of members of both the Democratic and Republican parties. Usually public hearings are held on bills in committee to obtain additional input from experts outside Congress or from the public.

3. *Report of the committee.* The chairman of the committee reports on whether the committee views the bill favorably or unfavorably and indicates whether or not the committee recommends that the bill be passed into law.

4. *Debate on the bill.* The House of Representatives and the Senate can consider different versions of a bill at the same time. Once one house of Congress has completed its consideration of the bill, it is sent to the other house. It goes through the same four steps in the second house that it went through in the first house. If the bill is passed by the second house with no changes, it goes to the president for signature. If the bill is amended by the second house, it must be returned to the first house for adoption of the amendments. If the first house does not accept the amendments made by the second house, a **conference committee** consisting of members of both houses is appointed to develop a compromise bill that is returned to both houses for a vote.

5. *President's signature.* A bill that has passed both houses of Congress is submitted to the president for signature. If the president signs the bill, it becomes law. If the president refuses to sign the bill, it must be passed again in both houses by a two-thirds vote in order to become law.

Passing Laws as Political Activity.   Compromise is the first of many ways the lawmaking process is highly political. Compromise occurs in each stage of a bill's becoming a law. The legislative process requires that the bill be discussed in committees and by both houses of Congress. The political views of members of Congress represent a wide spectrum from extremely liberal to extremely conservative. If a member of Congress believes the federal government should restrict its role in helping a particular population, he or she might vote against any efforts that would require a substantial financial commitment on the part of the federal government. Another member of Congress might feel strongly about the importance of the federal government's involvement in social problems and vote for every social program, regardless of the financial commitment involved. Compromise implies that one member of Congress might have to agree to changes in the bill to obtain enough votes for the bill to pass. That means that a bill can be changed a great deal by the time it is finally passed.

The second reason lawmaking is so political is that input into drafting a bill and testifying at public hearings is not an equitable process. Those who know what legislation is being considered and are aggressive enough to let their congressional representatives know how they feel about the bill, or who have a special area of expertise, are most likely to influence the content and fate of a bill. Low-income people, the homeless, children, persons with disabilities, and others with income or physical restrictions often go unheard. These populations are unlikely to approach their congressional representatives personally but rather are dependent on advocacy groups to represent their interests. However, these advocacy groups rarely have access to the financial resources necessary to launch a full-scale lobbying effort. Our democratic system is a wonderful one if you can maneuver around the obstacles to actively participate in it.

Competing interests are a third reason the legislative process is so political. The strength of our democratic process is the opportunity it gives diverse groups of people to participate in the legislative process. Diverse groups have the right to expect that new laws will represent their special interests as well as those of the general population.

For example, if a law were passed that required testing all health care professionals for Acquired Immune Deficiency Syndrome (AIDS), we would see just how strong competing interests can be. Patients of the health care system might welcome such testing as a way to further prevent the spread of the disease. Physicians and nurses might resist mandatory testing, citing it as invasion of their privacy and suggesting that if they must be tested, all their patients should be tested as well. Which of these competing interests prevails is often determined by who has the greater influence on the legislative system. Physicians and nurses who have strong lobbying groups in Washington, D.C., might have more organized, effective influence than people who have no lobbying group to represent their interests.

Rule Making. A law provides basic guidelines and authority for the development of a program. **Promulgating the rules** is the second step in transforming a law into a program. In promulgating the rules, the intent of the bill is translated into specific statements of how the law will be implemented and enforced (Haynes & Mickelson, 1991).

The rule-making process is usually allocated to the government agency that has staff expertise in the area. For example, national legislation on child support enforcement would be assigned to a subdivision of the Department of Health and Human Services for promulgation of the rules. The Office of Management and Budget, under presidential supervision, monitors all rule-making activities to ensure consistency and legality. Federal program rules are then published in the *Federal Register,* along with information regarding the public hearings to be held on the rules.

Even legislation that appears to be highly beneficial to clients can change dramatically in the rule-making process if it is not carefully monitored by its supporters. Social workers can influence the outcome of the rule-making process at two critical points. Professional contact with the staff members assigned to write the administrative rules through written or verbal suggestions is one way to influence the outcome of the rule-making process. Another is to testify at the public hearings through which public input is sought.

The Budgetary Process. When a bill becomes law, it does not automatically become a program or provide services. The budgetary process usually follows a two-step procedure (Jansson, 1990). First, legislative bodies authorize a maximum amount that may be allocated to a program within a given year. Second, the legislative body appropriates (or actually commits) a specific amount to a program. Frequently, the amount of money allocated to a program is significantly less than the amount authorized. The political battles that develop over how much money is allocated to a program can be at least as heated as the original legislative process. Even the most innovative legislation is useless without sufficient funds to implement it. In the past ten years, the federal government has had a difficult time funding existing programs as it struggles to deal with the growing national deficit. Funds are appropriated on the basis of the amount of tax money available. If not enough money is available to fund a program, either the program is not funded or taxes must be raised. However, to raise taxes, Congress must pass another bill that authorizes new taxes. Locating the funding for a program can be complicated.

THE INFLUENCE OF THE MEDIA

A political influence on social welfare policy that is often underestimated is the mass media. Television, radio, newspapers, books, and magazines exert a powerful influence on identifying social problems and on the outcome of pending social welfare legislation.

The media can also control the audience's perception of the seriousness or focus of a social problem. For example, if the media spotlights gay men and intravenous drug users when discussing AIDS, it is unlikely that additional money will be allocated for research and services to persons with AIDS (Shilts, 1987). Outside of some metropolitan areas, intravenous drug users and gay men are not a powerful enough political bloc to be considered. In addition to their small numbers, gay men and intravenous drug users may be seen by some as engaging in socially unacceptable behavior. Controlling the public's perception of the population infected with the AIDS virus can also manipulate the public to ignore, for instance, the number of children who are born with AIDS. These children have not engaged in any of the socially unacceptable behaviors that may be attributed to gay men or intravenous drug users. If the media does not draw attention to the infant AIDS population, that population may remain unserved.

Three major factors influence the media's selection of material: editorial policy, investigative reporting, and community service programming.

Editorial Policy

An **editorial** is a newspaper article or a television or radio broadcast that expresses the opinion of those who own or run the medium. Editorials can be a powerful means of influencing the opinions of the consumers of the news. According to Rystrom (1983), the real purpose of the editorial page in a newspaper is to encourage debate. Few major newspapers present only one position on an issue. Even if the editorial board of a newspaper characterizes itself as liberal, it may represent the conservative viewpoint through columnists and guest editorial writers.

The power of the editorial lies in the selection of issues for editorial attention. The content of editorials is determined by the composition of a newspaper's editorial board. The average newspaper reader glances at the editorial page headlines, only stopping to read if the topic is of interest. However, if a topic receives exceptionally in-depth coverage, the newspaper can create interest in a social issue. Editorials usually include information to which the average reader may not otherwise have access.

Consider the editorial shown in Figure 5.2 on out-of-wedlock pregnancy. The editorial is a combination of fact regarding the alarming rise in out-of-wedlock, especially teenage, pregnancies and strong opinion that despite a reader's beliefs about sexual activity among teenagers, children born to single mothers suffer for society's moralistic attitude toward the behavior of their parents. The editorial implores us to recognize that the poverty inflicted on these children is the most serious problem. Social problems are frequent topics of editorial comment. When they appear in newspapers with the prestige of *The New York Times*, they carry considerable influence.

Investigative Reporting

In the past 20 years, newspaper and television reporters have become more involved in **investigative reporting.** Investigative reporting is based on the assumption that things are not exactly as they appear to be and that information is being intentionally concealed from the public (Benjaminson & Anderson, 1990). Investigative reporters systematically examine all aspects of a story with an eye to what the public does not know. Most often the purpose of investigative reporting is to encourage public awareness and seek change.

Investigative reporting has been a powerful tool in raising the public's awareness about social welfare policy issues. In the late 1950s, John Kenneth Galbraith published a commentary, *The Affluent Society*, that depicted the United States as a relatively middle-class country full of workers who had prospered in the strong economy of the 1950s. In response to this book, Michael Harrington's *The Other America* drew such poignant attention to the plight of poor whites in Appalachia that it caught the attention of President John F. Kennedy. President Kennedy planted the seeds that later became the War on Poverty in 1964. Although President Kennedy did not live to see the official declaration of war on poverty, Harrington's book was instrumental in drawing his attention to the problem.

The Husband Vanishes

Children of unwed mothers may no longer suffer endless stigma. People no longer use terms like "born on the wrong side of the blanket." And the term "bastard" has long since been bleached of its power as an epithet. What illegitimate children now suffer is poverty. Today they constitute more than one of every four children born in the United States.

That figure is even more astonishing when compared with only 25 years ago. Then, the rate among whites was just over 4 percent and among blacks, 25 percent. By 1988 the black rate was 63 percent and the white rate had more than quadrupled to 18 percent.

What happened? For one thing, a sexual revolution. More than half of American teenagers are sexually active; most report having had two or more partners, and the age of first intercourse gets lower and lower. But America is reluctant to give adolescents easy access to contraceptive counseling—and also determined to bar access to abortion. Thirty-five states require parental involvement or a judicial bypass before minors can end unwanted pregnancies. "You play, you pay," it seems, is still at the back of many a mind.

When adolescent sexuality is treated with common sense and common decency, however, teenagers are far less apt to experience pregnancy.

In Baltimore, for instance, students at two inner-city schools—all of whom were poor and took early sex for granted—participated in a program conducted by the Johns Hopkins School of Medicine. A social worker and nurse gave individual and group counseling; medical and contraceptive services were provided at two nearby clinics. Students at two other schools got only Maryland's required sex education courses. After three years, the pregnancy rate at the first pair of schools had dropped 30 percent. At the second, it had gone up 58 percent.

Sadly, such public school programs are rare and seldom replicated. Even if there were more such programs, more contraceptive choices and more straight talk about sex and its consequences, there'd still be unwed mothers. Almost all of them—never mind the publicity about the occasional celebrity mother—would be poor.

"As long as people don't have a vision of a future which having a baby at a very early age will jeopardize," says Laurie Zabin, a Johns Hopkins professor, "they won't go to all the lengths necessary to prevent pregnancy."

Even so, a pregnant 15-year-old sees childbearing as very important, important enough to be shared with people she trusts, her family, her female relatives in particular, and not her child's father. A husband, she figures, would be just another mouth to feed. "They were like middle-class males of the 1950s," Jeanne Masarek, a Swarthmore College psychologist, says of teenage girls she has worked with in inner-city Philadelphia. They said they wouldn't marry until they could provide."

•

The rate of teenage sexual activity in this country rose sharply in the 1980s, but the teenage pregnancy rate changed little because more kids were using contraceptives. Even so, by age 20, a fifth of all women have had their first child.

Maybe marriage, as detractors claim, has become passe. Maybe society is changing the way it thinks about out-of-wedlock births. Meanwhile, though, millions of families consist of poor mother and child units. The fathers are occasional satellite figures, if they're present at all.

America can't legislate abstinence, contraception, or the family ethic. But it can face up to damage done by mindless, obsolete moralism. The task ahead is to give poor children, illegitimate or not, dreams and chances.

Figure 5.2 Example of an editorial
SOURCE: From "The Husband Vanishes," February, 19, 1991, in *The New York Times*.

Nursing home conditions have been a frequent topic for investigative reports. The inability of older people in nursing homes to change the conditions in which they live, the deplorability of those conditions, and the strong involvement of the federal government in regulating and funding nursing homes contribute to their ease as a target for investigative reporting. Public outrage regarding the conditions in nursing homes places public officials in a delicate position: The public and public officials now know what is going on. The public's anger and outrage when a powerful investigative piece is published can influence lawmakers to take action.

Community Service Programming

Radio and television stations are strongly encouraged by the Federal Communications Commission (FCC) to devote a portion of their news programming to community issues. In their regular reports to the FCC, stations include the amount of air time and the nature of the programming that covers a list of community issues identified by the FCC as serving the public interest (Whitley & Skall, 1988). Among these issues are the following:

+ Unemployment/employment training
+ Education
+ Drug and alcohol use/drunken driving
+ Children's welfare
+ Health care
+ Housing
+ Racism and prejudice
+ Teen issues (that is, pregnancy and drug and alcohol use)
+ Environmental issues
+ Neighborhood issues and community development
+ Poverty
+ People and government/taxes
+ Consumer issues

A station might not cover all the issues but choose instead to focus on an issue such as racism and prejudice. One aspect of this issue is what is being done on the legislative and policy level to decrease the amount of racism and prejudice. By exposing audiences to such social issues, electronic media can exert a powerful influence. An informed audience is more likely either to become involved in change or to contact legislators.

Community service programming also includes local and national **public service announcements** (PSAs). PSAs are short visual or audio spots devoted to nonprofit organizations such as the Red Cross or the Salvation Army. The purpose of the PSA is to give the nonprofit sector an opportunity to reach a wide audience without incurring the cost of a paid commercial. For example, a PSA would give the Red Cross the opportunity to solicit blood donors in times of shortages. The Salvation Army might use a PSA to request help with its holiday food programs for low-income families. Television and radio stations have absolute control over which local PSAs are shown and thus control which nonprofit agencies benefit from the free publicity. This control has its advantages and disadvantages. It is an advantage to noncontroversial organizations, such as child welfare agencies, youth recreational services, and general social service agencies. However, because of the controversial nature of what they do, it might place at a disadvantage reproductive health care clinics or agencies that serve people with AIDS.

THE COURT SYSTEM

The court system is rarely acknowledged for the powerful influence it exerts on the development of social welfare policy. The court system, be it local, state, or the federal Supreme Court, is a swift and powerful policy maker. The power to make policy is part of the judicial function (Birkby, 1983).

The Nature of Court Decision Making

Court decision making differs from the policy-making function of the legislature in several important ways (Birkby, 1983; Rubin, 1986). Courts must wait for issues to come to them; they cannot initiate changes in public policy. Legislative bodies can initiate legislation to address a certain issue; courts cannot (Birkby, 1983). Judges rule on specific cases with specific sets of facts and circumstances; therefore, not all legal rulings are applicable even to similar cases. Although the legal profession relies heavily on precedents set by other judges to support their cases, similarity does not mean cases will be handled the same way (Rubin, 1986). Judges cannot "not decide." Congress and the president can decide to ignore a bill, and it dies for lack of action. Court cases must be decided one way or another.

The power of the Supreme Court and lower courts lies in the judges' power to interpret laws. As we noted earlier, people's values determine what is defined as a social problem. Likewise, judges' personal and political values are powerful determinants of what cases will be heard and how laws will be interpreted.

The court system does not make laws. It rules on legal issues that refine the meanings and interpretations of certain laws. For example, in *Brown v. Board of Education of Topeka, Shawnee County, Kansas,* 347 U.S. 483 (1954), the Supreme Court ruled that "separate but equal" facilities for African-American and white students in public education were discriminatory because separate facilities were not actually equal. This ruling opened the door for the desegregation of public schools, one of the most powerful victories in the fight for equal opportunities for minorities.

Such rulings become part of law as a matter of **legal precedent.** This means that how previous judges have handled certain legal questions becomes part of the law. Precedents may have a powerful influence on future court

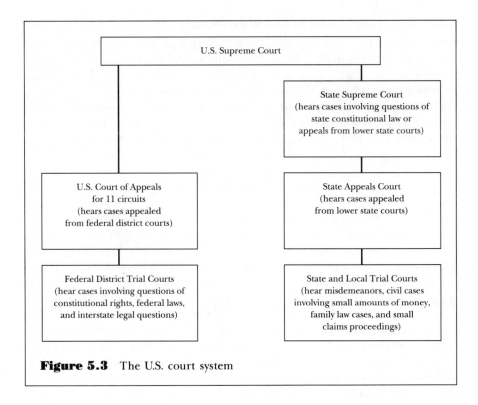

Figure 5.3   The U.S. court system

decisions, but court decisions are not "self-executing, meaning that judges
have relatively little direct power to enforce compliance with their decisions"
(Smith, 1991, p. 98).

The Structure of the Court System

Figure 5.3 illustrates the organization of the U.S. court system. Federal district
courts hear cases involving the U.S. Constitution, federal laws, and parties
who are citizens of different states. Appeals go from federal district courts
to circuit courts of appeals and then may advance to the U.S. Supreme Court.
Criminal cases involving misdemeanors (minor crimes with no injury to persons or involving no weapons) and limited-damage civil suits are usually
handled by city or municipal trial courts. State trial courts usually handle
larger civil suits involving large amounts of money, probate, divorce, and
felony cases.

Cases are appealed to another level of the court system when one
of the litigants is not satisfied with the ruling of the lower court. When a
case is appealed, the judge reviews the record of the lower trial court and
the briefs from each side of the case to see if a mistake has been made.
Although cases that have been heard before the U.S. Supreme Court are the
best-known cases, making it to the Supreme Court is a long process.

How the Court System Is Political

The court system is political in part because of the power of individual judges to interpret a law. Judges are either elected or appointed. If a judge is elected, it is because his or her approach (whether lenient on criminals or particularly strict) reflects the inclination of the voters. If a judge is appointed, it is by an elected official and therefore reflects the political orientation of that elected official. Supreme Court justices are appointed for life by the President of the United States. Democratic presidents have tended to appoint relatively liberal judges; Republican presidents tend to appoint conservative judges. Because justices are appointed for life, the political orientation of the Supreme Court outlasts presidential administrations.

How the Court System Determines Social Welfare Policy

As mentioned earlier, courts do not make laws but interpret the application of laws. Even if a state has passed a law through the traditional legislative process, the court system can overturn the law if it is found to be unconstitutional or illegal on the basis of other laws. Using the court system to achieve changes in social welfare policy is often a much faster way of making those changes. A Supreme Court ruling not only affects the state from which the case originates but serves as a valuable precedent for challenging laws in all states.

In *Griswold v. State of Connecticut,* 381 U.S. 479 (1965), the Supreme Court ruled in favor of Planned Parenthood of Connecticut. Planned Parenthood had been fined for giving a married couple information about contraception, which was at that time a violation of Connecticut law. The court rendered its decision on the basis that a law prohibiting the dissemination of information about contraception is in violation of the right to privacy, which is protected by the Bill of Rights. This is not to say that sexually active people did not use contraception before this ruling, but laws existed in states other than Connecticut that prohibited the dissemination of information about contraceptive techniques. A Supreme Court ruling allowed states to abolish many antiquated laws that had not been enforced in years.

One of the most famous U.S. Supreme Court cases that changed social welfare policy in the United States is *Roe v. Wade,* 410 U.S. 113 (1973), which is discussed in Chapter One. The Supreme Court determined that the Texas statute that prohibited elective abortions, except in cases of incest or rape, was a violation of the due process clause of the Fourteenth Amendment. Thirty-one states had highly restrictive abortion laws that could no longer be enforced after *Roe v. Wade* (Brieland & Lemmon, 1985). *Roe v. Wade* continues to be highly controversial, and it will probably be challenged again in the 1990s by those who oppose elective abortions. We may see national policy on elective abortions change again through the court system.

SUMMARY

This chapter examines how personal and social values define social problems in different ways. Although not a direct policy maker, the media can be important to the policy-making process in how they choose to expose their audiences to social issues that are later defined as social problems. This chapter also examines the most traditional form of policy making, the legislative process, and one of the more nontraditional methods, the court system.

Chapter Six examines the policy-making process in depth based on the problem-solving approach, the same basic model direct-service practitioners frequently use to assess problems and select intervention methods for individual clients. Using the example of the fictitious community of Cableton, Chapter Six shows how the legislative process, the media, and the courts affect the development of a social welfare policy.

DISCUSSION QUESTIONS

1. *Discuss how values might influence the development of an AIDS policy in the United States. How will people's different opinions about why AIDS is a problem suggest different solutions to the problem?*
2. *Review the process by which a bill becomes a law.*
3. *What social issues have been covered by investigative reporters in your local newspaper? What happened once an investigative story was published? Did public officials take action as a result of the story?*
4. *What social issues are presently before the U.S. Supreme Court? How does the political orientation of Supreme Court justices influence their decisions? Have decisions been overturned that were made by Supreme Court justices with different political orientations?*

SUGGESTED PROJECTS

1. Collect editorials on social issues from your local newspaper for several weeks. Can you identify the political orientation (conservative or liberal) of the paper's editorial board? Interview the editor of the paper and discuss how he or she determines what kinds of editorials the paper publishes. If your class has strong feelings about a social issue in your community, ask the editor if you may write a guest editorial.
2. As a class project, follow a piece of legislation through your state legislature or through the U.S. Congress. If you are following a piece of state legislation, interview a lobbyist to find out how he or she can influence the outcome of a bill.

3. Find out how local television or radio stations determine what community service programming they will air. Are they willing to air controversial public service announcements? What community service programming have they broadcast in the last year?

Notes

1. The literature on teenage childbearing is extensive. For further information that supports these five common statements, see *A State-by-State Look at Teenage Childbearing in the United States* (Flint, MI: Charles Stewart Mott Foundation, 1991); Cheryl D. Hayes (Ed.), *Risking the Future: Adolescent Sexuality, Pregnancy and Childbearing* (Washington, DC: National Academy Press, 1987); Elise F. Jones, *Teenage Pregnancy in Industrialized Countries* (New Haven, CT: Yale University Press, 1986); Gary E. McCuen (Ed.), *Children Having Children: Global Perspectives on Teenage Pregnancy* (Hudson, WI: McCuen, 1988); Kristin Moore and Martha R. Burt, *Private Crisis, Public Cost: Policy Perspectives on Teenage Childbearing* (Washington, DC: The Urban Institute, 1982); and Maris A. Vinovskis, *An "Epidemic of Adolescent Pregnancy"? Some Historical and Policy Considerations* (New York: Oxford University Press, 1988).

IMPORTANT TERMS AND CONCEPTS

conference committee	*promulgating the rules*
editorial	*public service announcement*
investigative reporting	*rational process*
legal precedent	

CHAPTER SIX

The Policy-Making Process:
The Problem-Solving Approach

*Since human wants are endless, and when one is satisfied
another immediately takes its place, we all are constantly involved in problem solving; although some of us, because we do
not understand how one problem solves effectively, make a great
mess of it.*

—BEULAH COMPTON & BURT GALAWAY, 1989, p. 308

Direct practitioners are well aware of the importance of approaching a client's problem in a systematic, organized fashion. In the midst of the emotional intensity that frequently accompanies a personal problem, practitioners can help to stabilize emotional chaos and steer clients toward meaningful decision making if they approach the problem through a series of rational steps leading to problem resolution. The **problem-solving approach** is the most familiar way of organizing our knowledge so we can analyze the causes of problems, propose solutions, and turn ideas into ac-tion plans in a logical and coherent fashion.

Although most commonly used in direct services, the problem-solving approach is equally useful for developing social welfare policy. This chapter includes the following:

♦ An explanation of the steps in the problem-solving model as it is used in direct services

+ Application of the problem-solving model to the development of a social welfare policy to address the problem of teenage pregnancy in the fictitious community of Cableton
+ A demonstration of the importance of a community social systems assessment in broadening our perspectives on the causes of social problems and their solutions

A systematic, organized approach to problem solving is not unique to social work practice. All physical and social sciences attempt to approach problem solving through a set of basic steps:

1. *Assessing the problem.* Gathering information about a problem to help define the problem precisely and establish general goals.

2. *Exploring alternatives.* Considering as many solutions to the problem as possible, using available resources and developing new ones. This stage also includes thinking through the consequences of the proposed alternatives.

3. *Selecting an alternative and developing an action plan.* Once an alternative is selected, it is necessary to carefully plan what must be done to reach the goals identified by the assessment. Goals must be translated into specific tasks to be accomplished.

4. *Implementing the action plan.* During this stage, the plans made in Step 3 are carried out.

5. *Evaluating the results.* If the goals of Step 1 have been achieved, the process is complete. If the goals have not been achieved, the evaluation process identifies how a new action plan might be developed.

Although most commonly associated with direct services, the problem-solving model is helpful in explaining the development of social welfare policies and programs. Continuing with the example of teenage pregnancy, this chapter uses the problem-solving model to develop a hypothetical social welfare policy that addresses the special needs of teen mothers and their children. Because this model can be used to develop any social welfare policy, this example serves as a general guideline for policy development.

THE COMMUNITY OF CABLETON

This exercise uses the example of a fictitious urban area, Cableton. Cableton has a population of 500,000 with a racial composition of 60% white, 40% African American, 8% Hispanic, and 2% Asian. Neighborhoods are highly segregated, with 90% of all racial and ethnic minorities living within a 2-mile radius of the downtown area. Seventy percent of all minorities have incomes below the poverty line, compared to 15% of the white population. Cableton was a highly industrialized city but has lost 50,000 jobs in the last 20 years as the economy has turned from manufacturing to service jobs.

Recently, a state study has indicated that Cableton has the second highest teenage pregnancy rate among minorities in the United States. Eighty percent of the teen mothers in Cableton keep their babies and—as single mothers—try to raise them. Most of these mothers have become dependent on public assistance and have swelled the public assistance rolls beyond the ability of Cableton County to provide assistance. When the state study was released, the local newspaper provided extensive coverage of both the study and teenage pregnancy in general. A series of articles focused on how much teenage parents and their children were costing taxpayers; public outrage over the issues resulted. Responding to public pressure, the mayor of Cableton appointed the Task Force on Teen Parenthood (TFTP) to make recommendations for local policies that would address the issue. Members of the task force included social workers, health care providers, and several city council members.

STEP 1: ASSESSING THE PROBLEM

Assessment involves gathering information about a problem, defining the problem precisely, identifying resources and obstacles, and setting goals. Assessment is the most important step in policy making because it is the foundation of the entire process.

The state report on Cableton did not surprise members of the TFTP, most of whom had been concerned about rising rates of teenage pregnancy for years. However, the state report gave the TFTP the most valuable component of policy making: information. The study had been done by researchers at the School of Social Welfare at the local state university, so it was considered reliable. Who conducts the study and for what purpose can bias a research study so that the information is useless. Not all policy-making groups are fortunate enough to have a dependable research study at their disposal. More commonly, policy makers must find out more directly what people need.

Needs Assessments

A **needs assessment** is a procedure for determining what services a community requires to meet basic human needs. Good planning and policy making require concrete information about the extent of the need for services and how well current services are meeting those needs. Policy makers cannot rely on what they *feel* people need; they must obtain statistical documentation. Professional intuition can be accurate, but specific facts and figures are required to convince city councils or state legislatures that a need truly exists.

Needs can be identified by a needs assessment survey. Surveys are questionnaires in which people are asked what they need and why existing services are inadequate to meet those needs. If carefully conducted, surveys provide the most accurate and current information about a community's needs. However, surveys are expensive and time consuming. The task of identifying and finding survey participants for a particular issue is a much bigger project than most communities can handle.

Using existing statistical information collected by a unit of government or a college or university can be a less expensive, more efficient way to obtain information about the social welfare needs of a community. The TFTP in Cableton decided to accept the results of the state survey. The survey summarized current population surveys conducted by the government, birth records, the records of the county department of social services, and other demographic data about Cableton to determine the teenage pregnancy rate in the city. The state report identified the neighborhoods, age groups, racial groups, and school districts in which unusually high teenage pregnancy rates occur. After sifting through all the information, the TFTP determined that the most serious problem existed among teenagers under the age of 18 who quit high school as soon as they became pregnant. Even if the young mothers did not want to receive public assistance as a means of financial support, few full- or part-time jobs were available to these high school dropouts that paid enough to enable them to support their children.

However, the Cableton TFTP was not satisfied simply with knowing that the high-risk group was high school dropouts. They wanted to know why Cableton, as opposed to other communities in the state, had such a high pregnancy rate. The members separated into two groups for the next step in the assessment process.

Group 1 researched the general topic of teenage pregnancy. The group wanted answers to the following questions:

+ What common characteristics do teen mothers in all communities share?
+ Who is most at risk to become pregnant?
+ What have other communities done to decrease the number of teenage pregnancies?

The best resource in the policy-making process is information. Using what other professionals have learned can save time and money when the Cableton leaders reach later stages in the problem-solving process.

Group 1 found the alarmingly high rates of teen pregnancy were not unique to Cableton. The United States has the highest teen pregnancy rate in the industrialized world (Jones, 1986). International studies have attributed this phenomenon to several factors unique to the United States. These factors include lack of access to health care for teenagers due to the private structure of health care in this country. In other major industrialized nations, the government is primarily responsible for providing health care; this eliminates the financial barriers to adolescents seeking contraceptive information. Health care in the United States is treated much like other private enterprises. People have access to health care if they can afford to pay for it or are poor enough to qualify for government Medical Assistance. The private model of health care is an example of the enduring American value of free enterprise. The American Medical Association is one of the strongest lobbying groups in Washington, D.C., and has effectively kept the federal government out of the business of providing health care. The financial interests of physicians may be reflected in this value, which has contributed to a higher rate of teenage pregnancy because of lack of access to health care for teens.

Jones (1986) also found that attitudes of repression and denial about adolescent sexuality contributed to high pregnancy rates. Adolescents lack accurate information about sex, which is portrayed in the United States as "romantic yet sinful and dirty; it is flaunted but also something to be hidden" (Jones, 1986, p. 223). Traditional American values identify marriage as the "right" context for sexual behavior. As a result, sexual activity among teenagers is seen as a problem in itself. The editorial presented in Figure 5.2 discusses the potential of people's attitudes to destine the children of teenage mothers to a life of poverty. Although behavior in the United States does not necessarily reflect that value, its persistence in people's minds makes it an obstacle to working with teens who are sexually active.

Group 1 also found that high levels of public assistance are not directly linked to the incidence of teen pregnancy. Other industrialized nations have more generous benefit levels than the United States but lower teen pregnancy rates and much lower poverty rates among teen parents. Experts speculate that more generous financial support for teen parents reduces the likelihood of lifelong poverty for the mother and child. The level of poverty in any country also directly correlates to pregnancy rates among teenagers. In the United States, public assistance payments do not bring recipients above the poverty line. This is a reflection of another American value, the importance and necessity of hard work and self-sufficiency. The American value system actively discourages public dependency. Unfortunately, the victims of the resulting poverty are children, who are powerless to change their own situations.

Finally, Group 1 discovered that the teenagers most likely to become pregnant were "those from emotionally as well as economically deprived backgrounds, who unrealistically seek gratification and fulfillment from having a child of their own" (Jones, 1986, p. 227). This finding suggests that whatever plan is developed for reducing teenage pregnancy in Cableton, it will be necessary to work with high-risk teens who lack goals and a vision for their own future.

Based on the wide variety of information they have reviewed, Group 1 identifies the following factors as important influences on the teenage pregnancy rates in Cableton:

1. Lack of access to contraceptive methods among teens
2. High levels of poverty, which contribute to the emotional and economic deprivation of teens who see having a baby as a way to change their lives for the better

Group 2 of the TFTP organized a series of community meetings involving teachers from local schools, health clinic nurses, social workers from youth centers in low-income neighborhoods, and teen parents. Group 2 heard several important points in the series of community meetings. First, teachers indicated that teens romanticize having and raising a child. Teachers saw teenagers who have no career aspirations and poor self-images as those at highest risk for becoming pregnant while still in school. Youth workers expressed concern about teenagers, both male and female, having access to contraceptive information and general health care and the "it will never happen to me" attitude of some teens. Social workers from the county department of social services blamed much of the problem on the lack of healthy role models for teens and poor parental supervision. County social workers also described how serious and debilitating unemployment had become during the last 20 years. Even high school graduates living in low-income neighborhoods could not find jobs that could support a family. Fathers of children did not marry the children's mothers because they could not provide as much support as public assistance. During these meetings community leaders in Group 2 heard a variety of reasons why the rate of teen pregnancy was so high in Cableton but nothing that contradicted researchers in other communities.

Teen parents had important contributions to make to the TFTP's understanding of teen pregnancy. Some parents indicated that although they knew about birth control, they either did not know where to obtain it or how to use it correctly. Others simply had not considered the possibility that they would become pregnant. Teen parents spoke openly about how different it was to be a parent from how they had envisioned it. They shared their frustrations about being isolated from their friends, having difficulty finding and paying for child care, and feeling that their lives were hopeless now that they had to care for a child. They cited a sense of total "aloneness" once they became parents, making it difficult, if not impossible, for them to resume their schooling or even to think about employment.

Figure 6.1 shows the social system assessment compiled by the TFTP. The assessment graphically identifies the elements in a teenage parent's social system and identifies the factors that influence them.

Defining the Problem and Setting Goals

After processing all the information from the literature search and the public meetings, the TFTP defines the problem as concisely as possible. Some teen pregnancies result from lack of information about or access to contraceptive information. Once a pregnancy occurs, teenagers are at high risk for dropping out of school, partly due to a lack of child care and support services. The depressed economic condition of low-income neighborhoods makes it difficult, if not impossible, for teen parents to work their way out of poverty and off welfare, even if they are highly motivated. The TFTP agrees on three main goals for their policy-making efforts that reflect their definition of the problem:

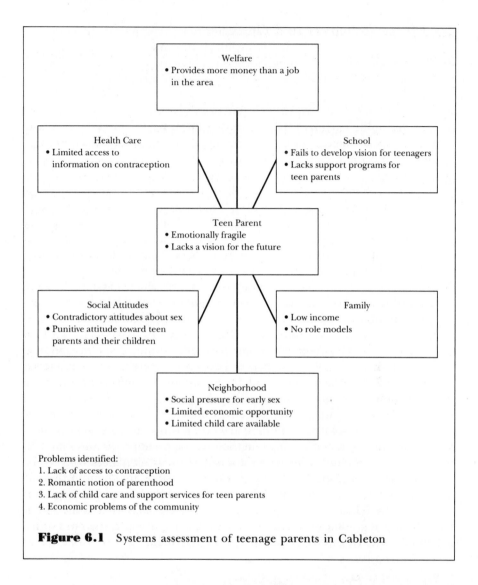

Welfare
• Provides more money than a job in the area

Health Care
• Limited access to information on contraception

School
• Fails to develop vision for teenagers
• Lacks support programs for teen parents

Teen Parent
• Emotionally fragile
• Lacks a vision for the future

Social Attitudes
• Contradictory attitudes about sex
• Punitive attitude toward teen parents and their children

Family
• Low income
• No role models

Neighborhood
• Social pressure for early sex
• Limited economic opportunity
• Limited child care available

Problems identified:
1. Lack of access to contraception
2. Romantic notion of parenthood
3. Lack of child care and support services for teen parents
4. Economic problems of the community

Figure 6.1 Systems assessment of teenage parents in Cableton

1. Launch an intensive, communitywide education effort aimed at parenthood awareness and encouragement of the use of contraceptives
2. Mobilize community resources to increase the number of support programs available to teen parents to help parents complete at least high school if a pregnancy occurs
3. Work with the city council to develop financial incentives for business and industry to locate in low-income neighborhoods, thus increasing employment opportunities for all residents

Identifying Resources and Obstacles

Before the Task Force on Teen Parenthood moves ahead toward developing a plan and identifies areas in which policies and programs must be developed, it is important for them to identify resources and the obstacles they anticipate in meeting the goals they have set as a task force.

Resources.   Examples of resources it might be helpful to mobilize include public health clinics geared to the special needs of adolescents, school nurses and guidance departments, social workers in the public assistance section of the county department of social services, day care centers, and child care providers. For years, the Cableton Economic Development Commission has considered presenting a tax-incentive business development plan to the city council. The work of the TFTP should speed up their efforts. Identifying existing community resources helps prevent expensive duplication of services and determine why existing services are not currently meeting identified needs.

Obstacles.   Once TFTP members identify resources, they must also identify obstacles they anticipate. For every obstacle that planners correctly anticipate, there are usually three or four they did not anticipate. Obstacles can include lack of public funds for new programs, community resistance to acknowledging teenage sexuality (doing so might be interpreted as encouraging it), racism aimed at minority teens in the community, and the skepticism of service providers who doubt that new programs will help reduce teenage pregnancy. The TFTP cannot improve the local economy by itself, but it can pressure organizations like the Cableton Economic Development Commission to come up with some ideas, if it determines that the commission is not an obstacle in itself. In this final part of the assessment process, the task force must acknowledge potential obstacles, brainstorm solutions to overcome them, and identify obstacles they cannot remove. For example, lack of public funds for new social welfare programs is a common obstacle facing groups trying to work with social problems. The task force will have to work within the existing service delivery system for more efficient service delivery or for a different kind of service rather than attempt to develop a completely new social program.

Assessment is lengthy and complicated, but it is the foundation of the policy-making process. A sound assessment lays important groundwork for the rest of the policy-making process.

STEP 2: EXPLORING ALTERNATIVES

Exploring alternatives involves discussing as many solutions as possible using available resources and considering the anticipated obstacles. As potential solutions are identified, the consequences must also be anticipated. Unfortunately, we can never know all the possible solutions to a problem, nor can we anticipate all the possible obstacles. This is a good example of what organizational theorists call *bounded rationality*, a term that describes the limits of our abilities to examine all options. Our exploration is limited by our knowledge and by the unforeseen consequences of our decisions.

All alternatives are presented together with the goals of the task force to ensure that the task force is working in conjunction with the goals established in the assessment process.

> *Goal 1:* Launch an intensive, communitywide education effort aimed at parenthood awareness and encouragement of the use of contraceptives.
>
> > *Option 1:* Mandatory sex education in all schools in the district.
> >
> > > *Advantages:* This plan, which covers all age groups, is the most aggressive in terms of coverage. It is efficient because it uses an existing service system, the schools. It would also focus on prevention by educating children before they become sexually active. Beginning sex education in high school might be too late.
> > >
> > > *Disadvantages:* Schools are already overburdened with responsibilities, and school boards might not be willing to require sex education of their students, fearing reprisal from parents and taxpayers. Mandatory sex education might be unacceptable to parents who want to provide sex education at home. This program does not reach teen parents who may not be in school.
> >
> > *Option 2:* On-site school health clinics that offer birth control information and provide contraceptives to minors.
> >
> > > *Advantages:* If clinics were available in high-risk neighborhoods through the school system, the basic problem of access would be solved. The same unit would provide education and service. Sex education and the learning function of the school system would be separate.
> > >
> > > *Disadvantages:* Cost is prohibitive. Parents and administrators might object to on-site clinics because they might seem to encourage sexual behavior among teenagers. Schools could be held liable if health problems developed because contraceptives were provided. The community might object to schools hosting health clinics that fall outside the function of public education. This option does not reach teen parents who have dropped out of school; they cannot benefit from any service offered by the public school system.
> >
> > *Option 3:* Aggressive sex education program in schools in high-risk areas and provision of basic birth control information when requested.

Advantages: This is a more efficient version of Option 1, in which high-risk areas are targeted for intervention. It is more feasible to work with 6 or 8 schools than with 60; therefore it would be more efficient. The program can still focus on junior high as well as high school students.

Disadvantages: Some parents might object to sex education programs and the provision of birth control information, but making the information available upon request might appease these objections. However, "upon request" limits access to this information if the teenager is too embarrassed to request it. Once again, this option does not reach teen parents who do not attend school.

Option 4: Public information campaign on radio stations and television stations using public service announcements (PSAs) to discuss adolescent sexuality and contraceptives.

Advantages: Radio and television broadcasts have a good chance of reaching teenagers both in and out of school. Public service announcements are a free service of radio and television stations. A wide variety of PSAs can be developed to meet the interests of a broad audience, including teenagers, teen parents, and adult members of the community.

Disadvantages: It might be difficult to obtain the cooperation of radio and television stations if station owners are not willing to develop PSAs on such a controversial topic. Stations might be afraid of alienating advertisers and viewers. Limited time is available for PSAs.

Option 5: Development of an aggressive, informative series in the local newspaper on teen parenthood, designed to educate everyone who reads the paper.

Advantages: This option reaches a wide audience, especially those outside of high-risk areas of Cableton. Publishing informative articles is one of the purposes of newspapers. This is an inexpensive way to distribute information.

Disadvantages: The newspaper might not be willing to publish the proposed series. Negative publicity on the part of the press created the public outrage about teenage pregnancy in the first place.

Goal 2: Mobilize community resources to increase the number of support programs available to teen parents to help them complete at least high school if a pregnancy occurs.

Option 1: Child care centers located in the schools.

Advantages: Child care centers located in the schools would be very convenient and would serve as a strong incentive to bring teen parents back into the classroom. The physical

facilities already exist, and school nurse services would be
accessible.

Disadvantages: The school system is already overburdened
with its responsibilities to students. Starting child care
centers is very expensive, and the school system cannot afford to completely subsidize a child care center. How would
TFTP decide which schools would have child care centers
and which ones would not? Where would the money come
from to pay child care workers when teachers are already
underpaid?

Option 2: Work with existing child care facilities to expand the
services available, making teenage parents a top priority for
new child care spots.

Advantages: This option takes advantage of existing services
and expertise in the community. It requires only an expansion, not the development of new services. It would not
be necessary to train new workers.

Disadvantages: Additional money will be required to expand
existing child care facilities. Many young mothers will require transportation to existing and expanded child care
centers; this requires additional funds. This approach addresses the need for additional child care but may not
prove sufficient to encourage teen mothers to return to
school.

Goal 3: Work with the city council to develop financial incentives
for business and industry to locate in low-income neighborhoods,
thus increasing employment opportunities for all residents.

Option: To work directly with the Cableton Economic Development Commission on long-term economic development. This
is a large-scale focus that will require the cooperation of a
number of organizations in addition to the TFTP and requires
expertise beyond that of the task force.

These options do not represent all the possible alternatives that the
TFTP could explore, but they give you an idea of how the process of exploring alternatives might look. Exploring alternatives requires discussing ideas
that might be clearly unacceptable to the community. If planners have some
idea of what the community will definitely not accept, it will help them
develop a more acceptable plan of action.

STEP 3: DEVELOPING AN ACTION PLAN

After carefully exploring alternatives, the TFTP decides to act on the original
goals in the following way:

Goal 1: Launch an intensive, communitywide education effort aimed at parenthood awareness and encouragement of the use of contraceptives.

> *Plan of Action:* Three junior and senior high schools have been targeted for intensive programs to begin within six months. Three television and seven radio stations will be approached to participate in developing public service announcements to begin airing within three months. The task force will approach the largest local newspaper to work on developing a monthly feature on teen parenting that will inform and educate the community on teen pregnancy.

Goal 2: Mobilize community resources to increase the number of support programs available to teen parents to help them complete at least high school if a pregnancy occurs.

> *Plan of Action:* The TFTP would like to develop three child care centers in the neighborhoods most acutely affected by teen pregnancy. These child care centers would provide child care for 180 more children than are currently being served. At the same time, teen mothers and fathers who have children in child care will be given the opportunity to attend job training or career counseling sessions.

Goal 3: Work with the city council to develop financial incentives for business and industry to locate in low-income neighborhoods, thus increasing employment opportunities for all residents.

> *Plan of Action:* The TFTP has set up three meetings in the next six months to work with the Economic Development Commission. Both the commission and the task force have been assigned general tasks to accomplish during the next six months. The problem-solving process will start all over again for this group.

In this example, the goals of the TFTP have been placed in action in quantifiable terms so that when the policy is evaluated in six months, the task force will be able to measure its results. When goals are specific, it is easier to break down the tasks that must be done and assign them to task force members, and the tasks are more likely to get done.

STEP 4: IMPLEMENTING THE ACTION PLAN

During this stage of the problem-solving approach to policy making, the goals are translated into specific tasks that must be done to achieve the goals. For example, a city council member and a social worker are assigned to approach the local newspaper about running a series of informative articles about teen pregnancy and teen parents. This team is chosen because the city council member is acquainted with a member of the paper's editorial board, her tennis partner. The social worker can help a reporter obtain the most recent and accurate information and connect her to teen parents who are willing to be interviewed by the paper.

Target schools for the parenthood education and birth control information campaigns will be approached by the public health nurses who work in the district in which the schools are located. Taking advantage of people's natural affiliations with others in the community can make the implementation of the action plan most efficient and effective.

It soon became evident that the development of the new child care centers would be a long-range goal. Four task force members were assigned to investigate child care development. These members included two city council members, two child care center workers, and a local businessperson. This part of the policy plan would require the biggest financial commitment. A detailed plan would be needed and financing would have to be secured before this portion of the plan could be implemented.

STEP 5: EVALUATING THE POLICY-MAKING EFFORT

Once a policy has been implemented, it is important to evaluate whether progress is being made toward achieving the goals. After six months, the TFTP meets again to assess how well they are moving toward achieving their goals. They find the school information project is going very well. School officials and parents in the targeted schools have been very cooperative.

A lawsuit was filed against the school district complaining about sex education in the public schools. The judge in the case determined that parents who objected to sex education in the schools had to be given the option of keeping their children out of sex education classes. However, as the classes progressed, many of these junior high and high school students wanted to take the classes. School officials and TFTP members agreed to reevaluate and perhaps expand the program in another six months. If the program continues to be successful, the school system will consider incorporating the cost of the program into the permanent school budget.

The six-month evaluation of the media educational program indicated that some changes in strategy would be necessary. Radio and television stations were helpful in producing public service announcements but aired them early in the morning, a time when the target audience (teenagers and teen parents) was not likely to be tuned in. The series of educational newspaper articles was slow in getting off the ground, but six articles were scheduled to run within the next three months. The TFTP decided to arrange for meetings with media people to try to correct these problems.

The subcommittee on child care development reported that it had succeeded in obtaining a grant for $100,000 from local industry to set up at least one child care center. A portion of that money would be used to set up career counseling for teen parents at the day care center, rather than in the school setting. Although career counseling was not part of the original plan, it was one of the original goals of the task force.

The task force members assigned to work with the Economic Development Commission reported that three tax incentive plans were under consideration in an effort to attract new jobs to low-income neighborhoods.

SUMMARY

This chapter shows how the problem-solving approach can be used to develop social welfare policy using the example of a large community's effort to address its high teenage pregnancy rate. Assessing a problem requires gathering information about the problem and establishing general goals. In the process of exploring alternatives, it is important to consider both feasible and impractical alternatives and the consequences of all possible choices. Once an alternative has been selected, it is important to act on the goals, which means translating them into a specific plan of action. Goals should be measurable so policy-making efforts can be meaningfully evaluated.

Chapter Seven discusses the ways practitioners and researchers analyze and evaluate proposed and current social welfare policy. Program and policy evaluation is the first step in identifying what we want to change when it becomes apparent that the policy is either insufficient or ineffective in meeting the needs of the client population for whom it was developed.

DISCUSSION QUESTIONS

1. *What are the steps in the problem-solving model? Which step do you feel is the most crucial to developing a workable social welfare policy?*
2. *What risk does a policy-making organization take if it does not assess needs before it develops a policy?*
3. *How does the inclusion of a systems assessment of policy issues broaden our understanding of the cause of a social problem and its solution?*

SUGGESTED PROJECTS

1. Find out whether a human services needs assessment has been conducted in your community in recent years. Who conducted the assessment, and how was the information used by those in decision-making positions? Did the group conducting the needs assessment in your community follow the problem-solving approach?

2. Select a committee or subcommittee in your community that is addressing a specific social problem. Interview committee members to assess how
   they plan to study the social problem and how they will identify a wide
   range of solutions to that problem.

IMPORTANT TERMS AND CONCEPTS

needs assessment   *problem-solving approach*
plan of action

Policy Evaluation, Research, and Analysis

We often design programs that seem curiously out of touch with the problems that arise in practice. . . . we seem unable to grasp the real nature of action, which remains hidden, tacit, and inaccessible. Clearly, there is more to understanding policy than the task of legitimizing action. At the least, we seek to discover meaning and purpose from our action.

—MARTIN REIN, 1983, p. xi

⬧ ⬧ ⬧

As Martin Rein indicates in the opening quote, social welfare policy is often "curiously out of touch with the problems that arise in prac- tice." The programs and policies developed and implemented in the ways discussed in the first six chapters might be inadequate to meet the real needs of the clients we serve. It is not difficult to find practicing social workers who shake their heads in disbelief at the impracticality or inefficiency of new social welfare policies and programs. It often seems as though policy makers develop policies in a political vacuum rather than in close consulta- tion with the clients and social workers who live with those policies.

On the other hand, the social work profession can legitimately be accused of offering only vague recommendations about the need for specific policies or improving current policies. Comments such as "somebody has to do something" or "it will never work with my clients" are offered rather than coherent, carefully composed suggestions for a more effective social welfare policy.

This chapter helps you develop the skills necessary to engage in program evaluation, policy research, and policy analysis. These are three ways of gathering empirical evidence to assess the effectiveness and efficiency of current and proposed social welfare policy. This text examines evaluation, research, and analysis separately because each has a specific role in policy assessment.

Specifically, this chapter includes the following:

+ A description of the program evaluation process in which an agency or staff member assesses the purpose and procedures of a program within an agency
+ An exploration of the process of social welfare policy research, the assessment of a policy or program conducted by administrative or academic researchers using the scientific method of examining the effectiveness and efficiency of large-scale social welfare policies
+ Introduction of the ANALYSIS model for evaluating policies and programs that directly affect your work with clients

PROGRAM EVALUATION

Program evaluation refers to "the critical and rigorous examination of a program's operation and outcomes with attention to the program goals and other effects, intended or unintended" (Rutman, 1977, p. 13). Program evaluation is conducted within a public or private agency to examine a program's efficiency and to determine whether a new program has achieved its goals for the service population. For example, a child welfare agency might want to assess the success of a specialized program to promote the adoption of children with special needs. By examining the components of the program's operation, the agency can determine whether the program is operating with the maximum amount of service and the minimum amount of waste or effort. By comparing the original goals of the program with the results, or outcomes, the agency can determine whether the goals were realized and thus determine whether a program should be continued, discontinued, or modified.

The Purpose of Evaluating Programs

Social welfare programs are evaluated for several reasons. First, a competent evaluation can assist the agency in future planning and management of the agency's programs (Portney, 1986). If the special-needs adoption program already mentioned is expensive to run and results in a small number of adoptions, management must decide whether the investment in personnel, marketing, and services is cost-efficient for the agency. Perhaps the money used to run the special-needs program might be more efficiently used in the treatment foster care program, providing special supplements to foster families for long-term care of children with special needs, rather than permanent adoption or institutionalization.

Programs are also evaluated as a means of maintaining accountability to funding sources. Purchase of service contracts, demonstration grants from sources outside the agency, and targeted funds from community sources may require agencies to evaluate a program. Funding sources have the right to know whether the funds are being used for their intended purposes and used in the most efficient way possible.

Programs are evaluated to determine whether the program has had unintended effects. As we know from Chapter Two, decisions are made within the constraints of bounded rationality, meaning that no one can know all possible alternatives or the consequences of those alternatives. A program begun with good intentions may have negative consequences that could not have been predicted. For example, the state of Wisconsin has a program called Learnfare, which requires that teenagers who receive AFDC or who are in families that receive AFDC must attend school on a regular basis or risk a reduction in the amount of their welfare checks. One of the unforeseen consequences of this program has been the increase in the number of teenagers receiving AFDC who apply for a waiver from the program. Because they cannot secure child care for their dependent children or transportation to day care, these teenagers are not required to attend school. Those on whom the program was meant to focus, teenaged parents, can be legitimately excused from school attendance. The demand for day care far exceeds the funds allocated to the Learnfare program to supplement existing resources for child care. This type of unforeseen consequence is an important part of evaluating the worth of a program such as Learnfare. Instead of saving the state of Wisconsin money on the AFDC program, it has resulted in an increase in the amount of state money allocated for day care, a very expensive and difficult program to run.

Programs are also systematically evaluated to obtain quantifiable and empirical descriptions of a policy's operation and outcomes. Vague and undocumented observations about a program's effectiveness are not helpful in making management decisions. Administrators need empirical observations— that is, numbers, specific case examples, and cost-benefit ratios on which to base sound management decisions.

Preevaluation Activities

Before evaluators engage in the full-scale evaluation of a program within an agency, four important questions must be answered.

First, *who will evaluate the program?* Programs are often evaluated informally within the agency by administrators or agency staff. Internal evaluations can take less time because staff know how the program operates and have access to the information necessary for the evaluation. It is unlikely, though, that internal evaluations of social welfare programs will be unbiased

(Rutman, 1977). The most comprehensive and credible program evaluations rely on outside evaluators, who are less likely to be biased about the program's operation. It is easier for outside evaluators to be objective because their jobs are not at stake should the evaluation reflect poorly on the program in question. They will not be affected by the pressure within the agency to evaluate a popular program positively or an unpopular one negatively. Their lack of preconceived notions about agency programs and staff can promote a more rigorous and critical evaluation of the program.

Second, *will the evaluation examine output or impact, or both?* If evaluators simply look at the numbers of clients served, hours of service, number of personnel, expenditure of funds, and other quantitative measures, the evaluation is referred to as an **output evaluation.** Output evaluations are primarily descriptive, not analytical. They report the numbers pertinent to a program's operation but do not analyze the effects of the program. Output evaluations are reports, not evaluations in the true sense of the word. **Impact evaluations** include the same quantitative materials as output evaluations but also include descriptive and analytical material about the nonquantifiable aspects of a program. The perception of a program in a community, the morale of staff and clients, the effect of a program on other programs in the community, and the effect of the program on specific clients are examples of materials included in an impact evaluation.

Some programs do not lend themselves to impact evaluation. When goals are poorly articulated or unmeasurable, only output measures can be assessed. Other programs may have small and unimpressive quantitative measures, but significant nonquantifiable impact on an agency or community.

Let's return to the example of a special-needs adoption program. For the purposes of discussion, let's say the demonstration program placed only six special-needs children in adoptive homes during the year of operation at a cost of $45,000. Permanent adoption saved the state more than $30,000 a year for each child placed in a permanent home rather than in an institution. That is a savings of $135,000 per year. The number of placements may not be impressive, but the cost savings certainly are. These figures are evaluations of output.

In addition, a greater number of couples from the community inquired about the special-needs adoptive process after they observed the support services offered by the agency in the adoptive process. The local newspaper cooperated by running a series of informative pieces on the adoptive process and about specific children to help find special-needs homes. This led to an increased sensitivity in the community to the importance of educational services for children with special needs through the local school system. These are components of an impact evaluation. If this evaluation had been restricted to the placement of six children, we would have missed the importance of the impact of those six placements on the process of special-needs adoption in the community.

Third, *how will the findings of the evaluation be used?* Evaluations are frequently conducted because decision makers request them, and the evaluation is connected to a political agenda (Palumbo, 1987; Rein, 1983). It is easy to evaluate a program with the specific intent of finding what is wrong with the program and minimizing its positive impact. It is just as easy to evaluate a program emphasizing its positive impact and minimizing its negative aspects.

For example, the Learnfare program in Wisconsin underwent a preliminary output evaluation in the fall of 1990 for the specific purpose of assessing the characteristics of the population affected by the Learnfare program (Quinn, Pawasarat, & Stetzer, 1992). The evaluation was preliminary and did not purport to analyze whether the goals of the Learnfare program had been met. It was useful, however, in identifying problems the strict attendance requirements of the Learnfare program had created for the individual student, the school system, and county departments of social services. It was also useful in identifying the number of AFDC teens who were exempt from Learnfare restrictions due to age, inability to obtain day care, or formal expulsion from school. A private research and evaluation firm was hired to conduct the evaluation to minimize the criticism that an evaluation was strictly politically motivated by the governor who had developed the program. The results were not those the governor had intended, and the report was discredited. The evaluators were accused of being hostile to the intent of the program and were referred to as liberals. As of this writing, another policy evaluation group has been contacted to evaluate the program. This is a particularly poignant example of the effect of politics on program evaluation.

Fourth, *can the program be evaluated at all?* Rutman (1977) contends that three conditions must be met before a program can be legitimately evaluated.

- ✦ Programs must be clearly articulated; that is, there must be a clear, concise statement of what the program entails.
- ✦ There must be a set of clearly specific goals or expected effects of the program.
- ✦ A rationale must link the program intervention to its expected goals or effects.

Returning to Learnfare, we see the rationale that students who complete at least high school are less likely to become dependent on welfare as adults. Students cannot complete school if they do not attend. Therefore, it seems logical that school attendance is linked to a reduction in current or future welfare spending. If AFDC teens do not attend school, the state reduces their assistance or assistance to their families, thus saving money. Either way, it appears that the state will save money by requiring students to stay in school. Or will it? This conclusion is based on an erroneous assumption that being in school ensures that a student will receive an education or attain the skills necessary to obtain and keep a job. Perfect attendance does not translate directly into the attainment of minimal literacy or job training skills. In this case, the program and its goals may have been clearly articulated, but there is no rational link of programs to their desired goals or effects. If the Learn-fare program is based on an erroneous set of assumptions, can it legitimately be evaluated?

These four questions constitute the preevaluation activities necessary for program evaluation. If the necessary conditions for conducting an evaluation cannot be met, the suitability or wisdom of initiating a program evaluation must be questioned.

Identifying Program Goals

The first step in the program evaluation process is identifying program goals and variables by which those goals can be measured. Comparing the output of a program with the original goals formulated during program development is the simplest and most straightforward way to evaluate a program. In fact, if all social programs had clear and measurable goals, program evaluation would be relatively simple.

Chapter Two discusses the difficulties inherent in articulating goals for social service programs because of the ambiguous technology of social work and the difficulty in quantifying social service intervention. These difficulties further compound the complexity of conducting impact and output evaluations in the social services field. How can we evaluate whether a program has achieved its goals if we cannot articulate or measure the goals?

In cases where program goals have not been clearly articulated, it may be necessary to reconstruct the goals before evaluating the program. The child welfare agency's special-needs adoption program already discussed may not have included quantifiable measures in its original goal statement; however, it might be possible, through conversations with administrators and workers, to reconstruct goals that can be used to measure its success. There is an inherent danger in doing so. It is difficult to reconstruct original intent, especially if one is pushing for a positive evaluation of a program.

Identifying Variables for Evaluation

The Object of Analysis.   Once the evaluator has either identified the original goals or reconstructed a set of goals, it is essential to identify the **object of analysis** (Tripodi, 1983). The object of analysis refers to the client, group, program, or organization that will be studied as a means of assessing the program under evaluation. In evaluating the special-needs adoption program, the clients and the program are the objects of analysis. It is important to observe the effects of the program on the children with special needs who are involved in it as well as to draw conclusions about the role of the program within the child welfare agency. In evaluating the Learnfare program, we would want to look at individuals, their families, the schools, and the AFDC program. All these objects of analysis are important to drawing conclusions about the program.

Selecting Variables for Analysis.   The second step in choosing variables is to identify exactly the quantifiable variables to be studied. For example, in the Learnfare program we would want to know attendance levels for AFDC families before the program as well as after. We would expect to examine the amount of money spent in AFDC grants to these families before and after the program went into effect. Quantifiable variables give us hard numbers to use in an evaluation; they are the strongest measure of both output and impact.

Variables should not be limited to measurable items. Equally important for a sound program evaluation is inclusion of nonquantifiable measures, such as the reaction of families on AFDC to the program, the experiences of the schools required to keep impeccable attendance records, and the reactions of the social workers who continue to be involved with families despite the actions of the Learnfare program. It is in these subjective areas that we can most often identify the unintended consequences of a policy decision.

Identifying Sources of Data.   **Data,** the information we need to assess a program, can be found in existing sources or can be gathered through a survey, a questionnaire, or interviews. Existing sources of data include public and private agency records and government data bases. For example, in evaluating the special-needs adoption program, we would want to examine the child welfare agency records, including the number of children adopted, the cost of adoptive services versus the cost incurred by the adoptive families, the cost of institutional placement for these children, the number of couples inquiring about special-needs adoption, and the like, both before and after the establishment of the special-needs program. The second source of information would be interviews or questionnaires sent to the adoptive families, the social workers who supervise the placements, and agency administrators. Questionnaires are a good source of nonquantifiable information and anecdotal evidence of a program's effectiveness.

Collecting and Analyzing Data

Once the data sources have been identified, data must be collected and analyzed. This can be a formal process involving computer data analysis or a simple computation of the results of the data collection, depending on the size of the program to be evaluated. In large-scale program evaluations, the methods discussed in the next section on policy research would be most appropriate. For small-scale program analysis, a simple description of the findings is sufficient.

An important part of the analysis of data collected for a program evaluation involves providing "before and after" information. If we assess the situation before the program began and again after the program was in operation, we are likely to obtain a more accurate, meaningful idea of the impact of the program. Thus, it is helpful to view the program as an intervention, much the same way we assess the importance of a social worker's

TABLE 7.1

Examples of Intended and Unintended Consequences in Selected Social Service Programs

PROGRAM	INTENDED CONSEQUENCES	UNINTENDED CONSEQUENCES
Aid to Families with Dependent Children	Single-parent families become more economically secure.	Two-parent families may break up to become eligible for support.
Child Support Enforcement	Both parents share financial support of child according to their ability to pay.	Unresolved issues around original divorce come up as dissension about money. May result in unwelcome contact with absent parent.
Food Stamps	Certain portion of monthly income must be spent on food for the family.	Program does not cover items such as diapers. May result in illegal sale of stamps to get cash to buy other necessities.
Medical Assistance	Children and parents have a way to pay for medical care even if they do not have insurance.	Without incentives, families may use hospital emergency room to receive routine care.

intervention in the life of a client. For the special-needs adoption program, it would be possible to assess the number of special-needs adoptions completed by the agency before the implementation of the special program. Then we could assess the number of special-needs adoptions and the increased interest in special-needs adoption after the program has been implemented. By comparing these numbers, we can draw some preliminary conclusions about the program's impact. This is looking directly at *intended* consequences of the program.

At this stage in program evaluation we need to examine *unintended* consequences of the program as well. Sometimes these are unexpected positive consequences, as is the case in the special-needs adoption program. Other times, the unintended consequences are negative, as in the example of the Learnfare program. Assessing the unintended consequences can be more indicative of the true worth of the program than assessing only the intended consequences. Even if a program meets its original goals and can demonstrate positive consequences, it might not be advisable to continue the program if the unintended consequences are serious and detrimental. Table 7.1 illustrates examples of the intended and unintended consequences in several common social welfare programs.

Reporting Evaluation Results

The final step in program evaluation is reporting the results of the evaluation. In informal evaluations, results are presented in a report to the program administration or a board of directors. Quality evaluations give equal weight to the positive and the negative findings of the evaluation. As in assessing the strengths and weaknesses of clients, it is important to report the strengths and weaknesses of a program. The observable strengths serve as the building blocks on which a program can be improved or modified; the weaknesses will need to be strengthened or eliminated.

Most program evaluations include recommendations based on the findings of the evaluation. Should the program be continued, discontinued, expanded, or contracted? What unintended consequences appear positive, and which are so negative they must be addressed? Does the expense of the program appear to be justified in view of the benefits derived from it? Does the program need more money to be effective? These questions are all examples of the recommendations that are usually included in the evaluation report.

In summary, program evaluation consists of six distinct steps, which are summarized in Box 7.1. First, the purpose of the evaluation must be clearly understood. Why and for whom is the evaluation being conducted? Second, several preevaluation activities must be completed, including deciding whether output or impact will be assessed, how the findings will be used, and assessing honestly whether the program is clearly articulated enough to be evaluated. Third, program goals must be identified either from program goal statements or through a process of reconstruction. Fourth, variables must be identified that will provide a meaningful evaluation of the program components to be assessed. Fifth, data must be collected and analyzed. Finally, the results of the evaluation must be presented in a format usable to those who have requested the evaluation or to decision makers.

Program evaluation is the most common kind of evaluative process you will participate in outside of your own professional or personal evaluation of a program. Next we examine large-scale policy evaluation, known as policy research.

POLICY RESEARCH

Large-scale policy research is most frequently the domain of professional policy and academic researchers and follows a more rigorous methodology than evaluation of a program within an agency. Policy researchers on this level are usually concerned about the effects of specific and general policies on a large number of people, not just those served by a particular agency. For example, researchers study the effects of national employment legislation on the abilities of AFDC recipients to obtain adequate employment or

---

BOX 7.1

Steps in Evaluating a Program

Step 1: Define the purpose of the evaluation.

Step 2: Complete preevaluation activities.

- ✦ Who will evaluate the program?
- ✦ Will the evaluation examine output or impact?
- ✦ How will the findings of the evaluation be used?
- ✦ Can the program be evaluated?

Step 3: Identify program goals.

Step 4: Identify variables for evaluation.

- ✦ What is the object of analysis?
- ✦ What variables will be observed and measured?

Step 5: Collect and analyze data.

- ✦ Identify intended consequences of the program.
- ✦ Identify unintended consequences of the program.

Step 6: Report the results of the evaluation.

- ✦ Identify the program's strengths and weaknesses.
- ✦ Describe the effectiveness of the program.
- ✦ Recommend changes if necessary.

---

the effects of deinstitutionalization from psychiatric facilities on the number of homeless, chronically mentally ill people. Large-scale studies on the use of food stamps, Medicaid, and income maintenance programs are common examples of large-scale policy research.

The Scientific Method and Policy Research

For policy research of this nature, researchers use the **scientific method,** a precise set of procedures by which traditional empirical research is conducted. These steps are summarized in Figure 7.1. The scientific method in policy research consists of six specific steps, which resemble the steps used in program evaluation. In the following description of conducting a research project, the effect of deinstitutionalization of the mentally ill on the number of homeless people will be used as an example.

Statement of the Research Problem.   The first step in empirical research on social welfare policy is stating the research problem; that is, the researcher

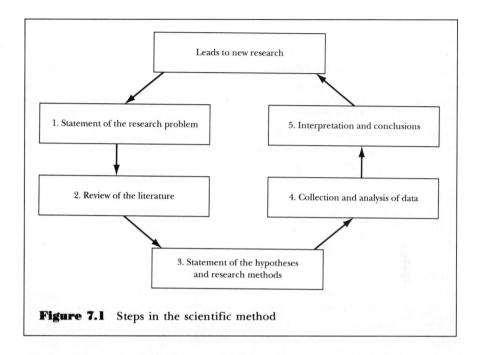

Figure 7.1   Steps in the scientific method

must clearly state the purpose of and reason for studying the research issue. What factors have prompted the research, and for what purpose might the research be used? In the case of the deinstitutionalization issue, the researcher might indicate that the number of homeless mentally ill appears to have grown significantly since mentally ill individuals were moved out of institutions into independent living arrangements beginning in 1961 (Johnson & Schwartz, 1991, p. 233). The researcher might indicate that a quantitative assessment of the number of people who were institutionalized and who now are home-less might give policy makers a clearer idea of the amount of money and kinds of programs that will be needed to provide community support for this homeless population.

The statement of the research problem is also a brief introduction to the research process that will be used. Indicating whether questionnaires, surveys, or existing sources of data will be used to gather data and the means by which that data will be analyzed provides a blueprint for the research.

Review of the Literature.   Once the general research statement has been articulated, the researcher must review existing research in this area. Have other studies addressed this same issue? If so, what were the results? What factors appear to be connected with the likelihood of ending up homeless after having been institutionalized? What programs and policies have been instituted to minimize the chance that someone will become homeless?

The review of the literature helps the researcher avoid repeating research that has already been done and directs the researcher's attention to factors that have been shown to be important in assessing the research question. If a researcher discovers that the size of the community has repeatedly been identified as a predictor of homelessness in the deinstitutionalized, this information should be included in the research question. If previous research has indicated that gender is not a factor in predicting homelessness, it may not be necessary to include it as a variable in future research. The review of the literature is helpful in providing the researcher with a solid assessment of what research has been done, what variables appear to be important in understanding the research question, and in what areas knowledge to date has been insufficient.

Extensive time and attention is spent on the review of the literature and statement of the research problem because empirical research of this nature is extremely expensive. Careful thinking before the research begins is imperative to avoiding costly mistakes and repeating research that has already been conducted.

Statement of the Hypotheses and Research Methods.   Once the literature has been thoroughly examined, the researcher can usually offer a number of **hypotheses,** or tentative statements about the relationships between variables. For example, a researcher might predict that the number of chronically mentally ill who are homeless is directly related to the geographical proximity of a psychiatric facility. This hypothesis is based on the conclusion that if people have been deinstitutionalized in a community, it is unlikely that they will move very far away from that community because they lack social support outside that community. Their only social support may be others who were hospitalized with them. Another hypothesis might be that the number of homeless mentally ill is directly related to the availability of single-room occupancy hotels, a source of affordable housing for individuals with low incomes (Lamb, 1984). With limited incomes and some difficulty in living with others, the chronically mentally ill might be restricted to these single-room occupancy hotels rather than to traditional apartment living. These hypotheses focus the research and guide the data collection.

Once hypotheses are stated, the researcher selects the **research methods** to be used; that is, how the researcher will obtain the information needed to determine whether these tentative statements about the relationship between two variables are valid. Hypotheses can never be proved. Rather, the best a researcher can say is that the findings of the research either support or fail to support the hypotheses. Examples of research methods include the use of surveys or existing data sets such as the Census or the General Social Survey. Original data may also be collected if existing data sets cannot be used. Planning the statistical and analytical methods to be used to evaluate data in relationship to the general hypotheses of a research project is an important part of determining the methodology to be used.

Collection and Analysis of the Data.   After collecting the data, the researcher applies the analytical methods described in the methodology section of the research. This section can include a descriptive summary of the data, such as the number of homeless persons studied, the length of previous institutionalization, and other factors that help us understand the basic characteristics of the population being studied. The analytical reports of the research include clear statements of the relationships of the findings to the original hypotheses. Does a statistically significant relationship exist between the geographical location of a psychiatric facility and the number of mentally ill homeless in a community? In communities with little or no low-income housing, are there significantly larger numbers of homeless mentally ill?

In this step of policy research, the researcher and the consumer of the research must be very careful not to suggest relationships between variables when the relationship is not strong enough to be meaningful. For example, most urban areas have both psychiatric facilities and homeless mentally ill. This relationship is only significant if the homeless mentally ill are prior residents of the hospitals in that area and can state with some certainty that they chose to stay in the area because of friendships with other former patients. The numbers must be large enough to be more than coincidental. The analysis of the data in relationship to the hypothesis must be rigorous and unbiased.

Interpretation and Conclusions.   The final step in policy research is interpreting the research findings and their relevance to social welfare policy. What variables identified in the research seem most closely associated with the growing number of mentally ill homeless people? What policy initiatives suggest themselves as solutions to the problem? What appears to be effective in minimizing the negative consequences of deinstitutionalization? In promoting the positive consequences? Answers to these questions can help policy makers and implementers determine what, if any, changes are necessary in the program.

Approaches to Policy Research

Three main approaches are used in policy research. Each examines a slightly different aspect of social welfare policy.

Researching the Policy-Making Process.   One approach to policy research assesses the policy-making process, which is discussed in detail in Chapter Six. The premise of this type of research is that understanding the process of making policy helps us understand why and how policy is made and how this process determines the final product (Portney, 1986). This approach to policy research is primarily descriptive rather than analytical. Although analysis about the policy-making process itself is included, it does not draw extensive conclusions about the impact of policy once it has been formulated. This kind of research is known as **formative policy research;** that is, it focuses on the formation of policy rather than on describing its impact on clients and agencies (Tripodi, 1983).

The problem-solving model used to describe the formation of the Task Force on Teen Parenthood in Chapter Six is a good model for this type of descriptive research.

The Cause and Consequences Approach.   A second, more analytical approach to policy is called the **cause and consequences** approach to policy analysis (Portney, 1986). This type of research assesses the process of going from identifying a social problem to implementing a policy and assessing the impact of that policy on the original social problem. The result is an evaluative assessment of the worth of social policy, similar to the process identified under program evaluation.

The actual policy can be either the independent or the dependent variable. As an independent variable, the policy is examined in terms of its impact on an existing social problem. In other words, the research examines the consequences of the policy once it has been implemented. Policy can also be seen as a dependent variable—that is, as an examination of the antecedents in terms of social problems that resulted in the formation of a policy. This type of policy research is known as **summative policy research**, which is descriptive and analytical, and can be generalized to other, similar policies.

The Prescriptive Policy Research Approach.   A third approach used in policy research is the **prescriptive policy approach** (Portney, 1986). The prescriptive approach recommends or prescribes a policy based on previous information about the impact of existing policies with a projection about the continuing effectiveness of these policies into the future. The intent is to quasi-scientifically suggest the best course of action for future policy decisions. Prescriptive policy research is often the domain of research institutes connected to colleges and universities that have access to sophisticated computer modeling techniques.

THE ANALYSIS MODEL

The methods of program evaluation and policy research discussed in this chapter are most often used by professional policy analysts who are hired specifically for that purpose. Both methods require training well beyond the scope of this book. What about you, the social work practitioner who must evaluate the importance and impact of social welfare policy every day in your work with clients? As stressed throughout this book, no social work practitioner remains untouched by the implications of social welfare policy both for the clients they serve and for the environment in which they work, the social service agency.

Unfortunately, practitioners too often rely on personal reactions to a policy and its effectiveness instead of carefully examining a policy in a systematic, critical manner. It is difficult to be a critical consumer of social welfare policy without first understanding the policy.

Luke into.

The model that follows is designed specifically for social work prac-titioners. It provides an easy way to remember the kinds of questions that should be asked both in evaluating policy as it is being proposed (formative policy evaluation) and in assessing the impact of policy once it has been im-plemented (summative policy evaluation). The eight areas of importance are easy to remember using the acronym ANALYSIS as a mnemonic device.

A (Approach)

As we have seen both in program evaluation and policy research, a brief sum-mary of the program to be evaluated is important in setting the stage for the evaluative process. It is important to understand first the basic *approach* of the policy being evaluated. Is the program a cash, in-kind, or service pro-gram? Does the program have eligibility requirements (means tested) or is it available to all regardless of income and assets (universal)? Is the policy designed to meet an immediate need, a **consumption approach,** or is it aimed at long-range goals, an **investment approach?** What are the stated goals of the program? Answering these basic questions helps you understand the dynamics of the program and helps set the stage for the rest of the ANALYSIS approach to policy assessment. Many of the criticisms of current social wel-fare policy result from a poor understanding of the policy and its original intentions.

What *attitudes* and values are reflected in the policy? Society's at-titudes and values shape much of the social welfare policy we have today. Now and in the future, these attitudes and values will continue to shape those policies. What attitudes does a policy such as Learnfare address? Clearly, the attitudes of social control and punishment are reflected in the policy. If AFDC families do not care enough to insist that their children attend school, the state will give them a financial incentive to do so. However, will an attitude of social control or punishment effectively address this issue in the long run?

It is also important to assess the policy in terms of the attitudes and values of the social work profession. The Code of Ethics of the National Association of Social Workers (see Appendix A) outlines the basic set of pro-fessional values that guides the social work profession. More often than not, social welfare policy operates in contradiction to those values (Prigmore & Atherton, 1986). For example, Learnfare is in direct contradiction to the social work value of client self-determination. It violates the principle of respect-ing the right of clients to make decisions for themselves. Often the practi-tioner's negative reaction to social welfare policy results from feeling uneasy about these value conflicts. Identifying specifically what attitudes are reflected in the policy under consideration can help us refine our professional assess-ments of the policy.

N (Need)

The second step in the ANALYSIS model is to carefully assess what *need* the policy is intended to meet; that is, what social problem prompted the development of the policy? Has the need been carefully documented, or was the policy a legislator's impulsive reaction to constituents' demands? Is the need widespread or isolated? For example, federal energy assistance is an important program in states with severe winters and makes the difference between life and death for many low-income families. However, it has far less relevance to those in warm climates where it is unlikely that a low-income family would freeze if their power were disconnected.

How is the need addressed by the program defined? If we determine that teenagers in low-income families need an education, does mandatory school attendance address that need? It is not clear that lack of marketable skills and inability to get a job are directly linked to school attendance. It is more logical that the need is addressed by intensive skills training and job development. Once teenagers have an education, can they do anything with it? Will sitting in school help students who have not been able to benefit from the traditional educational model?

In assessing the need, you will want to ask whether the policy is rationally connected to meeting that need. In the case of the Wisconsin Learnfare program, mandating school attendance as a means of minimizing future public dependency appears to be rationally connected until we examine the issue more carefully. We know that just attending school does not guarantee getting an education. But does the Learnfare program address the issue of why these children are not attending school or whether, once they graduate from high school, they could find a job anyway? Although based on good intentions, the program may not make the best connection between an identified need and a program to meet that need.

A (Assessment)

The first two steps in the ANALYSIS model are primarily descriptions of the basic premise and operation of the program or policy and the scope of the need addressed by the policy. The evaluative component of the ANALYSIS model begins with a preliminary assessment of the effectiveness of the program. By identifying concrete evidence of both the strengths and weaknesses of the program or policy, we can begin to draw preliminary conclusions about its effectiveness.

Identifying Program Strengths.   Although we may disagree with a proposed or existing policy, it is important to acknowledge that most social welfare policies and programs are developed with good intentions. However, we can recognize the good intentions of a program without condoning its operation. For example, the Wisconsin Learnfare program appropriately identified the significant connection between education and economic self-sufficiency. Young people cannot achieve any level of financial security without at least a high school education. Addressing this connection is the strength of the program. An additional strength is that forcing teenagers back into the classroom has helped school systems identify many of the problems that cause students to drop out of school in the first place, such as special learning needs and inadequate day care.

Continuing with our identification of program strengths, we need to know if there is empirical evidence that the policy has accomplished its original goals. What can we learn from program records or conversations with program participants? The Learnfare program could be assessed by comparing graduation rates of AFDC teenagers before and after the inception of the program with the number of teenagers graduating from high school who eventually become economically self-sufficient. This method, although impractical for the practitioner, is the ideal. A more practical alternative would be to speak with high school guidance counselors, principals, public assistance workers, and a small sample of teenagers affected by the program. Although such an assessment is not considered scientific, it can give you a preliminary idea of the program's strengths and weaknesses. This is a more professionally responsible approach than simply considering your personal reaction to a policy as a valid policy assessment.

Identifying Program Weaknesses.   The primary reason for you to engage in policy or program analysis is to identify elements of a policy that must change to serve your clients better. What are the indicators that the policy or program has not accomplished its goals or has had dangerous unintended consequences? Is the program a threat to a client's legal or ethical rights? When you gathered information about the program or policy, what weaknesses or problems did program participants identify?

The assessment phase of the ANALYSIS model is analogous to the assessment stage of the problem-solving model used in social work practice. Assessing policy weaknesses helps us identify what needs to be changed, whereas program strengths serve as the building blocks for change.

L (Logic)

Are the goals of the policy under consideration logically connected to the program designed to meet those goals? Does the intervention intended follow the logic of how people behave? Our knowledge of human behavior indicates that we cannot force people to change unless they want to change. Does it logically follow that a child who does not want to be in school can be forced to stay there? Every student knows exactly what to do to be expelled if he or she does not want to be in school. Every parent knows that he or she can force children to do some things and cannot force them to do others, including going to school. Can a parent convince a child that it is more desirable to stay in school, at least through high school, to increase the odds of obtaining minimum-wage employment after graduation than to quit school and become involved in the underground economy for fast and easy money now? Some policy decisions simply make no sense from the perspective of the logic of human behavior.

Is the program a logical expression of what we know about effective delivery of services? How the service is delivered or the program is administered has a powerful effect on its chances for success. In-kind programs, such as food stamps, have been very effective in targeting money for food for low-income families yet restricting recipients' choices about how they spend their monthly income. Cash income maintenance programs allow recipients freedom of choice about where their incomes will be spent but cannot guarantee a family will not face eviction for failing to include rent as part of monthly expenses. Learnfare employs a punishment (loss of some portion of AFDC benefits) for not complying with program requirements (attendance in school). Some behaviorists contend that the threat of punishment is more effective in influencing behavior; others believe people respond more consistently to rewards. The Learnfare program could just as easily raise the amount of monthly benefits for families whose children attend school regularly. Which do you believe would be more effective?

Y (Your Reaction as a Practitioner)

Part of the process of maturing as a professional social worker is learning to trust your intuition and judgments about both clients and social welfare policy. In this aspect of the ANALYSIS model, you are asked to carefully consider what you think, independent of anyone else's comments or insights about social welfare policy. Does the policy make sense to you? In what ways have you seen it affect clients and social workers? What problems or benefits has the program resulted in for the social service agency in which you work?

What concerns or impresses you about the policy? Have you seen unintended consequences of the policy that have been more detrimental than beneficial to the client population? Has the policy also had unintended positive consequences? What do your clients say about the policy? Combining your own feelings and insights with more empirical data about the policy can make the process of policy analysis much more meaningful for you.

S (Support)

From where, if anywhere, does the money to implement the policy come? Some policies do not involve additional services but are regulatory, designed to enforce rules rather than to provide services. If the program is funded by a grant from an outside source, its existence can be precarious. Therefore, the program will be carefully scrutinized before it is funded again or designated for a long-term funding commitment on the part of the social service agency. Other programs are required by state or federal law, and their fiscal allocation is tied to more conventional funding sources. How does the source of funds dictate what can and cannot be done with the program? How is the program financially accountable to outside sources?

A second aspect of evaluating financial support is assessment of whether a program is cost-effective in terms of what is accomplished. If a program is extremely expensive and serves only a few clients, its cost-effectiveness will be challenged. If a program requires a lot of tax dollars but saves money in the long run, its cost-effectiveness will be much easier to justify.

A third aspect of support is the general support of the program by those who are paying for it. Some people have such strong beliefs about the immorality of abortion that they would rather pay to support a child on public assistance for 18 years than have tax dollars go to pay for an abortion for a low-income woman. Their assessment of the cost-effectiveness of a program has little to do with financial considerations.

I (Innovation)

Innovation refers to the channels through which changes can be achieved in the program. Does the program appear to be working well but need more staff or more money? Can the program be improved with minor changes, or does it appear to need a comprehensive overhaul to be more effective? Can these changes be made on the agency level, or must other regulatory bodies make changes in administrative law to correct the flaws?

S (Social Justice)

Is the policy or program consistent with the social work profession's commitment to social justice? Does the policy address past inequities in treatment or opportunities for those who have been oppressed by society (that is, women, minorities, gays, and lesbians)? If social welfare programs and policies perpetuate inequities or create obstacles for those already powerless in society, as practitioners we cannot placidly accept these programs and policies. Inadequate child care for working AFDC mothers is not tolerable, even if the employment program is excellent. Discriminating against women in favor of male heads of households in designing employment training programs is not acceptable, no matter how many families are helped. Current and proposed social welfare policy *must* be sensitive to issues of social justice. It is in drawing attention to and advocating on behalf of those who suffer from social injustice that we perform our most important professional function. It is our professional role to speak for those who have no voice.

Summarizing the ANALYSIS

In considering all of the elements of the ANALYSIS model, what conclusions can you draw from your perspective as a social work practitioner? What improvements, changes, or decisions would you recommend? Who needs to know about your conclusions? Have you analyzed the policy so you can understand it better?

SUMMARY

This chapter explores three major types of social welfare policy assessment. Program evaluation entails assessing the effectiveness of a specific program,

BOX 7.2

The ANALYSIS Model of Policy Evaluation

A (Approach): Brief description of the methods used in the current or proposed policy. What attitudes or values are expressed in the policy? Is the policy consistent with acceptable values for helping people to meet their needs?

N (Need): What need does the policy attempt to address? How has the need for intervention been documented? What are the indications that the policy has met these needs?

A (Assessment): What are the program's or policy's strengths and weaknesses? What is the evidence from public records or from the experiences of professionals and program participants of the program's success or failure?

L (Logic): Does the proposed or current policy logically address the connection between the need and a means of solving the problem, based on what we know about human behavior and acceptable means of delivering services to clients?

Y (Your reaction): From your professional experiences, does the policy seem effective? Have you or your clients had especially good or bad experiences with the policy?

S (Support): What is the financial support for the program? Are the finances sufficient to meet the goals of the program? Are sources of program financing stable?

I (Innovation): What provisions have been made for changing the program if necessary? Is there sufficient opportunity for feedback on the program?

S (Social justice): Does the program address the important issue of social justice as expressed by society and the social work profession?

---

usually within a single agency or community. Policy research requires using the scientific method to systematically assess the relationship between empirical observations and hypothetical statements about policies. The ANALYSIS model offers a series of questions you should ask about policies being proposed or about policies that have been implemented. Box 7.2 recaps the ANALYSIS model. All three approaches require you to carefully formulate questions to gather the information necessary to assess whether a program has been effective in reaching its original goals.

If these approaches to evaluating policies identify a policy that is inadequate, ineffective, or unjust, it is our professional responsibility to work toward changing that policy. Chapter Eight explores the practitioner's role in influencing change in public policy at any level.

DISCUSSION QUESTIONS

1. *Which of the models of policy evaluation would be most appropriate in evaluating the following programs?*
   a. *A state-sponsored work program for AFDC recipients*
   b. *A city program for the homeless mentally ill*
   c. *The effect on retirees of an increase in Social Security benefits*
2. *What is meant by* object of analysis *in program analysis? How would changing the object of analysis change the purpose and usefulness of the evaluation?*
3. *Why are preevaluation activities critical to a comprehensive program evaluation?*
4. *What are the six steps in the scientific method? Which step do you feel is most important?*
5. *What is the difference between the summative and prescriptive approaches to policy research?*

SUGGESTED PROJECTS

1. Obtain a copy of a program evaluation done recently at a social service agency in your community. Compare the evaluation report with the elements of program evaluation discussed in this chapter. What information is missing? What information does the report contain that is not discussed in this chapter?
2. Following the steps of the scientific method, design a policy research process on some area of social welfare policy that interests you. Where could you find a data set that would provide the information you need to complete the project?
3. Select a policy or program in your community, and analyze that policy using the ANALYSIS model.

IMPORTANT TERMS AND CONCEPTS

causes and consequences approach

consumption approach

data

formative policy research

hypothesis

impact evaluation

investment approach

object of analysis

output evaluation

prescriptive policy approach

program evaluation

research methods

scientific method

summative policy research

The Practitioner's Role in Influencing Public Policy Change

Never doubt that a small group of thoughtful and committed citizens can change the world.

—Attributed to MARGARET MEAD

O ne of the most important reasons for analyzing social welfare policy and evaluating social service programs is to identify what needs to be changed for services to become more equitable and effective. Although changing the world may be more than the social worker can accomplish, the quotation that opens this chapter reminds us that a strong, organized, and committed group of people can accomplish amazing things when they work together. Social work is a profession committed to social change and social justice, but most practitioners shy away from this arena because they are skeptical about the possibility of change and lack the skills and knowledge needed to inspire change. Our profession and our clients suffer as a result.

Practitioners working with families and children tend to focus on promoting changes within the family or individual rather than focusing on the environmental factors that create or maintain many family problems. We cannot ignore the external elements in the environment that help perpetuate poverty, discrimination, substance abuse, unemployment, and family violence. When we focus only on the individual or family, we are tacitly asking clients to adjust to injustice rather than working to change an unjust society. In *The Politics of Therapy*, Halleck (1971) reminds all therapists that we can do only one of two things for the clients who seek our help. We can work to help clients accept things as they are, even if social conditions are the cause of many of their present problems, or we can work with clients to change those conditions.

This chapter is designed to encourage you to develop change-agent skills that go beyond the individual or family focus. This chapter covers the avenues by which you can work to influence change in social welfare policy on the local, state, or federal level. Chapter Nine discusses how to change program policy at the agency level. We might not aim to change the world, but we can focus on interventions that will change the parts of the world that directly affect our clients and ourselves as practicing social workers.

Specifically, this chapter includes information about the following:

+ How to identify sources of information on current and proposed social welfare and agency policy
+ Specific ways you can influence the political policy-making process to make it more responsive to clients and social workers
+ How to involve the client in the process of challenging and changing social welfare policy

FINDING OUT ABOUT SOCIAL WELFARE POLICY

Throughout this text, we have discussed various levels on which social welfare policy is made and implemented. Some social programs are authorized and funded on the federal level by federal legislation such as the Social Security Act of 1935. Others are unique to individual states, like Wisconsin's Learnfare program or Massachusetts' Employment and Training Program (ET). Still others, such as General Assistance payment levels, are the product of county-level decisions. Cities may also have their own policies regarding city welfare programs or services to homeless people. Other policies are set on the social service agency level with minimal influence from any unit of government.

The first step in understanding and eventually changing social welfare policy is to *find out on what level the policy is made.* That level, whether it is local, state, or federal, will be the target for gathering information and directing change efforts. If this book does not contain information on the program you want to study, you can research the policy in your college or university library. For more information, see the section entitled "Using Library Resources," which appears later in this chapter.

Local Governmental Policies

City-Level Policies.   If a policy has been identified as a city-level policy, more information on the policy can be obtained from a member of either the city council or another unit of city government. City council members represent a specific geographic area of a city. To find out who your city council member is, call City Hall. The mayor or city manager's office is another good source of information about city-level policies. The mayor's staff can give you information or direct you to a specific agency or office that has information about the policy in question.

Zoning is an example of a city-level policy that has implications for social work practice and planning. Certain areas of cities are designated for residential, multifamily, recreational, or commercial use only. If a community agency is developing residential facilities for people with AIDS, the agency must find out whether the zoning regulations permit the location of a group home in the neighborhoods being considered. Resistance to changing zoning restrictions from single-family homes to the special zoning permission required for group homes has been one way neighborhoods have prevented group homes for people with AIDS and other disabilities, and mental health halfway houses from locating in their areas. Community resistance is often based on people's fears that these facilities pose a threat to the safety and well-being of local residents. City council members are the key political connections when it comes to zoning regulations. You must work with the neighborhood residents as well as city-level politicians to make zoning changes. Other examples of city-level policies are the availability of fire and police protection, sanitation services, city-funded transportation systems, property taxes, public housing, and public health services. The following are examples of areas covered by city or town policies:

Animal control
Building codes
Economic development
Elections
Fire and police protection
Municipal court
Neighborhood libraries
Neighborhood rehabilitation
Parking
Playgrounds and parks
Public health
Public housing
Real estate taxes
Recreation programs
Road maintenance
Sanitation and sewers
Schools
Sexually transmitted diseases
Traffic
Water works
Zoning

County-Level Policies.   Most counties in the United States are governed by an elected county board of supervisors. Policies that affect social services are made by a committee of the county board that oversees the county department of social services, the largest employer of social workers in the public sector. In conjunction with state government, the county board is extremely powerful in determining eligibility and work requirements for public assistance recipients, as well as funding allocations for mental health, alcohol and drug, developmental disabilities, aging, and protective services programs.

Individual supervisors or the county government offices are the appropriate resources for information on county-level policies. County boards routinely hold public hearings to explain changes in policy and answer questions.

Many policies that affect county departments of social services are actually made on the state level but are implemented with some discretion on the county level. For example, the Social Security Act of 1935 allows, but does not require, states to provide for General Assistance (GA) payments to individuals and families who may not qualify for AFDC. Some states have responded with relatively generous GA payments; others provide no program benefits under General Assistance. Some states have programs geared specifically to able-bodied single persons; others have programs only for families with children. Regardless, individual counties retain the right to determine levels of such payments because the money comes from local property taxes.

County units of government also govern decisions about countywide transportation systems, county parks, the sheriff's office, county public health offices, road construction, county library systems, county court operations, and the county jail. The following are examples of areas covered by county-level policies:

Aid to Families with Dependent Children
Alcohol and Other Drug Abuse programs
Child support enforcement
County court system
County department of social services
County parks and recreation system
County public hospitals
District Attorney
Emergency government
Family Court Commissioner
Food stamps
Foster home licensing
General Assistance
Mental health centers
Nutrition programs for older adults
Protective services
Sheriff's department
Small claims court

State-Level Policies

State Legislators. The first source of information on state-level policies is your state representative's office, which is usually located in the state capitol. All states except Nebraska have a bicameral state government, usually consisting of a state assembly and a state senate through which legislation must pass before it becomes law. Either of your state legislators can help you find information on existing or proposed policies. A legislator may send you an exact copy of the pending or passed legislation and his or her position on the legislation.

State government administrators and legislators set AFDC payments, design and implement the food stamp program, regulate licensing of foster, group, and nursing homes, devise the rules for juvenile corrections facilities, subsidize many public health programs, and formulate the requirements of the state's public schools. The state government has a great deal of power over many of the health and social services programs in the state because the federal government has delegated a wide range of powers to state governments. This allows state governments to design and determine the kinds of programs best suited to the needs of the state's residents. However, it also results in disparity among states in the quantity and quality of human services available. The following are examples of areas covered by state-level policies:

> Community-based residential facilities
> Consumer protection
> Corrections
> Day care licensing
> Employment and training programs
> Labor relations
> Legislative hotlines
> Meat and food inspection
> Natural (environmental) resources
> Public Defender's office
> Refugee services
> State-mandated educational regulations
> State sales and income taxes
> State employment service
> Unemployment compensation
> Vocational rehabilitation
> Work permits
> Workers' Compensation

The State Office of the National Association of Social Workers (NASW). Information on an existing or proposed policy is just that—information. An analysis of the impact of the proposed legislation, however, may not be available from a legislator. The state office of the National Association of Social Workers exists primarily to follow and influence the legislative process as it affects social workers and their clients. Professional staff are routinely involved in watching licensure legislation, legislative changes in public assistance, third-party reimbursements for private practitioners, housing, and health care. State offices monitor the state budget to assure that adequate funds have been allocated for client services, the core of social work services. NASW's analysis of a piece of legislation can help the inexperienced policy analyst identify avenues for change. State chapters of NASW publish newsletters that identify critical pieces of legislation under consideration. Frequently, they identify where letters should be sent or who should be contacted to encourage the passage or defeat of legislation.

Federal Policies

Congressional Offices. The representative from your congressional district and the senator from your state are the first sources to help you obtain information about a federal policy or law. Lawmakers have offices in their home districts and in Washington, D.C. Traditionally, the local office handles constituents' problems, much the same way social workers help clients. This approach, however, reflects the philosophy of the individual legislator and might differ from district to district. Some members of Congress have staff who help constituents solve problems with Social Security, housing, veterans' benefits, medical benefits, and other government entitlement programs. Other representatives and senators place less emphasis on direct problem solving and simply refer constituents to community agencies.

Copies of existing and proposed federal legislation are available from the Washington, D.C., office of a member of Congress. Along with copies of the legislation, congressional staff can provide position papers on various issues reflecting the legislator's views. These position papers often contain valuable analyses of the adequacy of existing programs as well as suggestions for improvement, but be aware that the analyses contained in position papers reflect the legislator's liberal, moderate, or conservative political inclination. The following are examples of areas covered by federal-level policies:

> Agriculture (food stamps)
> Commerce and fair trade
> Consumer product safety
> Federal health care programs
> Federal housing
> Post Office
> Small Business Administration
> Social Security Administration
> Veterans' Affairs

The National Office of NASW. Like the state offices of NASW, the national office in Washington, D.C., stands as the professional voice of social workers in the federal legislative arena. In its monthly publication, *NASW*

News, NASW provides in-depth analysis of federal legislation and policies that affect practitioners and clients. NASW lobbies for pertinent social service legislation through nationwide letter-writing campaigns, expert testimony, and public education. The National Center for Social Policy and Practice specifically researches social welfare policies that directly affect social work practitioners.

During election years, NASW provides a political analysis of candidates' positions on public assistance, education, domestic spending, gender equity, entitlement programs, civil rights, and family policy issues. In sum, NASW is an excellent resource for finding out about any federal social welfare policy.

Think Tanks.   **Think tanks** are organizations devoted specifically to large-scale policy research and analysis, as discussed in Chapter Seven. Most think tanks are located in Washington, D.C., or nearby major research universities. The Heritage Foundation, American Enterprise Institute, Brookings Institution, and the Urban Institute are examples of think tanks that conduct research on political and social issues. These institutions represent a wide variety of political positions, from the most conservative to the most liberal. Their analyses of current policies can provide you with a solid overview of social welfare policies as well as current research about the effect of proposed changes in policy on client populations. The Institute for Research on Poverty at the University of Wisconsin–Madison and the Center for Social Research at the University of Michigan are examples of university-based think tanks that routinely produce discussion papers and research reports on current issues in social welfare programs.

In summary, a wide variety of resources exist to help you learn about social welfare policy on the agency and government levels. These resources can also help you gather statistical evidence either to support or to refute existing policy; this is the second step in influencing social welfare policy. Obtaining reliable information about the breadth of an existing social problem and assessing whether the existing or proposed policy can be effective in addressing that problem is the next step in preparing for change.

USING LIBRARY RESOURCES

Facts, not feelings, are the important weapon of the practitioner trying to change social welfare policy. The next section examines how to become politically involved in changing policy. Part of that process is finding facts and figures to support your recommendations for policy change. This section examines library resources that contain the kind of statistical information you must present to policy makers. These resources are available in most university and city libraries. See the Reference list in this text for complete publishing information about these resources.

Two useful professional resources are the *Social Work Dictionary* (Barker, 1987) and the *Encyclopedia of Social Work* (National Association of

Social Workers, 1991), both available in college and university libraries. The *Social Work Dictionary* includes brief descriptions of terms used in social work. *The Encyclopedia of Social Work* contains longer entries about important topics in social work, with historical and current perspectives on these issues. These resources are especially useful to novices in understanding policy issues.

The *County and City Data Book* (U.S. Department of Commerce, 1988), published periodically by the Bureau of the Census, contains demographic information on counties and cities throughout the United States. Based on U.S. Census information, this reference is geared to small-scale policy research. A similar document, *The Congressional District Data Book* (United States Bureau of the Census, 1973) is organized by congressional district, so it is tailor-made for the researcher trying to gather information for presentation to a congress-person. If neither of these resources contains the kind of information you need, consult *State and Local Statistics Sources* (Balachandian & Balachandian, 1991) for a list of state, local, and federal sources of information on public welfare, health care, law enforcement, environmental issues, labor, taxation, and the like.

The U.S. Bureau of the Census publishes summary information on population demographics regularly. Some information is based on the U.S. Census of the United States, conducted every ten years; other statistics are gathered from a small sample of the population. *The Statistical Abstract of the United States* (U.S. Department of Commerce, 1992) is a concise and comprehensive compilation of statistics on a broad range of topics, including social and demographic issues. It contains detailed information on employment, housing, poverty, education, and voting. One of the most helpful sections of the *Statistical Abstract* is its federal budget summary, which is updated every year. *The Census Catalog and Guide* (U.S. Department of Commerce, 1992) identifies all the data available in print or in computer-readable format from the Bureau of the Census. Census information is valuable because it allows you to compare various areas of the country when discussing a social problem.

Government agencies routinely collect information on the population; this information is printed in the *Monthly Catalog of United States Government Publications* available from federal government bookstores and the U.S. Superintendent of Documents, Government Printing Office. To identify officials in the federal government, consult the *United States Government Manual* (General Services Administration, 1992), which identifies members of the staff in all federal government offices.

INFLUENCING THE POLITICAL PROCESS

Once you have identified a policy issue, researched it thoroughly, and come to your own conclusions about what policy is needed or how a policy should be changed, it is time to take action. It is time to become part of the political process.

As a private citizen, you have the right to become involved in the political process in any way you choose, be it through letter writing, lobbying, testifying at a public hearing, organizing a voter registration drive, campaigning for a particular candidate, or seeking legal action. However, as an employee of a public or private agency, you might have some restrictions on how closely you may identify yourself with your employer.

Employees of private nonprofit social service agencies may not identify their affiliation with the agency in a direct endorsement of political candidates without risking the loss of the agency's nonprofit status. Likewise, private nonprofit agencies cannot require their employees to support a particular candidate. These restrictions protect both the agency and the employee. Consult your supervisor for your agency's specific restrictions.

The Hatch Act

Employees of public agencies are subject to the provisions of the Political Activities Act of 1939, better known as the **Hatch Act.** The Hatch Act regulates expenditures by and contributions to political parties by prohibiting federal employee participation in partisan political activities (Kruschke & Jackson, 1987). Although the Hatch Act has been heavily criticized as interfering with citizens' involvement in the political process simply because they work for the government, it has remained in force. State and local governments may enforce provisions similar to the Hatch Act, so it is imperative that you consult your supervisor or agency attorney to determine how legal restrictions might affect your role in political activities.

Written and Verbal Communication with Legislators

Writing letters to legislators is the most common way to let them know how you feel about a piece of pending legislation or an existing policy. Letters should be addressed to the appropriate lawmaker and contain concise, accurate information about your views and what you expect the legislator to do to support them. If you are writing to request that a legislator vote a certain way on a bill, indicate the number and name of the bill to avoid confusion. Staff at legislative offices indicate that original letters, not form letters or postcards, are most effective. Legislators are most influenced by constituents in their own districts rather than by lobbyists being paid to act on behalf of a professional organization.

Our role in participating in or organizing letter-writing campaigns should also include enabling clients to participate in the political process. Empowering clients to act on their own behalf when policy decisions are made helps move them toward solving their own problems. "The introduction of macro-level solutions in turn helps to reinforce in clients the idea that their problems may not be caused by their own inadequacies" (Haynes & Mickelson, 1991, p. 51). However, many clients will need to be educated about the issue at hand and the political process before they feel comfortable writing a letter to a legislator.

For example, a group of students in a large southern city was working with older adults at a senior center when a critical piece of legislation came up for vote in the state legislature. The proposed legislation dealt with the state subsidy of programs for older adults funded by the Older Americans Act. State legislators were expected to allocate only the federal minimum required to maintain federal funding of older-adult nutrition programs despite the overwhelming evidence that such programs had improved the physical and psychological health of the state's elderly. As low-income minority adults, the senior center members did not see themselves as actors in the political arena and reacted apathetically to the field students' efforts to promote political action on their part. By presenting an aggressive educational campaign at all the local senior centers, the social work students were able to convince older adults to write and call their state legislators and insist on an increase in the state subsidy.

By threatening to withdraw their voter support for the state legislators, the older adults made their wishes known. To reinforce their point, many of the older adults showed up at the capitol the day of the vote. Once they became aware of the importance of their communication with state legislators, it took little encouragement on the part of the social work field students to keep them active and motivated. The result was that the state budget allocation was increased for senior nutrition programs, allowing expansion, rather than contraction, of existing programs. An organized group of constituents who had a vested stake in the political issue of funding for their own nutrition programs was more effective in securing change than the group of field students might have been on their own.

Phone calls can also be effective in registering opinions on a legislative or civic matter. The opinions registered in a legislator's local office are routinely forwarded to them at the state or national capitol. Some states have legislative hot-lines with toll-free numbers for constituents to call to indicate how they want their legislator to vote. A phone call is a simple way to let a legislator know how you feel, and it is especially effective on the day of the critical vote.

Lobbying

A **lobbyist** is a person paid to represent an organization with government officeholders and agencies (Mahaffey, 1989, p. 361). The primary responsibility of a lobbyist is to represent the interests of the organization when important pieces of legislation are being considered for passage. Lobbyists contact legislators directly to ensure that bills that benefit the organization pass and those that could undermine an organization's interest do not. Lobbyists maintain continuing relationships with legislators and the legislative process and report to the employing organization with information and technical expertise on how to succeed in its work. Lobbyists also train the organization's members in how to influence the political process.

NASW performs many of the lobbying functions for the social work profession. It monitors state and federal legislation that affects the profession and aggressively seeks to educate its membership about important political issues. Because NASW exists outside of federal, state, or local restrictions on partisan politics, it can represent the issues of all social workers, public and private.

Public Hearings

As social work practitioners, few of you will be directly involved in lobbying either because of the restrictions imposed by your agency or because professional lobbyists are handling the work. However, public hearings remain an important way for you to make your and your clients' positions on important issues known to decision makers.

The **informational hearing** is one type of public hearing. At an informational hearing, the public hears a legislator or public officials describe a proposed or adopted policy. This type of hearing is specifically educational; it answers questions about new policies and procedures. A second type of hearing allows the public to express its opinions so legislators or public officials can hear how residents or constituents feel on important and controversial issues. Many issues require a public hearing by law. If no public hearing has been scheduled on a controversial issue, the public may demand one if sufficient interest exists. The individual written or oral comments are known as **testimony** and become part of the official proceedings of a public hearing. One need not testify at a hearing to make his or her position known. Most hearings have a sign-in sheet on which those who attend register their positions on issues without addressing the hearing.

The League of Women Voters (1972) has identified pointers for offering testimony at public hearings. These pointers, listed in Box 8.1, are appropriate to both professional and client testimony.

Professionals, including social workers and executive directors of social service agencies, frequently testify at public hearings, but rarely does their testimony have the effect of a client's words. A young working mother struggling to raise four children may be able to present a very convincing case for the need for quality day care in a community. An older adult who is isolated in his or her own home is in an excellent position to testify on the benefits of a subsidized transportation program for older adults. A recovering alcoholic can speak about the need for community-based alcohol and drug treatment programs much more effectively than the professionals who staff these agencies. An additional benefit of client testimony is the sense of empowerment it gives the client. Making clients aware of their rights and responsibilities is an important part of motivating clients to own their role in change.

Using the Media

As explained in Chapter Five, the media has a role in formulating policy. The way the media handles a policy issue can affect how the public responds to proposed or adopted policies. If you are advocating a change in public policy, involve the media through press conferences, letters to the editors of

---

BOX 8.1

Pointers for Offering Testimony at Public Hearings

1. *Ask to be scheduled to present testimony.* If officials know how many individuals would like to address the hearing, they can set time limits and schedule presenters; this increases the chances that you will be heard.

2. *Submit your testimony in written form, even if you are able to address the hearing orally.* This gives officials time to review what you have said more carefully and for you to document your sources if you present testimony that includes statistics.

3. *Keep your testimony succinct and informative.* The most effective testimony is short and to the point. Loading your testimony with lengthy and drawn-out personal opinion will irritate rather than inform officials.

4. *Lively testimony makes the news!* Giving dramatic examples or particularly impassioned testimony often catches the eye of the media and can affect the general impression the media has of the issue. Do not underestimate the emotional atmosphere of the hearing.

---

newspapers, appearances on television and radio talk shows, and press releases. A well-organized, professional presentation of an issue can bring public attention to important policy issues.

Supporting a Political Candidate

Another approach to influencing the political process is to become directly involved with the selection of the legislators or public officials who make policy. The media's coverage of political candidates often leaves an individual more, rather than less, confused about how to choose a candidate to support. Selecting a candidate for whom to cast your vote requires more than absorbing political campaign messages.

Campaign Information.   It is important to become a critical consumer of political campaign commercials. Rather than address substantive issues, most political messages attempt to project a strong media image of the candidate. Ask yourself what, if anything, you have learned about the candidate's stand on issues, especially those of importance to the social work profession and the clients we serve. Do not assume that everything you hear about or from a candidate is completely true. Consider other sources of information.

Pamphlets, flyers, and other mailed information can sometimes be more help in identifying a candidate's position on a certain issue. Often candidates will compare their views with those of the other candidates, especially when they want to appeal to a particular voting audience. The National Association of Social Workers and other professional social work organizations routinely send information on candidates with an analysis of which candidate might offer the best choice for the profession and our clients.

Televised or radio-broadcast debates give you direct exposure to candidates. Debates focus on specific issues and give you a good idea whether a candidate has taken a stand on a particular issue. In national elections, public assistance, education, crime, housing, and employment are always topics of discussion. These issues are crucial to the clients we serve, so it is important to critically assess how candidates stand on these issues. Not only can you identify where the candidates stand, but you can obtain substantive information about what is currently perceived as wrong with policies in the area.

No candidate is likely to espouse all of your opinions, so it is important to identify several issues to which you are committed. For instance, if a strong national health care policy is important to you, follow the candidates' positions on this issue. Gather as much information as you can, and study it carefully before the election. Compare the candidates' positions before deciding. It may also be helpful to contact an organization such as NASW for its analysis of a candidate's position on an issue.

Political Polls.   Political polls are conducted by candidates and by organizations that have a vested interest in the popularity of a candidate. However, it is easy to distort the results of a poll to show whatever the sponsoring organization feels is important. Be a critical consumer of information from opinion polls. Know how many people were polled, who collected the information, and the breadth of issues included in the poll.

It is also helpful to note who endorses a political candidate. All major newspapers publicly endorse candidates close to the election and state in their editorial pages why they endorse that candidate. Finding out who endorses a candidate can help you identify the candidates who appear to best serve the interests of social workers and their clients.

Voting

When voters become disillusioned by the tactics of a campaign, their reaction may be simply not to vote. To relinquish this precious political right and responsibility is to vote for apathy, the root cause of a political system sadly out of touch with the citizens who must live within it. No candidate is perfect, and the rigors of political life can make even the candidate with the most integrity appear untrustworthy. But armed with the best information possible, it remains critical that you voice your political position by voting and by encouraging your clients to do the same.

Be wary of single-issue candidates, who occupy most of their time with and talk about only one issue. Candidates with a single issue are dangerous because often they do not have well-considered positions on other issues. Single-issue politicians usually appeal to a large bloc of voters and may be too single-minded to be effective legislators.

Going to Court to Change Policy

Sometimes no amount of pressure on legislators results in laws and regulations that reflect the best interests of the client or the social work profession. When all other avenues of change fail, **litigation**—action within the court system—may be the only route left to accomplish change. Sometimes even the threat of filing a lawsuit against an individual or organization results in immediate action or at least facilitates the organization's willingness to talk.

Initiating court action is not a route to be taken lightly. Several factors must be considered before proceeding with litigation. First, you must consider carefully whether all possible routes of initiating change have been completely explored. In a litigious society, filing a lawsuit seems to be the easy way out; in fact, it should be a last resort. Second, determine whether the change you would like to see is actually the kind of issue the court system will take seriously. Lawsuits do not have to be heard by the court if they appear to be frivolous or inconsequential. The court system is already bogged down with more cases than it can handle, and judges are not receptive to insignificant suits. Third, keep in mind that litigation is extremely expensive and time consuming. Although many organizations provide low-cost legal advice for certain issues, a full-blown lawsuit can be very expensive. Think carefully about whether your organization or clients might lose more than they gain.

If you have answered these questions and still find court action advisable or necessary, consult an attorney or an organization that specializes in the kind of litigation you are considering. Only an attorney can advise you on building a case and presenting it in court.

SUMMARY

This chapter makes clear that it is not enough for you simply to understand how current social welfare policy is made and implemented. As part of the social work profession's commitment to the clients' well-being, it is critical to be aware of and committed to political change. We have this obligation not only to our clients, but to ourselves. We can more effectively empower our clients if we can empower ourselves to change what needs to be changed in our environment.

Change can occur on a broad level through full participation in the political process or on the agency level through the agency hierarchy. Both kinds of change require a willingness to gather as much information as possible, explore obstacles and resources, develop and carry out an action plan, and continuously evaluate our efforts. Chapter Nine discusses how practitioners can approach policy change within their most immediate environment, the social service agency.

DISCUSSION QUESTIONS

1. *Where would you find more information on the following policies?*
   a. *Policies regarding the licensing of foster homes*
   b. *Changes in AFDC work requirements*
   c. *Zoning laws*
   d. *Public housing*
2. *What restrictions on political activity might exist for social workers who work in public agencies?*
3. *When is litigation appropriate?*
4. *Why is it important to involve clients in presenting testimony at public hearings?*

SUGGESTED PROJECTS

1. Invite someone from your local office of NASW to describe NASW's activities regarding important social service legislation in your state.
2. Identify several issues you feel are important to social workers and their clients, and research the positions of your local legislators on those issues.
3. Attend a public hearing on an important social service issue in your community.
4. Conduct a voter registration drive on your campus or in the neighborhood in which your college or university is located.

IMPORTANT TERMS AND CONCEPTS

the Hatch Act   *lobbyist*
informational hearing *testimony*
litigation   *think tank*

The Practitioner's Role in Changing Agency-Level Policy

*I used to work for an agency that required its workers to
account for all of their daily activities in ten-minute increments
and indicate what case we were working on during each of those
intervals. We all thought it was ridiculous but were told that it
was the only way to bill the worker's time to the appropriate
case under the agency's numerous purchase of service contracts.
When one of my clients died and I requested the afternoon off to
attend the funeral, the agency told me to bill my time at the
funeral to the client's case. Several weeks later I left that agency.
I couldn't work for a social service agency that I thought valued
its own financial survival over compassion and concern about
clients and their families. I thought my resignation would shake
up the agency and force them to change some of their policies. It
didn't. I know now after 15 years of practice that I should have
stayed at the agency and made a personal investment in being
part of changing that policy. But at the time I just did not
think that was my job or my responsibility. If it wasn't mine,
whose was it?*

—FIFTEEN-YEAR VETERAN IN THE FIELD OF CHILD WELFARE

———◆•◆———

It seems appropriate that our approach to integrating social welfare
policy and social work practice returns to where it began—the practitioner within the social service agency. As the political sands shift

because of our efforts (or in spite of them), the social work profession's connection to the primary or secondary organizational setting remains consistent. As the opening comments of the child welfare worker indicate, organizational policies can be a source of anger and frustration. Social work field students frequently complain to educators that their placement agencies have policies that seem to contradict the values of the social work profession. Instead of respecting the uniqueness of the individual, some agencies insist on providing methodical and uniform services even when a worker determines this is not the best way to serve a client. Instead of supporting the professional commitment to client self-determination, agencies usurp that right with rigid philosophies of service or casework methods that limit, rather than expand, client choices.

We know from Chapters Two and Three that organizational survival is one of the primary goals of the social service agency. When the agency becomes insensitive to its basic mission, however, it is a classic case of goal displacement. Nonetheless, organizations can and do change. The child welfare worker quoted understands in retrospect that walking away from a policy he considered inappropriate did nothing to change the policy. The key to surviving successfully within the agency setting while maintaining integrity in providing services to our clients is to be an active part of the change process.

Specifically, this chapter includes the following:

+ Ways you can find out about an agency's policies and how these policies were developed
+ A description of your role as a social work practitioner in initiating organizational change
+ A discussion of why organizational change is so often resisted
+ Methods to help you change attitudes and behaviors as well as organizational structure

FINDING OUT ABOUT AGENCY-LEVEL POLICIES

Several valuable resources exist within the agency to help you find out more about a policy. The first source is your direct supervisor. Supervisors who are familiar with an agency policy and have seen it in operation for a long time can offer valuable insights into the rationale followed in the policy's development. Supervisors can help you understand whether the policy is the product of formal or informal agency practice. Sometimes the day-to-day policies of an agency are simply procedures, not policies, and are not as rigid as you might assume. Your supervisor can help you identify how much latitude you have in implementing a policy.

For example, imagine you are an adoption worker for Children's Friend Society, a statewide child welfare agency. It is agency policy to deny more than one healthy infant adoption per family; that is, if a family adopts through Children's Friend, they cannot be considered for a second placement by the agency. You feel the policy is unfair and would like to see it changed. As long as couples go through all the steps required for being placed on the agency waiting list, you consider it unfair to deny couples an opportunity for a second placement. Your direct supervisor should be your first source of information. If he or she cannot give you a satisfactory explanation, the executive director might be helpful. Executive directors are in a unique position to speak on behalf of both the agency staff and the board of directors. Minutes of past board of directors' meetings can also provide insight into why policies were initially adopted and whether the board's original intent is reflected in the policy as it is implemented.

Another source of information is the agency manual of policies and procedures. Most agencies identify in the manual general operating procedures, the day-to-day activities within the agency, as well as the policies reflecting the philosophy of the agency. Employees should routinely be given a copy of the manual as part of their orientation.

Private, nonprofit agencies, such as Children's Friend Society, may be restricted by their **agency charter,** the legal document that authorizes them to provide child welfare services. To be licensed as a child welfare agency, agencies must meet certain legal requirements and undergo periodic relicensing procedures. The legal restrictions might explain the existence of certain policies, and the absence of others, within an agency. The same holds true for public agencies, which, by law, must provide certain services and refrain from providing others.

ORGANIZATIONAL-LEVEL CHANGE

Chapters Two and Three explore the social service agency as the context for practice and the implementation of policies generated within and outside the agency. One of the most common complaints of social workers and clients is that bureaucracies are cumbersome to operate within and that they seem too impersonal to adequately meet the needs of employees and clients. The inability to be responsive to people's needs implies the need for change. You can be a vital force in initiating change within the organization.

Organizational change refers to "modification of formal policies, programs, procedures, or management practices" (Resnick & Patti, 1980, p. 5). Organizational change is usually attempted because it improves services to clients. However, it may also result from employees' efforts to improve their working environment. Change usually occurs from the top of the organization to the bottom. This chapter describes how change occurs from *the bottom to the top* with the social work practitioner as the agent of change.

The Practitioner's Responsibility for Organizational Change

If the practitioner's responsibility is to provide services to clients, shouldn't organizational change remain the responsibility of administrators and boards of directors? Resnick and Patti (1980) say definitely not. Practitioners are in a unique position to see the need for change because they are familiar with how day-to-day operations of the agency affect the client. It is the practitioner, not the administrator or board of directors, who provides the actual service to the client. Therefore, the practitioner is in a better position to assess whether the organizational structure serves the welfare of clients—the primary purpose of the organization. As shown in Chapter Two, in an effort to survive, organizations may displace goals, so that the importance of survival supersedes service to the client. If we are bound by our professional code of ethics to the primacy of client welfare, we are similarly bound to pursue organizational change if necessary to meet the needs of the client population (Resnick & Patti, 1980).

A second reason Resnick and Patti (1980) believe the practitioner has an appropriate role in organizational change is that engaging in methods to improve the context of service delivery is critical to worker morale and work satisfaction. It is difficult to empower our clients to make changes in their lives if we do not feel competent to attempt to change our own professional working environment. It is impossible to provide the best services possible if we know there is a serious flaw in the organization.

Third, social work practitioners are the vital link between the administrative structure and the clients the agency serves. Practitioners play an important role in providing the information the organizational structure needs to adapt to the changing character of the populations we serve. For example, 20 years ago, social workers relied heavily on an older person's family to provide care in the case of serious illness or disability. Families remained geographically close to one another and many women did not work, so daughters and daughters-in-law became unofficial service providers for dependent older adults. Today, three-fourths of American women work part- or full-time outside the home. American families are more mobile than ever before, rarely remaining in the same towns and cities in which they were raised. The implications for social services to older adults are significant. Instead of providing services that focus on coordinating family resources to cope with an older person's dependency, geriatric social workers must often find and fund resources to replace those once provided by family. As a result, maintaining older adults in their own homes is more expensive and requires intensive case management and reliance on a complex network of nonfamily support networks. The continuing experience of practitioners involved in providing hands-on service positions them to anticipate changes in the service delivery environment.

Changing Individuals' Attitudes and Behavior within the Organization

The quality of an organization's operation is the product of its members' performance. Complaints about inefficiency, ineffectiveness, and nonresponsiveness may be leveled at the members of the organization, not at the structure or operating procedures. Although practitioners may not be in the position to make changes in administrative personnel, they can work toward changing the attitudes and behavior of colleagues.

One of the concerns frequently expressed by social work students is the fear of burning out in the social work profession. Students are concerned that the rigors of working with clients and taxpayers' chronic lack of commitment to social problems will result in the student's personal disillusionment and bitterness toward helping people at all. It does not take the new practitioner long to identify workers in social service agencies who appear burned out, or at least so skeptical about their jobs that they cease to be effective. These attitudes are the first focus of organizational change.

Research supports the conclusion that workers who participate in important decisions that affect their work with clients are less likely to become apathetic in their jobs (Arches, 1991). Becoming active in the decision-making process and encouraging one's colleagues to do the same is the most important way to change organizational attitudes. This can be accomplished by the use of **quality circles** or other employee-centered mechanisms for organizational decision making. The quality circle concept originated in private business out of a concern about employees' alienation from the life of the organization. Management quickly surmised that employees would be more likely to remain loyal to an organization, and therefore become more productive, if they were given opportunities to influence decisions in the workplace and an outlet for expressing their frustrations with the organization.

For example, a group of social workers at a shelter for runaways had long been frustrated with their lack of input about scheduling work hours and the kind of group therapy techniques the shelter used. The house manager scheduled hours for professional and volunteer staff without consulting them, employing a system beset with favoritism. Workers also felt that the traditional rap-group therapy format reflected the interests of the executive director, a skilled group worker trained in the 1960s, rather than those of the more recently educated group workers. These group workers were more skilled in confrontational and existential techniques, which they were never allowed to use.

To address these concerns, the social workers formed their own quality circle to support each other and to identify how they might change the scheduling and group therapy problems. Instead of simply lodging a complaint with the executive director about the scheduling problem, they devised their own system of staff rotation in which all workers would receive an equal chance to work with residents and families and have weekends off on a regular basis. This system offered an element of diversity that had been missing for the staff and met the needs of the agency to have adequate staff coverage. Likewise, the social workers carefully constructed a case to persuade the executive director that it was time for a change in the group therapy techniques employed by the agency. They compiled research findings about the effectiveness of various group therapy techniques and compared them with their experiences with the current format. Much to their surprise, the executive director enthusiastically accepted both their scheduling and group therapy recommendations. Scheduling had been done without consultation simply because the house manager had never considered another scheduling method and was not aware of the problem it had caused. The rap-group format continued to be used for the past 20 years because no social worker had ever suggested a different format, and the executive director had assumed the old format was working.

In this example, attitudes were changed simply by providing new information to those in service and decision-making positions. Like individuals and families, the organizational system needs new input to thrive and grow. Input can take the form of inservice training, staff retreats, training in new techniques, or simply a staff meeting dedicated to information exchange. Changing the behavior of individuals within the organizational setting might also depend on providing current information to those in decision-making positions. Changing the focus of the therapy group sessions was instigated by group workers. These workers were not convinced that the current rap-group format, relatively unstructured and focused on feelings, was the most effective way to encourage change in runaways. They saw the rap-group approach as unresponsive to the more demanding needs of teens who run away in the 1990s, as opposed to the reasons teens ran away in the 1960s. Many of the home's residents were dealing with physical and sexual abuse, highly dysfunctional families, pregnancy, and gang problems. Different group therapy techniques were needed to respond to the changing severity of adolescent problems.

Why Is There Resistance to Change?

Convincing others in a social service agency to change their attitudes or behavior is rarely as easy as it appears in the foregoing example. More frequently, people resist changing old habits. Things are always easier once a routine has been developed; initiating change implies an investment of time and energy that some organizational members may not be willing to make.

Others resist change because they interpret the suggestion of change as a questioning of their competency. It would have been easy for the executive director simply to refuse to change the group approach on the basis that it had worked fine for 20 years and did not need changing. Changing practices in which individuals have a strong personal investment requires a great deal of political finesse to avoid creating defensiveness and resistance.

Individuals resist change that threatens their values or beliefs (Neugeboren, 1985). For example, until recently it was widely accepted that running away was a sign of individual pathology in the runaway. Something was wrong with the adolescent who could not tolerate living in the family. However, after working with runaway adolescents in a group setting for 30 years, members of the profession are more likely to accept the theory that for many teens, running away may be a healthy response to an intolerable situation. The pathology is no longer seen as lying exclusively within the child, but rather, it may be traced to the individual's family. If one staff member at the agency for runaways were to persist in believing in individual pathology as the reason teenagers run away, it might be difficult to change his or her views. Changing one's beliefs can be very threatening to an individual.

Force or Persuasion?

Executive directors and supervisors can force staff to change the organization, but direct service providers do not have the authority to demand changes in attitudes or behavior. The practitioner must rely on persuasion to influence change from a position of little power. Information, cooperation, and sensitivity to the reasons for resistance to change are the practitioner's most valuable tools in promoting change. Many of the same techniques we use in encouraging change in our clients can be equally effective in working with colleagues.

Changing Organizational Goals, Structure, or Procedures

The second major type of organizational change is aimed at organizational goals, structures, or procedures. This type of change is more substantive and cannot be achieved by the efforts of the direct services practitioner alone. Once the practitioner has identified an area in which change is needed or justified, he or she must work with the agency structure and governing bodies to achieve that change. As Chapter Four indicates, private and public agencies have different decision-making and authority structures.

Private Agencies. Private agencies have boards of directors who, in addition to the executive director, are responsible for major changes in organizational orientation or procedure. It is wise for the practitioner's own organizational survival to respect the organizational chart when pursuing change. First work with the supervisor, then with other area supervisors, then with the executive director. To simply go above everyone's head to the board of directors is courting disaster.

However, you can develop good relationships with board members without threatening the agency's authority structure. Staff members are usually assigned to work with board members on committees; this is a good way to develop working relationships with board members around specific areas. Board members rely on input from agency staff members to make sound, informed decisions. If you find the traditional authority structure resistant to change, working closely with board members through the committee structure might allow you to communicate information to board members without being insubordinate to the chain of command.

Boards of directors vary in their receptiveness to working with staff members. As discussed in Chapter Four, some boards see their function as that of endorsing the suggestions of the executive director; others take a more active role in developing policy for the agency. The latter type of board is much more receptive to input from staff than the former. Passive boards can be extremely resistant to feedback from staff and might interpret any uninvited input as inappropriate.

Public Agencies.   Much of what public agencies can and cannot do is determined by legislative mandate or the actions of a unit of government. Therefore, organizational change in public agencies is more complicated than in private agencies. We have already discussed techniques for changing policy established by legislative bodies. Through lobbying, aggressive letter-writing campaigns, and appearances at public hearings, social work practitioners can directly affect the policy-making process in legislative bodies.

Public agencies often have community advisory committees that do not make policy but may have a powerful influence on certain issues within the agency. Working with the advisory committee is a back door to suggesting and working toward changes not only for employees of the public agencies but for workers from outside the agency who would like to see changes in the operation.

For example, county departments of social services establish the eligibility requirements for General Assistance clients. In a large urban area, a group of social workers from the homeless shelter were constantly frustrated by the fact that, to receive General Assistance, individuals had to have an address. But without General Assistance, most homeless individuals did not have the money to pay the security deposit on an apartment. There seemed to be no way to break this cycle for homeless people. Workers from the shelter aggressively advocated for the homeless with the advisory committee of the local county department of social services to change the residency requirement. As part of a compromise, the homeless shelter volunteered to be a temporary address for homeless people applying for General Assistance. Once individuals had secured housing, their names would be transferred to their new addresses. By offering a compromise combined with a logical presentation of the reasoning behind the change, workers were able to persuade the advisory committee to recommend the change to the county board of supervisors. A solid presentation, combined with communitywide pressure generated by the media, resulted in the recommended change in the residency requirement.

Making changes in the day-to-day operations of a public agency may require informal as well as formal techniques. The practitioner's reputation in the agency may be the most powerful tool for change. If supervisors and administrators perceive a staff member as loyally committed to the goals of the agency, that person's efforts to change the organization will be more positively interpreted than the efforts of a disgruntled employee. A positive reputation within the agency can be effective in what Pierce (1984) refers to as **organizational shaping,** which means initiating a series of minor but important changes in organization operation that are often less threatening than initiating major changes all at once.

THE PROBLEM-SOLVING MODEL AND ORGANIZATIONAL CHANGE

To illustrate how the practitioner can instigate organizational change, the problem-solving model is used in the example of a social work practitioner attempting to change a specific aspect of service in an intermediate care facility for developmentally disabled adults. Just as the problem-solving approach is helpful in identifying clients' needs and possibilities for service, the problem-solving approach is also helpful for the practitioner who is anticipating organizational change.

Assessing the Need for Organizational Change

Dan is a social worker at Hillcrest, a residential treatment center for developmentally disabled adults. He has been working at Hillcrest for three years and knows intimately how the agency operates and what he would like to see change. He is concerned about the recreational activities available to residents. Dan works with higher functioning adults who can learn simple tasks and have learned to read and write. Although most of his clients hold jobs outside the home, they spend their leisure time with other residents, who may not have all the same intellectual abilities they possess. At present, a recreational therapist has designed a leisure activity program that is intended to meet the needs of both higher-level functioning residents *and* the most severely impaired.

Higher functioning residents rarely attend the leisure activities because they find them too simple and feel they are being treated like children. The current leisure program appears to be working well for the more impaired residents, but it does not serve the needs of all of Hillcrest's residents. As a result, Dan's clients simply sit and watch television every night and do not participate in any structured leisure activity. In this stage of assessing the problem, Dan identifies specifically the clients who need more stimulating activities, based on client self-reports, his observations as the social worker, and the recommendations of the Hillcrest psychologist.

Problem Definition and Goal Setting.   Clearly stated, the problem is that the current recreational program does not meet the needs of higher functioning residents. Hillcrest's recreational therapist, Tom, is available to residents only two hours a day because of financial restrictions imposed by the agency. Tom designed the program within this limited context to meet the needs of the lowest functioning residents; he hoped that higher functioning residents would derive at least some benefit from the program. Tom is resistant to changing the program because he feels he does not have the time or interest to change it given current financial restrictions.

Dan's goal is to work toward establishing a separate recreational program for his higher functioning clients that will recognize their need for more rigorous stimulation in leisure activities. Ideally, Dan would like to see the range of therapeutic recreation services expanded at Hillcrest, but he is willing to compromise by using the agency's allocation of recreational services differently. Dan has engaged in one of the first and most important aspects of organizational change—committing both to making what would be a perfect change *and* to identifying what compromise, if necessary, is acceptable.

Identifying Resources.   Dan has identified the problem and has established a preliminary goal for his change effort. Now it is important that he begin to identify resources that will work with the change effort before he goes to the executive director of Hillcrest for an executive decision on his plans. Dan identifies the following resources:

1. *The presence of a therapeutic recreation program in the agency.* Half the battle has already been won. Hillcrest already employs a recreational therapist, so the agency is aware of the importance of leisure activities for its residents and committed to providing them.

2. *A cooperative attitude on the part of the psychologist and the clients affected by the change.* Residents and the psychologist agree that a new recreational program is needed. They will become important allies in Dan's efforts to persuade the executive director. Developing committed allies is essential to initiating organizational change.

3. *Dan's own professional reputation in the agency and his good relationship with administration.* Just as the quality of the social worker's relationship with a client can help foster change for the client, the worker's reputation and working relationship with the administration and with those affected by any proposed change are important in promoting organizational change.

Determining the Organization's Receptiveness to Change.   Because the worker is employed by the agency, he or she faces certain risks should the organizational change effort be particularly unpopular with administrators, colleagues, or clients. Workers may risk being fired or ostracized by colleagues if they are not particularly thoughtful in the early stages of organizational change.

If the proposed changes are in direct contradiction to the stated goals and purpose of the agency, one cannot expect an enthusiastic reception for the idea. A series of smaller, less threatening changes might accomplish the same end without threatening the basic integrity of the agency.

Who will the winners and losers be if the change occurs? If a proposed change is seen as a direct threat to an administrator's integrity or to one's colleagues, you can expect significant resistance. Dan needs to create a win-win situation in which clients, staff, and administration all benefit from the change.

The agency could be changed in many ways, so Dan must carefully select the issues he chooses to take on. If Dan appears to be the kind of worker who constantly complains about how an agency runs its program, no one will take him seriously when he attempts to facilitate change. He does not want to get the reputation of being a chronic malcontent.

Identifying Obstacles. Just as it is important to identify the strengths we bring to the change effort, it is likewise important to be aware of the obstacles that might present themselves. Dan has identified Tom's resistance to an expansion in the recreational program, financial constraints, the lack of room at Hillcrest to run a separate recreational program for residents, and an unknown attitude on the part of the administration as the most immediate obstacles to organizational change.

After carefully thinking through the obstacles, Dan decides he can work on Tom's attitude if he can either convince administration of the financial need or show Tom how he can run programs for both lower and higher functioning adults within the same time frame. Dividing the current facility used for recreational programs or having recreational activities away from Hillcrest might overcome the obstacle of inadequate space. Now Dan must carefully explore alternatives and develop an action plan to present to the administration.

Exploring Alternatives. Dan's first alternative is to secure additional funding from the administration to develop an off-site recreational program designed specifically for the needs and interests of Hillcrest's higher functioning residents. The advantage of such an approach is that it opens up the possibilities for a wide range of recreational activities, including field trips, camping, sporting events, and other community activities. The disadvantages are that such a program is expensive and will require additional staff.

Dan's second alternative is to expand the existing recreational program at Hillcrest but have separate time slots for recreational programming depending on the residents' abilities. The same facility within Hillcrest could be used, but the programs would be held at different times. The advantages of this approach include its being the best use of current space and requiring a smaller outlay of money on the part of the agency. The disadvantage is that the program will still require money for extra staff and materials.

The third alternative is to have both recreational programs running simultaneously in the same room but simply designing the program for two, rather than one, recreational activity. Neither additional therapist's time nor additional space would be needed. This is the last-resort alternative for Dan and not one that he will necessarily suggest to administration—unless the first two alternatives fail.

Dan has carefully thought through three realistic possibilities, anticipating the resources and obstacles he will encounter in his change effort. Most important, he is thinking in terms of compromise, an essential element in promoting and realizing organizational change.

Developing an Action Plan

Dan presents all three alternatives in a proposal to be discussed with the executive director and Tom, the recreational therapist. Each plan is accompanied by a detailed explanation of its costs and benefits. In his proposal, Dan includes letters of support from the staff psychologist and from residents who would participate in the proposed program. He is now ready to go to the executive director. He will present the first two plans in detail to give the executive director and Tom some room for bargaining—an important part of advocating for organizational change.

Implementing the Action Plan

In Dan's meeting with the executive director and Tom, he finds out that finances are extremely tight and that it is unlikely that the recreational program can be expanded with additional paid staff. The administration is not resistant to Dan's suggestions, but its hands are tied by the financial restrictions. If Dan can find additional money or volunteers to assist with the program, the administration and Tom are willing to try the program on an experimental basis.

Dan's first move is to approach a local men's club both for financial assistance and for volunteer help. After presenting his case with the help of clients, he secures a small amount of money to be used for supplies and persuades the men's club to commit ten hours a month in volunteer time to assist in off-site field trips. After six months, the men's club will consider making another financial contribution. In view of these developments, the executive director agrees to start the program. Although Tom is hesitant, he agrees to work with Dan on developing alternative recreational outlets.

Evaluating the Organizational Change

Dan knows that if the program is successful and residents react enthusiastically, both Tom and the executive director will have a difficult time disbanding the improved recreational program, although doing so remains a possibility. He also knows that it is imperative that residents actively participate in the program or else his original contention that residents watch television because they find the existing program boring will not be supported. He also knows that the men's club's time and money must be expended wisely, or they will be unwilling to make an additional commitment.

These are the issues Dan must address in his continuing evaluation of the expanded recreational program and in the process of stabilizing the change effort, similar to the way this is done with clients. Organizations are dynamic, changing organisms. Dan may need to adjust his approach or the kind of program that develops, depending on other factors that arise in the external or internal environment of the social service agency.

SUMMARY

As practitioners, one of our professional tasks is to sensitize our clients to the importance of working toward change in their own lives by empowering them with both a more positive attitude and the skills needed to initiate change. Whether we are working with a young mother who struggles to balance the demands of work and family or an older adult coming to terms with declining health and financial resources, we help clients gain more control over their own personal environments. The organization is the social worker's professional environment, and, like our clients' environments, sometimes it needs to be changed. This chapter discussed how the practitioner can identify and change a policy. Approaching organizational change through the problem-solving approach is a natural, familiar technique for the social work practitioner. Assessing strengths and weaknesses, exploring alternatives, implementing an action plan, and continually evaluating the change effort brings a sense of logical order to organizational change.

DISCUSSION QUESTIONS

1. *Why do social work practitioners have a responsibility to pursue organizational change?*
2. *Discuss the difficulties involved in changing attitudes as opposed to organizational structure. How do the techniques for approaching these two kinds of change differ?*
3. *What are quality circles? On what behavioral principles are they based? Would they be appropriate to social service agencies? Secondary social work settings?*
4. *What are the similarities between a client's resistance to change and that of the members of an organization?*
5. *Discuss the similarities between applying the problem-solving model to change client behavior and applying it to change organizational policy.*

SUGGESTED PROJECTS

1. Following the problem-solving example used in this chapter, initiate a change in your social work program or within the college or university (both organizational settings).
2. Find out if any agency or business in your community uses quality circles or another intensive employee participation model, and invite a representative to speak to your class.

3. Occupational or industrial social work involves helping people cope with the stresses and challenges of their jobs. Interview an occupational social worker and find out how he or she helps people cope with the organizational environment. Does he or she play a role in encouraging employees to initiate changes in the organization?

IMPORTANT TERMS AND CONCEPTS

agency charter   *organizational shaping*
organizational change   *quality circle*

CODE OF ETHICS
National Association of Social Workers

PREAMBLE

This code is intended to serve as a guide to the everyday conduct of members of the social work profession and as a basis for the adjudication of issues in ethics when the conduct of social workers is alleged to deviate from the standards expressed or implied in this code. It represents standards of ethical behavior for social workers in professional relationships with those served, with colleagues, with employers, with other individuals and professions, and with the community and society as a whole. It also embodies standards of ethical behavior governing individual conduct to the extent that such conduct is associated with an individual's status and identity as a social worker.

This code is based on the fundamental values of the social work profession that include the worth, dignity, and uniqueness of all persons as well as their rights and opportunities. It is also based on the nature of social work, which fosters conditions that promote these values.

In subscribing to and abiding by this code, the social worker is expected to view ethical responsibility in as inclusive a context as each situation demands and within which ethical judgement is required. The social worker is expected

to take into consideration all the principles in this code that have a bearing upon any situation in which ethical judgement is to be exercised and professional intervention or conduct is planned. The course of action that the social worker chooses is expected to be consistent with the spirit as well as the letter of this code.

In itself, this code does not represent a set of rules that will prescribe all the behaviors of social workers in all the complexities of professional life. Rather, it offers general principles to guide conduct, and the judicious appraisal of conduct, in situations that have ethical implications. It provides the basis for making judgements about ethical actions before and after they occur. Frequently, the particular situation determines the ethical principles that apply and the manner of their application. In such cases, not only the particular ethical principles are taken into immediate consideration, but also the entire code and its spirit. Specific applications of ethical principles must be judged within the context in which they are being considered. Ethical behavior in a given situation must satisfy not only the judgement of the individual social worker, but also the judgement of an unbiased jury of professional peers.

This code should not be used as an instrument to deprive any social worker of the opportunity or freedom to practice with complete professional integrity; nor should any disciplinary action be taken on the basis of this code without maximum provision for safeguarding the rights of the social worker affected.

The ethical behavior of social workers results not from edict, but from a personal commitment of the individual. This code is offered to affirm the will and zeal of all social workers to be ethical and to act ethically in all that they do as social workers.

The following codified ethical principles should guide social workers in the various roles and relationships and at the various levels of responsibility in which they function professionally. These principles also serve as a basis for the adjudication by the National Association of Social Workers of issues in ethics.

In subscribing to this code, social workers are required to cooperate in its implementation and abide by any disciplinary rulings based on it. They should also take adequate measures to discourage, prevent, expose, and correct the unethical conduct of colleagues. Finally, social workers should be equally ready to defend and assist colleagues unjustly charged with unethical conduct.

Summary of Major Principles

I. The Social Worker's Conduct and Comportment as a Social Worker

A. *Propriety.* The social worker should maintain high standards of personal conduct in the capacity or identity as social worker.

B. *Competence and professional development.* The social worker should strive to become and remain proficient in professional practice and the performance of professional functions.

C. *Service.* The social worker should regard as primary the service obligation of the social work profession.

D. *Integrity.* The social worker should act in accordance with the highest standards of professional integrity.

E. *Scholarship and research.* The social worker engaged in study and research should be guided by the conventions of scholarly inquiry.

II. The Social Worker's Ethical Responsibility to Clients

F. *Primacy of clients' interests.* The social worker's primary responsibility is to clients.

G. *Rights and prerogatives of clients.* The social worker should make every effort to foster maximum self-determination on the part of clients.

H. *Confidentiality and privacy.* The social worker should respect the privacy of clients and hold in confidence all information obtained in the course of professional service.

I. *Fees.* When setting fees, the social worker should ensure that they are fair, reasonable, considerate, and commensurate with the service performed and with due regard for the clients' ability to pay.

III. The Social Worker's Ethical Responsibility to Colleagues

J. *Respect, fairness, and courtesy.* The social worker should treat colleagues with respect, courtesy, fairness, and good faith.

K. *Dealing with colleagues' clients.* The social worker has the responsibility to relate to the clients of colleagues with full professional consideration.

IV. The Social Worker's Ethical Responsibility to Employers and Employing Organizations

L. *Commitments to employing organizations.* The social worker should adhere to commitments made to the employing organizations.

V. The Social Worker's Ethical Responsibility to the Social Work Profession

M. *Maintaining the integrity of the profession.* The social worker should uphold and advance the values, ethics, knowledge, and mission of the profession.

N. *Community service,* The social worker should assist the profession in making social services available to the general public.

O. *Development of knowledge.* The social worker should take responsibility for identifying, developing, and fully utilizing knowledge for professional practice.

VI. The Social Worker's Ethical Responsibility to Society

P. *Promoting the general welfare.* The social worker should promote the general welfare of society.

THE NASW CODE OF ETHICS

I. The Social Worker's Conduct and Comportment as a Social Worker

A. *Propriety.* The social worker should maintain high standards of personal conduct in the capacity or identity as social worker.
   1. The private conduct of the social worker is a personal matter to the same degree as is any other person's, except when such conduct compromises the fulfillment of professional responsibilities.
   2. The social worker should not participate in, condone, or be associated with dishonesty, fraud, deceit, or misrepresentation.
   3. The social worker should distinguish clearly between statements and actions made as a private individual and as a representative of the social work profession or an organization or group.

B. *Competence and professional development.* The social worker should strive to become and remain proficient in professional practice and the performance of professional functions.
   1. The social worker should accept responsibility or employment only on the basis of existing competence or the intention to acquire the necessary competence.
   2. The social worker should not misrepresent professional qualifications, education, experience, or affiliations.

C. *Service.* The social worker should regard as primary the service obligation of the social work profession.
   1. The social worker should retain ultimate responsibility for the quality and extent of the service that individual assumes, assigns, or performs.
   2. The social worker should act to prevent practices that are inhumane or discriminatory against any person or group of persons.

D. *Integrity.* The social worker should act in accordance with the highest standards of professional integrity and impartiality.
   1. The social worker should be alert to and resist the influences and pressures that interfere with the exercise of professional discretion and impartial judgement required for the performance of professional functions.
   2. The social worker should not exploit professional relationships for personal gain.

E. *Scholarship and research.* The social worker engaged in study and research should be guided by the conventions of scholarly inquiry.
   1. The social worker engaged in research should consider carefully its possible consequences for human beings.
   2. The social worker engaged in research should ascertain that

the consent of participants in the research is voluntary and informed, without any implied deprivation or penalty for refusal to participate, and with due regard for participants' privacy and dignity.

3. The social worker engaged in research should protect participants from unwarranted physical or mental discomfort, distress, harm, danger, or deprivation.

4. The social worker who engages in the evaluation of services or cases should discuss them only for the professional purposes and only with persons directly and professionally concerned with them.

5. Information obtained about participants in research should be treated as confidential.

6. The social worker should take credit only for work actually done in connection with scholarly and research endeavors and credit contributions made by others.

II. The Social Worker's Ethical Responsibility to Clients

F. *Primacy of clients' interest.* The social worker's primary responsibility is to clients.

1. The social worker should serve clients with devotion, loyalty, determination, and the maximum application of professional skill and competence.

2. The social worker should not exploit relationships with clients for personal advantage.

3. The social worker should not practice, condone, facilitate, or collaborate with any form of discrimination on the basis of race, color, sex, sexual orientation, age, religion, national origin, marital status, political

belief, mental or physical handicap, or any other preference or personal characteristic, condition or status.

4. The social worker should avoid relationships or commitments that conflict with the interests of clients.

5. The social worker should under no circumstances engage in sexual activities with clients.

6. The social worker should provide clients with accurate and complete information regarding the extent and nature of the services available to them.

7. The social worker should apprise clients of their risks, rights, opportunities, and obligations associated with social service to them.

8. The social worker should seek advice and counsel of colleagues and supervisors whenever such consultation is in the best interest of clients.

9. The social worker should terminate service to clients, and professional relationships with them, when such service and relationships are no longer required or no longer serve the clients' needs or interests.

10. The social worker should withdraw services precipitously only under unusual circumstances, giving careful consideration to all factors in the situation and taking care to minimize possible adverse effects.

11. The social worker who anticipates the termination or interruption of service to clients should notify clients promptly and seek the transfer, referral, or continuation of service in relation to the clients' needs and preferences.

G. *Rights and prerogatives of clients.* The social worker should make every effort to foster maximum self-determination on the part of clients.

1. When the social worker must act on behalf of a client who has been adjudged legally incompetent, the social worker should safeguard the interests and rights of that client.
2. When another individual has been legally authorized to act in behalf of a client, the social worker should deal with that person always with the client's best interest in mind.
3. The social worker should not engage in any action that violates or diminishes the civil or legal rights of clients.

H. *Confidentiality and privacy.* The social worker should respect the privacy of clients and hold in confidence all information obtained in the course of professional service.

1. The social worker should share with others confidences revealed by clients, without their consent, only for compelling professional reasons.
2. The social worker should inform clients fully about the limits of confidentiality in a given situation, the purposes for which information is obtained, and how it may be used.
3. The social worker should afford clients reasonable access to any official social work records concerning them.
4. When providing clients with access to records, the social worker should take due care to protect the confidences of others contained in those records.
5. The social worker should obtain informed consent of clients before taping, recording,

or permitting third party observation of their activities.

I. *Fees.* When setting fees, the social worker should ensure that they are fair, reasonable, considerate, and commensurate with the service performed and with due regard for the clients' ability to pay.

1. The social worker should not accept anything of value for making a referral.

III. The Social Worker's Ethical Responsibility to Colleagues

J. *Respect, fairness, and courtesy.* The social worker should treat colleagues with respect, courtesy, fairness, and good faith.

1. The social worker should cooperate with colleagues to promote professional interests and concerns.
2. The social worker should respect confidences shared by colleagues in the course of their professional relationships and transactions.
3. The social worker should create and maintain conditions of practice that facilitate ethical and competent professional performance by colleagues.
4. The social worker should treat with respect, and represent accurately and fairly, the qualifications, views, and findings of colleagues and use appropriate channels to express judgements on these matters.
5. The social worker who replaces or is replaced by a colleague in professional practice should act with consideration for the interest, character, and reputation of that colleague.
6. The social worker should not exploit a dispute between a colleague and employers to obtain a position or otherwise

advance the social worker's interest.

7. The social worker should seek arbitration or mediation when conflicts with colleagues require resolution for compelling professional reasons.

8. The social worker should extend to colleagues of other professions the same respect and cooperation that is extended to social work colleagues.

9. The social worker who serves as an employer, supervisor, or mentor to colleagues should make orderly and explicit arrangements regarding the conditions of their continuing professional relationship.

10. The social worker who has the responsibility for employing and evaluating the performance of other staff members, should fulfill such responsibility in a fair, considerate, and equitable manner, on the basis of clearly enunciated criteria.

11. The social worker who has the responsibility for evaluating the performance of employees, supervisees, or students should share evaluations with them.

K. *Dealing with colleagues' clients.* The social worker has the responsibility to relate to the clients of colleagues with full professional consideration.

1. The social worker should not assume professional responsibility for the clients of another agency or a colleague without appropriate communication with that agency or colleague.

2. The social worker who serves the clients of colleagues, during a temporary absence or emergency, should serve those clients with the same consideration as that afforded any client.

IV. The Social Worker's Ethical Responsibility to Employers and Employing Organizations

L. *Commitments to employing organization.* The social worker should adhere to commitments made to the employing organization.

1. The social worker should work to improve the employing agency's policies and procedures, and the efficiency and effectiveness of its services.

2. The social worker should not accept employment or arrange student field placements in an organization which is currently under public sanction by NASW for violating personnel standards, or imposing limitations on or penalties for professional actions on behalf of clients.

3. The social worker should act to prevent and eliminate discrimination in the employing organization's work assignments and in its employment policies and practices.

4. The social worker should use with scrupulous regard, and only for the purpose for which they are intended, the resources of the employing organization.

V. The Social Worker's Ethical Responsibility to the Social Work Profession

M. *Maintainint the integrity of the profession.* The social worker should uphold and advance the values, ethics, knowledge, and mission of the profession.

1. The social worker should protect and enhance the dignity and integrity of the profession and should be responsible and vigorous in discussion and criticism of the profession.
2. The social worker should take action through appropriate channels against unethical conduct by any other member of the profession.
3. The social worker should act to prevent the unauthorized and unqualified practice of social work.
4. The social worker should make no misrepresentation in advertising as to qualifications, competence, service, or results to be achieved.

N. *Community service.* The social worker should assist the profession in making social services available to the general public.
1. The social worker should contribute time and professional expertise to activities that promote respect for the utility, the integrity, and the competence of the social work profession.
2. The social worker should support the formulation, development, enactment, and implementation of social policies of concern to the profession.

O. *Development of knowledge.* The social worker should take responsibility for identifying, developing, and fully utilizing knowledge for professional practice.
1. The social worker should base practice upon recognized knowledge relevant to social work.
2. The social worker should critically examine, and keep current with emerging knowledge relevant to social work.
3. The social worker should contribute to the knowledge base of social work and share research knowledge and practice wisdom with colleagues.

VI. The Social Worker's Ethical Responsibility to Society

P. *Promoting the general welfare.* The social worker should promote the general welfare of society.
1. The social worker should act to prevent and eliminate discrimination against any person or group on the basis of race, color, sex, sexual orientation, age, religion, national origin, marital status, political belief, mental or physical handicap, or any other preference or personal characteristic, condition, or status.
2. The social worker should act to ensure that all persons have access to the resources, services, and opportunities which they require.
3. The social worker should act to expand choice and opportunity for all persons, with special regard for disadvantaged or oppressed groups and persons.
4. The social worker should promote conditions that encourage respect for the diversity of cultures which constitute American society.
5. The social worker should provide appropriate professional services in public emergencies.
6. The social worker should advocate changes in policy and legislation to improve social conditions and to promote social justice.
7. The social worker should encourage informed participation by the public in shaping social policies and institutions.

Glossary
of Terms and Concepts

Administrative hearing A meeting between a representative of the regulatory agency and a client or agency, during which both sides have a chance to discuss an area of disagreement.

Administrative regulations Procedural requirements for the provision of services or conduct of activities imposed by an authoritative body.

Affirmative action An active effort on the part of an organization to address inequities in racial and gender composition of its employees. Affirmative action plans for organizations must identify the steps an organization will take to give preferential treatment to the hiring of groups that have been discriminated against in the past.

Agency charter The legal authorization for a private group of persons to be approved by the state for the provision of specific social services contingent on meeting a set of requirements established by state administrative agencies.

Agency policy The set of operational procedures used to run the day-to-day operation of a social service agency, maintain agency accountability to its funding sources, and provide the framework within which social welfare policy, developed outside the agency, is implemented.

Authority The position in which an individual's right to exert power over others is recognized and supported by those who grant that power and those over whom the power is exerted.

Blaming the victim A phrase created by Ryan (1976), which describes the practice of attributing the fault for the development and maintenance of a social problem to those who are the victims, not the perpetrators, of the problem. This activity shifts the blame for the development of a social problem away from its true cause to its victims.

Bounded rationality A characteristic of decision making in which the decision maker's inability to consider all possible choices and their consequences results in the consideration of only a limited number of possible decisions. The decision maker attempts to be as rational as possible within these limitations.

Cause and consequence approach An approach to policy analysis that assesses the process of going from identifying a social problem to implementing a policy and assessing the impact that policy has on the original social problem.

Coalition A short-term agreement between organizations to work together on a specific issue. Organizations neither give up their specified domains nor trade their services to another agency; they simply agree to a division of responsibilities in handling a particular joint interest.

Conference committee A bipartisan committee representing both the House of Representatives and the Senate that meets to develop a compromise bill when neither house will accept the other's version of a piece of legislation.

Consumption approach An approach to policy designed to meet an immediate need, such as food stamps.

Data Information needed to assess a program or conduct an empirical study.

Delegation doctrine A legislative practice in which laws are developed within a very broad framework of intended policies while the specific rules and procedures for implementing programs are delegated to administrative agencies.

Diversification of resources An active effort by an organization to secure income from a number of sources to minimize damage to the organization should one source of income be terminated.

Eclectic profession Any occupation in which knowledge is borrowed from a wide range of disciplines. Social work is an eclectic profession borrowing knowledge from psychology, sociology, anthropology, economics, and political science.

Editorial An article or report that appears in the media and expresses a specific opinion about an issue but does not pretend to be unbiased.

External environment of a social service agency All the elements outside the agency's internal environment that influence the type of service provided by the agency. These elements include characteristics of clients, the availability of human resources, the influence of regulatory agencies, interorganizational relationships, financial resources, and the sociocultural characteristics of the community in which the agency is located.

Federated fund-raising organizations Fund-raising organizations, such as United Way, that are made up of member agencies. A single fund-raising campaign is organized, and its proceeds are allocated to member agencies. This type of fund-raising is considered more efficient and effective than a large number of small fund-raising efforts.

Formative policy research   Policy research that focuses on the formation of policy rather than on a description of its impact on clients and agencies.

Goal displacement   A tendency on the part of organizations to concentrate on the means of service rather than the end it hopes to accomplish. How the service is provided becomes the goal rather than the achievement of previously stated goals.

Hatch Act   The Political Activities Act of 1939, which regulated the expenditures by and contributions to political parties by prohibiting federal employee participation in partisan political activities.

Horizontal power   Power in relationship to others in the same tier of the organizational structure.

Human resources   The people who staff social service agencies and other organizations.

Hypothesis   Tentative statement about the relationship between variables.

Impact evaluation   An evaluation of a social service program; it includes all the quantitative components of the scope of a program's operation as well as an assessment of the nonquantifiable aspects of the program.

In-kind program   A service provided as the service itself rather than as the cash to purchase the service. Examples include food stamps (vouchers), Medical Assistance (health care services), and public housing (low-cost housing).

Informational hearing   A hearing in which the public hears a legislator or public official describe a proposed or adopted policy.

Internal environment   Factors within the social service agencies such as organizational technology, goals, and authority and power structures, which influence the daily operation of the organization.

Institutional model of social welfare   A service provision system in which the federal government of a country has determined that social welfare and other human services will be provided as a basic function in people's lives. Continuing needs throughout the life cycle are anticipated rather than addressed as they develop. Institutional social welfare systems expect individuals to have trouble meeting the complex needs of modern living and provide a comprehensive set of social services to assist individuals.

Interorganizational relationships   The interactions between organizations established in the interest of coordinating activities.

Investigative reporting   Media reporting aimed at systematically examining all aspects of a current news story, with a focus on information that is not known by the public but that contributes to a clearer understanding of an issue. Most often the reporting is based on the assumption that things are not exactly as they appear to be and that certain information is being intentionally concealed from the public.

Investment approach   An approach to policy designed to meet a long-term need such as education; this approach invests in the individual's ability to secure employment in the future.

Involuntary clients   Individuals who are referred to or forced into services because they are required by law to receive them, not because they have chosen to participate.

Legal precedents   Actions taken in court decisions that become part of subsequent case law.

Litigation   Legal action that results in bringing a case to court.

Lobbyist   An individual paid to represent an organization's interests with government officeholders and agencies. The primary responsibility of a lobbyist is to represent the interests of the organization when important pieces of legislation are being considered for passage.

Means-tested program   A social or financial service that requires an applicant to prove financial need in order to receive the service.

Mission statement of an agency   A broad statement about the scope of problems addressed by the agency and a general description of how the agency intends to address those social problems.

Mythology of autonomous practice   The erroneous belief that social workers operate independently, outside of the restrictions of agency and social welfare policy. The term was coined by Jansson (1992). Social work practitioners are actually restricted in practice by agency policies.

Needs assessment   A procedure for determining what services a community requires to meet basic human needs; includes research, surveys, questionnaires, and public hearings.

Nonprofit agency   A private social service agency that is not operated with the interest of generating a profit beyond the actual cost of running the agency. If a profit is generated, it is reinvested in services provided by the agency.

Object of analysis   The client, group, program, or organization that is studied as a means of assessing the effectiveness of a program under evaluation.

Organizational change   The intentional effort to modify existing organizational practices or structures, undertaken to improve the efficiency or functioning of the organization.

Organizational shaping   Initiating a series of minor but important changes in organizational operation that are often less threatening than initiating major changes all at once.

Organizational technology   "A set of systematic procedures used by an organization to bring about predetermined changes in its raw material"

(Hasenfeld & English, 1977, p. 279). In social service agencies, organizational technology includes the various social work roles, such as broker, advocate, mediator, resource coordinator, or therapist.

Output evaluation   An evaluation that examines the number of clients served, hours of service, number of personnel, expenditure of monies, and other quantitative measures of a program's operation.

Output goals   A subsection of program goals, output goals include the number of units of service a program hopes to provide.

Philosophy of service   The value orientation of a social service agency, which determines the approach, kind, and quantity of agency service.

Political   A term applied to any activity devoted to seeking and using power over the allocation and distribution of resources, which requires compromise, negotiation, and inevitably conflict. Activities are considered political when they imply that one party has more power than another and when a shift in that power distribution is the ultimate goal of the activity.

Power   The ability to influence people to do things, usually associated with authority.

Prescriptive policy approach   Policy research that recommends or prescribes a social welfare policy based on previous information about the impact of existing policies, with a projection of the continuing effectiveness of these policies into the future.

Primary social work setting   Agencies or organizations in which social work is the primary purpose of the organization and social work is the dominant profession. Examples include child welfare agencies, family service agencies, and homeless shelters.

Private social service agencies   Denominational or nondenominational providers of social services that are not intended to generate a profit or where the profit is not distributed to stockholders but reinvested in the agency. A volunteer board of directors runs the agency through an executive director.

Private for-profit social service agencies   Providers of social and health care services that are organized and run as profit-generating businesses with a paid board of directors and stockholders who hold a financial interest in the organization.

Problem-solving approach   A systematic way to identify a client, group, or community problem, explore alternatives, develop an action plan, implement that plan, and evaluate the intervention effort.

Program evaluation   The examination of a social service program's operation and outcomes, with a particular emphasis on the intended and unintended effects of services.

Program goals   The ends that individual programs within a social service agency hope to accomplish by providing services to clients. Effective program goals should be measurable.

Promulgating the rules   The process of transforming a piece of legislation into a specific program or policy by identifying the specific guidelines and operating procedures to be used in administering the program.

Public social service agencies   Organizations that provide social and financial service under the authorization of local, state, or federal agencies.

Public service announcement   A short visual or audio media announcement, devoted to a nonprofit organization, that gives the nonprofit sector an opportunity to reach a wide audience without incurring the cost of commercial advertising.

Purchase of service agreement   An arrangement whereby one social service agency contracts with another to provide a service.

Quality circle   An employee-centered organizational decision-making group.

Rational process   A decision-making process in which all choices and all consequences of those choices are known, and decisions are made on the basis of achieving the greatest good with the least harm.

Research method   The means by which a researcher obtains the information needed to determine whether hypotheses are valid.

Residual model of social welfare   A system of social welfare and other human services that are developed piecemeal as a reaction to the development of social problems, rather than in anticipation of them. Family and work are seen as the first line of defense for individuals experiencing problems. The government is viewed as a last resort for service provision.

Scientific method   A precise set of procedures by which traditional empirical research is conducted, including statement of the research problem, review of the literature, statement of the hypotheses and research methods, collection and analysis of data, interpretation, and conclusions.

Scope of services   The range of services offered by a social service agency, determined by its funding services and the purpose of the agency.

Secondary social work setting   An agency or organization in which social work functions in conjunction with another profession, such as medicine. The other profession plays the dominant role in the general work of the organization. Examples include hospitals, nursing homes, alcohol and drug treatment centers, and community centers.

Self-determination   The social service client's right to be an active participant in the course of action selected to address an identified client problem. Self-determination is considered one of the most important values in the social work profession.

Service eligibility requirements   Personal, financial, or social criteria a potential service client must meet to receive social services from a public or private agency.

Summative policy research   An examination of the effect of a policy, in which the social policy can be the independent or dependent variable. As an independent variable, the policy is examined in terms of its impact on an existing social problem. As a dependent variable, the antecedent social problem that resulted in a particular policy is examined.

Testimony   Written or oral comments presented at a public hearing or court procedure.

The working poor   Individuals who hold full- and part-time jobs but work at such low wages that they rarely earn much above the poverty line.

Think tank   A private or university-based organization that engages in large-scale policy research.

Universal program   Service provided to people without a means test. Social security benefits, public education, and police protection are examples of universal programs in the United States.

Vertical authority   The formal position of any person in the hierarchy of formal authority, from those with the most power to those with the least.

References

ABRAMOVITZ, M. (1986). The privatization of the welfare state: A review. *Social Work,* *31*(4), 257–264.

ADAMS, P. (1982). Policies and social work practice: a radical dilemma. In M. A. Mahaffey & J. Hanks (Eds.), *Practical politics: Social work and political responsibility.* Silver Spring, MD: National Association of Social Workers.

ARCHES, J. (1991). Social structure, burnout and job satisfaction. *Social Work, 36*(3), 202–207.

BALACHANDIAN, M., & BALACHANDIAN, S. (1991). *State and local statistics sources 1990–1991.* Detroit, MI: Gale Research.

BARKER, R. L. (1987). *The social work dictionary.* Silver Spring, MD: National Association of Social Workers.

BENJAMINSON, P., & ANDERSON, D. (1990). *Investigative reporting* (2nd ed.). Ames: Iowa State University Press.

BIRKBY, R. H. (1983). *The court and public policy.* Washington, DC: Congressional Quarterly.

BLUMBERG, R. L. (1987). *Organizations in contemporary society.* Englewood Cliffs, NJ: Prentice-Hall.

BRIAR, K. H. & BRIAR, S. (1982). Clinical social work and public policies. In M. A. Mahaffey & J. Hanks (Eds.), *Practical politics: Social work and political responsibility.* Silver Spring, MD: National Association of Social Workers.

BRIELAND, D., & LEMMON, J. A. (1985). *Social work and the law.* St. Paul, MN: West.

BURT, M. A. (1985). *Testing the social safety net: The impact of changes in support programs during the Reagan administration.* Washington, DC: Urban Institute Press.

CHARLES STEWART MOTT FOUNDATION. (1991). *A state by state look at teenage childbearing in the United States.* Flint, MI: Author.

COMPTON, B. (1980). *Introduction to social welfare and social work.* Homewood, IL: Dorsey Press.

COMPTON, B., & GALAWAY, B. (1989). *Social work processes.* Belmont, CA: Wadsworth.

CORMAN, R. P. (1987). The realities of profitization and privatization in the non-profit sector. In B. J. Carroll, R. A. Conant, & T. A. Easton (Eds.), *Private means—public ends.* New York: Praeger.

DAFT, R. L. (1989). *Organization theory and design* (3rd ed.). St. Paul, MN: West.

DANE, B. O., & SIMON, B. L. (1991). Resident guests: social workers in host settings. *Social Work, 36*(3), 208–213.

DEMONE, H. W., JR., & GIBELMAN, M. (1987). Privatizing the acute care general hospital. In B. J. Carroll, R. A. Conant, & T. A. Easton (Eds.), *Private means—public ends.* New York: Praeger.

DEMONE, H. W., JR., & GIBELMAN, M. (1988). The future of the purchase of services. In H. W. Demone & M. Gibelman (Eds.), *Services for sale: Purchasing health and human services.* New Brunswick, NJ: Rutgers University Press.

DINITTO, D. M. (1991). *Social welfare: Politics and public policy* (3rd ed.). Englewood Cliffs, NJ: Prentice-Hall.

DYE, T. R., & ZEIGLER, L. H. (1989). *American Politics in the Media Age.* Pacific Grove, CA: Brooks/Cole.

EIKIN, N. (1987). Privatization in perspective. In B. J. Carroll, R. A. Conant, & T. A. Easton (Eds.), *Private means—public ends.* New York: Praeger.

EINHORN, E. S., & LOGUE, J. (1989). *Modern welfare states: Politics and policies in social democratic Scandinavia.* New York: Praeger.

GALBRAITH, J. K. (1958). *The affluent society.* Boston: Houghton Mifflin.

GALPER, J. (1975). *The politics of social services.* Englewood Cliffs, NJ: Prentice-Hall.

HALLECK, S. (1971). *The politics of therapy.* New York: Science House.

HARRINGTON, M. (1962). *The other America.* New York: Penguin.

HARTMAN, A. (1991). Social worker-in-situation. *Social Work, 36*(3), 195–197.

HASENFELD, Y. (1983). *Human service organizations.* Englewood Cliffs, NJ: Prentice-Hall.

HASENFELD, Y., & ENGLISH, R. A. (1974). *Human service organizations.* Ann Arbor: University of Michigan Press.

HAYES, C. D. (Ed.). (1987). *Risking the future: Adolescent sexuality, pregnancy and childbearing.* Washington, DC: National Academy Press.

HAYNES, K., & MICKELSON, J. S. (1991). *Affecting change: Social workers in the political arena.* (2nd ed.). New York: Longman.

HELMS, L. B., HENKIN, A. B., & SINGLETON, C. A. (1989, June). The legal structure of policy implementation: Responsibilities of agencies and practitioners. *Social Services Review,* 180–198.

HICKSON, D., PUGH, D. C., & PHEYSEY, D. C. (1969). Operations technology and organizational structure: an empirical reappraisal. *Administrative Science Quarterly, 14*(3), 378–397.

JANSSON, B. S. (1990). *Social welfare policy: From theory to practice.* Belmont, CA: Wadsworth.

JOHNSON, L., & SCHWARTZ, C. L. (1991). *Social welfare: A response to human need.* (2nd ed.). Boston: Allyn & Bacon.

JONES, E. (1986). *Teenage pregnancy in industrialized countries.* New Haven, CT: Yale University Press.

KADUSHIN, A. (1976). *Supervision in social work.* New York: Columbia University Press.

KETTNER, P. M., & MARTIN, L. L. (1987). *Purchase of service contracting.* Newbury Park, CA: Sage.

KRAMER, R. M. (1981). *Voluntary agencies in the welfare state.* Berkeley and Los Angeles: University of California Press.

KRUSCHKE, C. R., & JACKSON, B. M. (1987). *Dictionary of Public Policy.* Santa Barbara, CA: ABC/Clio.

LAMB, H. R. (1984). *The homeless mentally ill: a task force report of the American Psychiatric Association.* Washington, DC: American Psychiatric Association.

LEIBY, J. (1978). *A history of social welfare and social work in the United States.* New York: Columbia University Press.

LEVITAN, S., & SHAPIRO, I. (1987). *Working but poor: America's contradiction.* Baltimore, MD: Johns Hopkins University Press.

LEWIS, H. (1988). Ethics and the private non-profit human service organization. In M. Reisch & A. C. Hyde (Eds.), *The future of non-profit management and the human services.* San Francisco: San Francisco State University Monograph.

LUBOVE, R. (1975). *The professional altruist.* New York: Atheneum.

MAHAFFEY, M. (1989). Lobbying and social work. In I. S. Colby (Ed.), *Social welfare policy: Perspectives, patterns, and insights.* Chicago: Dorsey Press.

MARCH, J. G., & SIMON, H. (1958). *Organizations.* New York: Wiley.

MARCUS, L. J. (1988). Processes of new organizations: a case study. *Administration in Social Work, 12*(3), 91–106.

MASON, D. E. (1984). *Voluntary non-profit enterprise management.* New York: Plenum Press.

MCCUEN, G. E. (Ed.). (1988). *Children having children: Global perspectives on teenage pregnancy.* Hudson, WI: McCuen.

MOORE, K., and BURT, M. A. (1982). *Private crisis, public cost: Policy perspectives on teenage childbearing.* Washington, DC: The Urban Institute.

NATIONAL ASSOCIATION OF SOCIAL WORKERS. (1991). *Encyclopedia of social work.* New York: Author.

NEUGEBOREN, B. (1985). *Organization, policy, and practice in the human services.* New York: Longman.

OFFICE OF THE FEDERAL REGISTER, NATIONAL ARCHIVES AND RECORDS SERVICES. (1991). *The United States government manual.* Washington, DC: U.S. Government Printing Office.

PALUMBO, D. (1987). *The politics of program evaluation.* Newbury Park, CA: Sage.

PERROW, C. (1979). *Complex organizations: A critical essay.* Glenview, IL: Scott, Foresman.

PIERCE, D. (1984). *Policy for the social work practitioner.* New York: Longman.

PORTNEY, K. (1986). *Approaching public policy analysis.* Englewood Cliffs, NJ: Prentice-Hall.

PRIGMORE, C. S., & ATHERTON, C. R. (1986). *Social welfare policy: Analysis and formulation.* Lexington, MA: D. C. Heath.

QUINN, L., PAWASARAT, J., & STETZER, F. (1992). *Evaluation of the impact of the Wisconsin Learnfare experiment on the school attendance of teenagers receiving Aid to Families with Dependent Children.* Milwaukee: University of Wisconsin-Milwaukee, Employment and Training Institute.

REID, W. J. (1965). Inter-agency coordination in delinquency prevention and control. In M. N. Zald (Ed.), *Social welfare institutions.* New York: Wiley.

REIN, M. (1983). *From policy to practice.* Armonk, NY: M. E. Sharpe.

REISCH, M. (1990). Organizational structure and client advocacy: Lessons from the 1980s. *Social Work, 35*(1), 73–74.

RESNICK, H., & PATTI, R. J. (1980). *Change from within: Humanizing social welfare organizations.* Philadelphia: Temple University Press.

RUBIN, E. R. (1986). *The Supreme Court and the American family: Ideology and issues.* New York: Greenwood Press.

RUTMAN, L. (1977). *Evaluation research methods.* Beverly Hills, CA: Sage.

RYAN, W. (1976). *Blaming the victim.* New York: Vantage Books.

RYSTROM, K. (1983). *The why, who and how of the editorial page.* New York: Random House.

SHILTS, R. (1987). *And the band played on: Politics, people and the AIDS epidemic.* New York: St. Martins Press.

SMITH, C. E. (1991). *Courts and the poor.* Chicago: Nelson-Hall.

STOECZ, D. (1988). Human service corporations and the welfare state. *Society, 25,* 53–58.

TRIPODI, T. (1983). *Evaluation research for social workers.* Englewood Cliffs, NJ: Prentice-Hall.

UNITED STATES DEPARTMENT OF COMMERCE. (1991). *Bureau of the Census catalog and guide.* Washington, DC: U.S. Government Printing Office.

UNITED STATES DEPARTMENT OF COMMERCE, BUREAU OF THE CENSUS. (1972). *County and city data book.* Washington, DC: U.S. Government Printing Office.

UNITED STATES DEPARTMENT OF COMMERCE, BUREAU OF THE CENSUS. (1973). *Congressional district data book.* Washington, DC: U.S. Government Printing Office.

UNITED STATES DEPARTMENT OF COMMERCE, BUREAU OF THE CENSUS. (1991). *Statistical abstract of the United States* (111th ed.). Washington, DC: U.S. Government Printing Office.

UNITED STATES DEPARTMENT OF HEALTH AND HUMAN SERVICES, OFFICE OF RESEARCH AND STATISTICS. (1989). *Social security programs throughout the world 1989.* (Research Report No. 62). Washington, DC: U.S. Government Printing Office.

VINOVSKIS, M. A. (1988). *An "epidemic" of adolescent pregnancy? Some historical and policy considerations.* New York: Oxford University Press.

WALLENDORF, M. (1979). Understanding the client as consumer. In G. Zaltman (Ed.), *Management principles for nonprofit agencies and organizations.* New York: American Management Association.

WALLER, D. (1989). *Learnfare teen school requirement: A summary.* Madison: Wisconsin Department of Health and Human Services.

WEINBACH, R. W. (1990). *The social worker as manager.* New York: Longman.

WHITLEY, J. W., & SKALL, G. P. (1988). *The broadcasters survival guide: a handbook of FCC rules and regulations for radio and TV stations.* New York: Scripps Howard Books.

WILENSKY, H. L., & LEBEAUX, C. N. (1965). *Industrial society and social welfare.* New York: Free Press.

WILSON, J. A. (1979). Management of mental health in nonprofit organizations. In *Management principles for nonprofit agencies and organizations.* New York: American Management Association.

Index

A

Abramovitz, M., 48
Action plans
  developing, 108–109
  implementing, 109–110
Adams, P., 10
Administrative hearing, 55
Administrative rules, 55
Affirmative action, 46
Agency. *See* Social service agencies
Agency charter, 151
Aid to Families with Dependent Children
    (AFDC), 9, 75, 77
AIDS, 88–89
American Federation of State, County, and
    Municipal Employees (AFSCME), 47
ANALYSIS model of program evaluation,
    13, 126–131. *See also* Social welfare
    policy, evaluation
Anderson, D., 90
Arches, J., 35, 153
Assessment in policy development,
    100–105
Atherton, C., 127
Authority
  defined, 28
  functions of, 29
  horizontal, 30
  informal, 31
  issues unique to social service agencies,
    31–33
  manifestations of, 29
Autonomous practice, myth of, 4

B

Balachandian, M., 141
Balachandian, S., 141
Barker, R., 140
Benjaminson, P., 90
Birkby, R., 93
Blaming the victim, 11
Blumberg, R., 16
Boards of directors, 67, 151
Bounded rationality, 33–34, 106
Briar, K., 13
Briar, S., 13
Brieland, D., 95
Brown v. Board of Education of Topeka, 93
Burt, M., 84, 97

C

Cash assistance, 77–78, 130
Causes and consequences approach, 126
Clients
  and community values, 57
  competition for, 42
  empowerment of, 142–143
  involuntary, 25
  perceptions of an agency, 43
  potential population, 41
  referrals, 42
Coalitions, 53–54
Code of Ethics, National Association of
    Social Workers, 12, 25, 127
Community advisory committees, 156
Complementary resources, 52
Compton, B., 26, 63

Conference committee, 86–87
Congress, United States, 85–89
Consumption approach, 127
Corman, R., 67, 72
County departments of social services, 63, 75
Courts
  decision making in the, 93–94
  determining policy within the, 95
  litigation in the, 147
  political character of, 95
  structure of, 94
  use of legal precedent in, 93

D

Dane, B., 19
Data, 119–120
Decision making
  and bounded rationality, 33–34
  environment, 34
  and job satisfaction, 34–35, 153
  in the organization, 33–35
  in private social service agencies, 155–156
  in public social service agencies, 156
  and quality circles, 153
  as a rational process, 82
Delegation doctrine, 54
Demone, J., 71, 73
Department of Health and Human Services, United States, 54, 55, 64, 68
DiNitto, D., 82
Diversification of resources, 50–51
Dye, T., 86

E

Eclectic profession, 26
Eikin, N., 74
Einhorn, E., 7
Editorial, 90
Employment and Training Program (ET), Massachusetts, 135
English, R., 26, 27, 57
Equal Pay Act of 1963, 46
Executive director, 151
Executive Order 11246, 46
Executive Order 11375, 46
External environment, social service agency
  defined, 16
  economic and financial environment, 48–52
  human resources, 43–48
  local economy, 48–49
  potential client population, 41–42

External environment, social service agency (*continued*)
  relationships with regulatory agencies, 54–56
  sociocultural environment, 56–58

F

Federal Communications Commission (FCC), 92
Federal policies, 139–140
Federal Register, 88
Federated fund-raising organizations, 51
Financial environment, social service agency, 48
Formative policy research, 125–126
For-profit agencies. *See* Social service agencies, for-profit

G

Galaway, B., 26
Galper, J., 10, 14, 62
General Assistance, 75, 77
General Social Survey, 124
Gibelman, M., 71, 73
Goals
  ambiguity of, 25
  conflicting, 25
  discrepancy between social worker's and organization's, 32
  displacement of, 24
  identifying program, 22, 118
  mission statement as, 22
  output, 22
  in program evaluation, 114
  setting, 103
  social service agency, 21–25
Griswold v. State of Connecticut, 95

H

Halleck, S., 10, 134
Harrington, M., 90
Hartman, A., 31
Hasenfeld, Y., 26, 27, 51, 57
Hatch Act, 142
Hayes, C., 97
Haynes, K., 82, 88, 142
Helms, L., 54
Henken, A., 54
Hickson, D., 26
Horizontal authority, 30
Human resources
  and agency reputation, 47–48
  availability of staff, 46
  defined, 43

Human resources (*continued*)
   and legislative mandates, 45–46
   staff qualifications, 46
   unionization, 47
Hypotheses, 124

I

Impact evaluation, 116
Informational hearing, 144
In-kind services, 78, 130
Institutional model of social welfare, 6–7
Intended consequences of a program, 120
Internal environment, social service
      agency
   agency goals as part of, 21–25
   authority and power in the, 21–25
   decision making in the, 33–35
   defined, 17
   elements of, 20–36
   organizational technology in the, 26–28
Interorganizational relationships
   conditions for creating, 52
   developing coalitions in, 53–54
Investigative reporting, 90–92
Investment approach, 127

J

Jansson, B., 4, 89
Johnson, L., 67
Jones, E., 11, 97, 101, 102

K

Kadushin, A., 33
Kettner, P., 71
Kramer, R., 50

L

Lamb, H., 124
League of Women Voters, 144
Learnfare, Wisconsin, 115, 117, 118, 128,
      129, 130, 135
Lebeaux, C., 6
Legal precedent, 93
Legislation
   budgetary process, 89
   lawmaking, 85–88
   as a political process, 87–88
   rule making in, 88
Legislative mandates, 45–46
Leiby, J., 19
Lemmon, J., 95
Letter-writing campaigns, 142–143
Levitan, S., 41
Lewis, H., 48
Library resources, 140–141

Litigation, 147
Lobbying, 143–144
Local fund-raising, 50
Local governmental policies
   city-level policies, 135–136
   county-level policies, 136–137
Logue, J., 7
Lubove, R., 19

M

McCuen, G., 97
Mahaffey, M., 143
March, J., 33
Marcus, L., 30
Martin, L., 71
Mason, D., 47, 50
Means-tested programs, 76–78
Media
   community service programming, 92–93
   editorial policy, 90
   influence on social welfare policy, 89–93
   investigative reporting, 90–92
   role in the political process, 144–145
Medical Assistance, 5, 8, 63, 75, 78
Medicare, 5, 75
Mickelson, J., 82, 88, 142
Moore, K., 84, 97
Mythology of autonomous practice, 4–5

N

NASW News, 139–140
National Association of Social Workers,
      12, 138, 139–140, 143, 146
National Center for Social Policy and
      Practice, 140
Needs assessment, 100–101, 127–128
Neugeboren, B., 26, 52, 154
New York Times, 90, 91

O

Office of Management and Budget, 88
Old Age, Disability, and Survivors'
      Benefits, 8
Organizational chart, 29–30
Organizational-level change, 149–161
   changing individual attitudes and
      behavior, 152–153
   defined, 151
   developing an action plan for, 160
   evaluating, 160
   informal techniques in, 156
   input as part of, 154
   organizational shaping, 156
   practitioner's responsibility for,
      151–152

Organizational-level change (*continued*)
  problem-solving model in, 157
  resistance to, 154
  using persuasion versus force, 155
Organizational shaping, 156
Organizational technology
  defined, 26
  people as raw material of, 27
  sequence of activities in, 27
Output evaluation, 116
Output goals, 22–23

P

Palumbo, D., 117
Patti, R., 151, 152
Pawasarat, J., 117
Perrow, C., 28, 34, 79
Pheysey, D., 26
Philosophy of service, 69–70
Pierce, D., 156
Policies and procedures, manual of, 151
Political Activities Act of 1939, 142
Political economy, school of, 30
Political polls, 146
Political process, 10–13
  defined, 10
  Hatch Act and the, 142
  influencing the, 147
  lack of client power, 11
  letter-writing campaigns, 142–143
  lobbying, 143–144
  media's role, 144–145
  public hearings, 144–145
  social work ethics and, 12
  social work's role, 10
  working for political candidates, 145
Portney, K., 114, 125, 126
Power
  compared with authority, 28
  functions of, 28
  horizontal, 30
  informal, 31
  issues unique to social service agencies,
    31–33
  manifestations of, 29
  over resources and rewards, 30
  vertical, 29–30
Preevaluation activities, 115–118
Prescriptive policy research, 126
Prigmore, C., 127
Primary social work settings,
  defined, 17–18
  influence on policy, 20
Problem definition, 83–85, 103–104

Problem-solving model
  application of, in policy development,
    100–111
  assessment in, 100–105
  defined, 98
  defining problems, 103–104
  developing an action plan in, 108–109
  evaluation of policy using, 110–111
  exploring alternatives, 105–108
  identifying resources and obstacles, 105
  implementation of action plan in,
    109–110
  setting goals in, 103–104
Program evaluation
  ANALYSIS model, 126–131
  data collection and analysis in, 119–120
  identification of goals in, 118
  impact and output evaluations, 116
  preevaluation activities in, 115–118
  purpose of, 114–115
  reporting results in, 121
  selecting variables in, 118–119
  summary of steps in, 121
Program goals, 22–23
Promulgating the rules, 88
Public hearings, 144–145
Public service announcements (PSAs), 92,
    107
Pugh, D., 26
Purchase of service contracts, 70–71, 115

Q

Quality circles, 153
Quinn, L., 117

R

Rational process, 82
Regulatory agencies
  administrative hearings, 55
  administrative regulations, 55
  client's right to appeal decisions of, 56
  delegation doctrine, 54
  prospective rule making, 54–55
  retrospective rule making, 54–55
Reid, W., 52
Rein, M., 113, 117
Reisch, M., 53
Reports in program evaluation, 121
Research methods, 124
Residual system of social welfare, 7, 9
Resnick, H., 151, 152
Review of literature, 123
Roe v. Wade, 95
Role ambiguity, 20

Rubin, E., 93
Rule making, 88–89
Rutman, L., 114, 116, 117
Ryan, W., 11
Rystrom, K., 90

S

Schwartz, C., 67
Scientific method, 122–125
Scope of service, 70
Secondary social work settings, 18–20
  devaluation of social work in, 19
  role ambiguity in, 20
  social work values in, 19
  token status of social work, 19
Self-determination, 17, 25, 127
"Separate but equal" doctrine, 93
Service eligibility requirements, 68–69
Shapiro, I., 41
Sickness and maternity benefits, 8
Simon, H., 19, 33
Singleton, C., 54
Skall, G., 92
Smith, C., 94
Social insurance, 8, 75
Social justice and social welfare policy, 131
Social Security Act of 1935, 135
Social Security Administration, 75
Social service agencies
  authority and power issues in, 31–33
  budget allocations in, 49
  context for practice, 3–5
  defined, 64
  diversification of resources, 50
  economic and financial environment, 48–52
  external environment, 16–35
  goals, 21–25
  internal environment, 20–35
  interorganizational relationships between, 52
  local economy, 48–49
  local fund-raising, 50
  mission statements, 22
  organizational change in, 149–161. *See also* Organizational-level change
  policy of, 4–5, 16
  program goals, 22–23
  redistribution of funds within, 51
  reputation of, 47–48
  unionization within, 47
Social service agencies, for-profit
  advertising by, 43
  defined, 64

Social service agencies, for-profit
  (*continued*)
  case for, 73
  criticisms of, 74
  within nonprofit agencies, 72–73
Social service agencies, nonprofit, 63, 67–68
  access to funds, 50
  agency-level policies, 151
  boards of directors, 67, 151
  decision making in, 155–156
  nondenominational, 67
  organizational change in, 156
  philosophy of service in, 69–70
  purchase of service contracts, 70–71
  scope of services, 70
  sectarian, 67
Social service agencies, public, 63–67
  compared with private nonprofit, 68–71
  decision making in, 156
  organizational change in, 156
  philosophy of service, 69–70
  purchase of service contracts, 70–71
  scope of services, 70
  service eligibility requirements, 68–69
  staff, 47
  strengths and weaknesses, 66–67
Social welfare policy
  direct services and, 3
  finding out about, 135–140
  institutional model of, 6
  intervention and values in, 85
  patchwork system of, 6–9, 62–81
  research. *See* Social welfare policy, research
  residual model of, 7
  Sweden and United States compared, 8
Social welfare policy, change
  practitioner's role, 134–147
  using the media, 144–145
  using the political process, 141–144
Social welfare policy, development, 83–95
  influence of the media, 89–93
  legislative arena, 85–89
  problem-solving approach, 98–111
  role of the court system, 93–95
Social welfare policy, evaluation, 110–111
  ANALYSIS model, 126–131
  program evaluation, 114–121
  research as a means of, 121–126
Social welfare policy, research, 121–126
  approaches, 125–126
  causes and consequences approach, 126
  identifying object of analysis, 118

Social welfare policy, research (*continued*)
  research methods, 122–125
  scientific method, 122–125
Social Work, 43
Social work (profession)
  burnout in, 153
  conservative nature of, 10
  devaluation of, 19
  dual role of supervision in, 32
  eclectic nature of, 26
  ethics and, 12
  knowledge base in, 26
  political role of, 10
  technology of, 27–28
  token status of, 19
Social work values
  client values and, 58
  compared with other professional
    values, 19
  conflict within for-profit agencies,
    73–74
  conflicting with organizational values,
    32
  conflicts with, 9, 127
  intervention and, 85
Sociocultural environment, 56–58
Staff
  availability of, 46–47
  character of, 48
  qualifications of, 46
  recruitment, 47
  unionization of, 47
State-level policies, 138–139
Stetzer, F., 117
Stoecz, D., 48
Summative policy research, 126
Supervision in social work, 32–33
Supplemental Security Income, 75, 77
Supreme Court, United States, 93, 94, 95
Surveys, 100–101
Sweden, social welfare policy in, 7
Systems assessment in policy, 103–104

T
Target efficiency, 78
Teenage pregnancy, 11, 101–103
  model social welfare policy for,
    103–111
  as a social problem, 83
  and social values, 84
Testimony, 144
Think tanks, 140
Title VII, Civil Rights Act of 1964, 46
Tripodi, T., 118, 125

U
Unemployment benefits, 8
Unintended consequences of a program,
  115, 120
United States Congress, 85–89
United States Department of Health and
  Human Services, 54, 55, 64, 88
United States Supreme Court, 93, 94,
  95
United Way, 48–49, 51
Universal programs, 76–78

V
Variables, selection of, 119
Vertical authority, 29–30
Vertical power, 29–30
Vinovskis, M., 84, 97
Voting, 146

W
Wallendorf, M., 58
Weinbach, R., 46
Whitley, J., 92
Wilensky, H., 6
Wilson, J., 16
Workers' Compensation, 8
Working poor, 41

Z
Zeigler, L., 86